# The Presidential
# Ca

Recent Titles in the
PRAEGER SERIES IN POLITICAL COMMUNICATION
Robert E. Denton, Jr., General Editor

Ethical Dimensions of Political Communication
*Edited by Robert E. Denton, Jr.*

Cordial Concurrence: Orchestrating National Party Conventions in the
Telepolitical Age
*Larry David Smith and Dan Nimmo*

Televised Presidential Debates: Advocacy in Contemporary America
*Susan Hellweg, Michael Pfau and Steven Brydon*

The Political Pundits
*Dan Nimmo and James E. Combs*

Visions of Empire: Hollywood Films on the Political Landscape of the 1980s
*Stephen Prince*

Postmodern Political Communication: The Fringe Challenges the Center
*Edited by Andrew King*

Enacting the Presidency: Political Argument, Presidential Debates, and
Presidential Character
*Edward A. Hinck*

Media and Public Policy
*Edited by Robert J. Spitzer*

American Rhetoric and the Vietnam War
*J. Justin Gustainis*

The Inaugural Addresses of Twentieth-Century American Presidents
*Edited by Halford Ryan*

The Modern Presidency and Crisis Rhetoric
*Edited by Amos Kiewe*

# The Presidential Campaign Film

## A CRITICAL HISTORY

### Joanne Morreale

*Praeger Series in Political Communication*

PRAEGER

Westport, Connecticut
London

**Library of Congress Cataloging-in-Publication Data**

Morreale, Joanne.
    The presidential campaign film : a critical history / Joanne
Morreale.
      p. cm.—(Praeger series in political communication, ISSN
1062–5623)
    Includes bibliographical references (p.  ) and index.
    Filmography: p.
    ISBN 0–275–93882–4 (alk. paper)—ISBN 0–275–95580–X (pbk. : alk. paper)
    1. Advertising, Political—United States.   2. Television in
politics—United States.   3. Presidents—United States—Election.
I. Title.   II. Series.
JK2281.M67   1993
324.7'3'0973—dc20   93–20129

British Library Cataloguing in Publication Data is available.

Library of Congress Catalog Card Number: 93–20129
ISBN: 0–275–93882–4
ISBN: 0–275–95580–X (pbk.)
ISSN: 1062–5623

First published in 1993

Praeger Publishers, 88 Post Road West, Westport, CT 06881
An imprint of Greenwood Publishing Group, Inc.

Printed in the United States of America

The paper used in this book complies with the
Permanent Paper Standard issued by the National
Information Standards Organization (Z39.48–1984).

10 9 8 7 6 5 4 3 2 1

# Contents

Series Foreword *by Robert E. Denton, Jr.*　　　　vii

Preface　　　　xi

Introduction　　　　1

**Part I: The Classical Form: The Expository Presidential Campaign Film**

1　Discursive Threads of the Presidential Campaign Film　　　　25

2　Instatement of a Genre: The Classical Presidential Campaign Film, 1952–1960　　　　45

3　Growth and Development of the Classical Presidential Campaign Film, 1964–1972　　　　69

4　The End of Exposition, 1972　　　　91

**Part II: The Modern Form: The Hybrid Documentary-Advertisement**

5　The Modern Period, 1976–1980　　　　111

6　The Generic Hybrid Ascends, 1984–1988　　　　137

7　Generic Transformation, 1992　　　　161

8  Afterword: The Presidential Campaign Film as Cultural
     Artifact                                            177

Filmography                                             181

Bibliography                                            183

Index                                                   189

# Series Foreword

Those of us from the discipline of communication studies have long believed that communication is prior to all other fields of inquiry. In several other forums, I have argued that the essence of politics is "talk" or human interaction.[1] Such interaction may be formal or informal, verbal or nonverbal, public or private, but it is always persuasive, forcing us consciously or subconsciously to interpret, to evaluate, and to act. Communication is the vehicle for human action.

From this perspective, it is not surprising that Aristotle recognized the natural kinship of politics and communication in his writings *Politics* and *Rhetoric*. In the former, he establishes that humans are "political beings [who] alone of the animals [are] furnished with the faculty of language."[2] And in the latter, he begins his systematic analysis of discourse by proclaiming that "rhetorical study, in its strict sense, is concerned with the modes of persuasion."[3] Thus, it was recognized more than twenty-three hundred years ago that politics and communication go hand in hand because they are essential parts of human nature.

Back in 1981, Dan Nimmo and Keith Sanders proclaimed that political communication was an emerging field.[4] Although its origin, as noted, dates back centuries, a "self-consciously cross-disciplinary" focus began in the late 1950s. Thousands of books and articles later, colleges and universities offer a variety of graduate and undergraduate course work in the area in such diverse departments as communication, mass communication, journalism, political science, and sociology.[5] In Nimmo and Sanders' early assessment, the "key areas of inquiry" included rhetorical analysis, propaganda analysis, attitude change studies, voting studies, government and the news media, functional and systems analyses, technological changes, media technologies, campaign techniques, and research techniques.[6] In a survey of the state of the field in 1983, the same authors and Lynda Kaid found additional, more specific areas of concern such as the presidency, political polls, public opinion, debates, and advertising, to name a few.[7] Since the first study, they also noted a shift away from the rather strict behavioral approach.

A decade later, Dan Nimmo and David Swanson argued that "political communication has developed some identity as a more or less distinct domain of scholarly work."[8] The scope and concerns of the area have further expanded to include critical theories and cultural studies. While there is no precise definition, method, or disciplinary home of the area of inquiry, its primary domain is the role, processes, and effects of communication within the context of politics broadly defined.

In 1985, the editors of *Political Communication Yearbook: 1984* noted that "more things are happening in the study, teaching, and practice of political communication than can be captured within the space limitations of the relatively few publications available."[9] In addition, they argued that the backgrounds of "those involved in the field [are] so varied and pluralist in outlook and approach, . . . it [is] a mistake to adhere slavishly to any set format in shaping the content."[10] And more recently, Swanson and Nimmo called for "ways of overcoming the unhappy consequences of fragmentation within a framework that respects, encourages, and benefits from diverse scholarly commitments, agendas, and approaches."[11]

In agreement with these assessments of the area and with gentle encouragement, Praeger established in 1988 the series entitled "Praeger Studies in Political Communication." The series is open to all qualitative and quantitative methodologies as well as contemporary and historical studies. The key to characterizing the studies in the series is the focus on communication variables or activities within a political context or dimension. As of this writing, nearly forty volumes have been published and numerous impressive works are forthcoming. Scholars from the disciplines of communication, history, journalism, political science, and sociology have participated in the series.

I am, without shame or modesty, a fan of the series. The joy of serving as its editor is in participating in the dialogue of the field of political communication and in reading the contributors' works. I invite you to join me.

Robert E. Denton, Jr.

# NOTES

1.  See Robert E. Denton, Jr., *The Symbolic Dimensions of the American Presidency* (Prospect Heights, IL: Waveland Press, 1982); Robert E. Denton, Jr., and Gary Woodward, *Political Communication in America* (New York: Praeger, 1985; 2d ed., 1990); Robert E. Denton, Jr., and Dan Hahn, *Presidential Communication* (New York: Praeger, 1986); and Robert E. Denton, Jr., *The Primetime Presidency of Ronald Reagan* (New York: Praeger, 1988).

2.  Aristotle, *The Politics of Aristotle*, trans. Ernest Barker (New York: Oxford University Press, 1970), 5.

3.  Aristotle, *Rhetoric*, trans. Rhys Roberts (New York: The Modern Library, 1954), 22.

4.  Dan Nimmo and Keith Sanders, "Introduction: The Emergence of Political Communication as a Field," in *Handbook of Political Communication*, ed. Dan Nimmo and Keith Sanders (Beverly Hills, CA: Sage, 1981), 11–36.

5.  Ibid., 15.

6.  Ibid., 17–27.

7.  Keith Sanders, Lynda Kaid, and Dan Nimmo, eds., *Political Communication Yearbook: 1984* (Carbondale: Southern Illinois University, 1985), 283–308.

8.  Dan Nimmo and David Swanson, "The Field of Political Communication: Beyond the Voter Persuasion Paradigm," in *New Directions in Political Communication*, ed. David Swanson and Dan Nimmo (Beverly Hills, CA: Sage, 1990), 8.

9.  Sanders, Kaid, and Nimmo, xiv.

10.  Ibid., xiv.

11.  Nimmo and Swanson, 11.

# Preface

This book came about as a result of research on Ronald Reagan's 1984 presidential campaign film, *A New Beginning*. While tracing the historical antecedents of this film, I became aware that campaign films comprise a largely unexplored yet surprisingly revealing genre of presidential campaign communication. I realized that these films are important cultural documents that provide a valuable archive of images of candidates, campaigns, and their cultural milieus. I also wanted to fill what I perceived as a gap in the campaign literature by concentrating on the visual aspects of presidential campaign communication. In today's post-literate world, it is imperative that we understand the subordination of the word to the image in political persuasion.

Thanks are due to the many people who made this work possible. A Research and Scholarship Development Grant from Northeastern University allowed me both the time and the resources to locate presidential campaign films and to talk with some of the persons involved in their production. The following people were extremely generous with their time, and I thank them for their patience: Gabriel Bayz, John Deardourff, Phil Dusenberry, Bo Goldman, Charles Guggenheim, Chris Kempferly, Jim King, Joe Napolitan, Dan Payne, Tom Roepke, Sig Rogich, Clay Rossen, Ed Spiegel, Russ Walton, Clifton White, and David Wolper.

I'd also like to express my appreciation to the librarians and archivists at the following research institutions: The Hoover, Roosevelt, Eisenhower, Kennedy, Johnson, Carter, and Ford Presidential Libraries, the National Archives (including the Nixon Presidential Materials division), the Audiovisual Materials room at the Library of Congress, the Political

Commercials Archive at the University of Oklahoma, the Public Affairs Video Archive at Purdue University, the Edmund Muskie Collection at Bates College, the UCLA Film Archives, the Minnesota Historical Society, the Cable News Network News and Tape Library, and the Audiovisual Materials department of the Republican National Committee.

I'd like to acknowledge Bruce Gronbeck, Arthur Miller, and the Obermann Fellows with whom I spent a month in the summer of 1991 discussing American self-images and presidential campaigns at the University of Iowa's Center for Advanced Studies. I'm grateful to the political scientists in the group for helping me to see from the vantage of their discipline, and I thank my fellow rhetorical critics for their enthusiastic support of my project.

Anne Kiefer, Richard Sillett, and Leesa Stanion made sure that this book turned from manuscript to printed page.

Finally, I thank Richard Lewis, not least for his unerring ability to articulate the word that I'm struggling to find, and Emma Lewis, whose presence helped me to complete this book.

# The Presidential Campaign Film

# Introduction

## TELEVISION AND PRESIDENTIAL IMAGE-MAKING

In 1948, victorious Democratic presidential candidate Harry S Truman proclaimed: "I traveled 31,000 miles, made 356 speeches, shook hands with a half million people, talked to 15 or 20 million in person" (Diamond and Bates 1984, 38). Truman popularized the whistlestop campaign tour, speaking from the rear platform of a train to crowds of supporters gathered at scheduled stops across the country. But four years later, the speechmaking tour was already becoming a cultural relic. The advent of television, both a symptom and facilitator of broader societal changes, marked a new era of presidential politics.

Television first became a factor in presidential politics in 1952, and its influence has steadily increased in subsequent elections. Today it is virtually unthinkable for a presidential candidate to conduct a campaign without benefit of the medium. Most campaigns recognize that viewers glean most of their knowledge about candidates from television: statistics suggest that watching television is Americans' most frequent activity after sleeping and working; television surpasses newspapers as the public's most credible source of information; and today over 60% of the population rely solely on television for their news. At the same time, more than 60 million Americans are functionally illiterate, and recent studies show that 44% of the population is aliterate—they have the capacity to read, but choose not to do so (Murray-Brown 1991, 19).

The television image is the fulcrum of the modern, visually oriented political campaign. Media specialists carefully research, process, and package candidates' images for television viewers. Polls and market research determine an appropriate image for the candidate to project, and an artful arrangement of visual, linguistic, and aural signs give this image form. I use *image* here in two senses: literally, the term refers to a visual impression, and more abstractly, it refers to the projection of personal qualities or traits that shape impressions of character.

Although crafting candidates' images is not new to political campaigns, television is a particularly apt mediator of images in both the visual and psychological senses of the term. The medium creates the impression of live, immediate, and transparent reproduction of the "real," and thus serves as a substitute for viewers' direct experience. Brief comments or political advertisements aimed at prime-time viewing audiences in critical media markets are more strategically important than personal appearances where candidates meet directly with their supporters. Now when candidates jet from city to city, they aim to deliver a terse, yet memorable sound bite that will play well on the local and perhaps national evening news.

In the age of television, campaigns increasingly focus upon character, and undecided voters frequently rely on perceptions of the candidate's personality. Television enables candidates to reach uninvolved or uncommitted voters in the privacy of their homes. It creates impressions, evokes feelings, and establishes identification between voters and candidates. Viewers can scrutinize candidates' facial expressions and features, while on-camera appearances simulate intimate one-on-one communication and enable viewers to feel that they "know" candidates. The need to better understand the mediated production of presidential candidates' images provides the impetus for this work.

## THE PRESIDENTIAL CAMPAIGN FILM

Most studies to date have focused on spot advertisements to assess televisual political image making and its place within American politics and culture (See Patterson and McClure 1976; Jamieson 1984; Diamond and Bates 1984; Mickelson 1989; Kern 1989; Biocca 1991). This book considers an often-overlooked genre of political campaign discourse, the presidential campaign film. These "documentary" films typically recapitulate the lives, accomplishments, and visions of presidential candidates. They are often representative anecdotes (Burke 1955, 59–61)—condensed accounts of a campaign that encapsulate the persuasive strategies and appeals made to voters within a particular social and historical milieu.

When campaign analyses mention these films at all, most consider them as advertisements. But presidential campaign films differ from advertisements in significant ways. Most simply, they are up to thirty minutes long and are more comprehensive than spot advertisements. As documentaries, they present "actual" persons and historical events in a seemingly factual manner. The films provide the fullest visual portrait of a candidate available in one package during an election; yet like all portraits, their details are arranged to impress an image upon the viewer. Joe Napolitan, founder of the American Association of Political Consultants, succinctly explained the differences between a campaign film and an advertisement: "A biographical film is the best way to give a complete portrait of a candidate. Spots can take on individual issues; they can create a skeleton. But a documentary puts flesh and muscle on a candidate."

Contemporary presidential campaign films are hybrid forms that encompass the traditional presentational modes of the American presidential campaign, the documentary film, and the product advertisement. In terms of presidential campaign traditions, the films are visual manifestations of the partisan print biographies of presidential candidates that first appeared in the 1820s. Andrew Jackson's biography, written anonymously by his friend John C. Eaton, is the prototype for the form.

The visual versions appeared along with the birth of film itself. The Lumiere Brothers produced a one-minute "actuality" film, *William McKinley at Home*, during his 1896 campaign (Ellis 1989, 11). The first presidential campaign film was *The Life of Calvin Coolidge*, produced in 1923, while *The Dewey Story*, a controversial film produced for Republican presidential candidate Thomas Dewey in 1948, was the first film shown both in movie theatres and on television. Virtually every presidential candidate in the age of television has had at least one campaign film, whether a filmed documentary meant for partisan audiences or a television documentary geared for heterogeneous audiences.

In their "classical" period from 1948–1972, documentary filmmakers, often unversed in politics, produced the presidential campaign films. These were primarily expository forms that aimed to inform and motivate the party faithful, and the campaigns screened them for informal gatherings of local party leaders and supporters. In some cases, these films also aired on television. As the presidential campaign films develop, they become a specifically televisual genre of political communication that departs from the representational modes of their predecessors. Many of the films produced from 1976 to the present, particularly those made for Republican candidates, comprise the modern period of the presidential campaign film. Filmmakers with backgrounds in advertising often produce them, aiming to attract and entertain a diverse television audience rather than a partisan group of supporters. These films often disregard literal representation and chronological ordering, the hallmarks of the classical films. Their trajectory vividly illustrates presidential campaigns' gradual incorporation of advertising aesthetics and marketing principles, as well as the declining influence of political operatives and the ascension of professional media consultants who foster the commercialization of candidates.

This development coincides with a shift from a "military" to "merchandising" model of campaigns (Westbrook 1983, 143–73). The old-style campaigns were organized much like military enterprises. They were concerned with gathering the troops—in terms of both financial contributions and party support, using volunteer campaign workers to mobilize the legions of the faithful party "soldiers." This strategy worked when elections were extremely competitive, voter turnout was high, and party affiliations were important aspects of personal identities. With post–World War II social and demographic changes, and the advent of television, campaigns now typically "sell" the candidate like a product to the vast numbers of voters not bound by party loyalty. The media campaign is far more important than assembling volunteers, local party organizers, or the elder statespersons of the party.

## THE TELEVISED PRESIDENTIAL CAMPAIGN FILM AS RHETORICAL GENRE

The campaign films produced for presidential candidates constitute a rhetorical genre that exemplifies the formation and transformation of American political discourse in the age of television. Describing televisual campaign films as a *rhetorical* genre underscores their instrumental aims. In the classical sense, rhetoric refers to the practice of persuasion and the strategies through which a speaker tries to influence an audience. In recent years, the study of rhetoric has broadened its scope to include the analysis and evaluation of all types of public discourse, including visual communication forms. From this wider perspective, all symbolic behavior is rhetorical insofar as it is designed to communicate; thus the rhetorical critic's task is to illuminate the nature and function of particular symbolic forms.

Presidential campaign films may be divided into three rhetorical sub-genres: the biographical film, concerned with establishing a candidate's identity; the resumé film, concerned with reiterating a candidate's accomplishments; and the visionary film, concerned with articulating a candidate's conceptions of America's future. These often overlap, so that the categorization of a film as one or the other is often a matter of degree.

I broadly define the term *biographical*; thus all of the films may be considered biographies of a sort. The notion of a biography is itself linear. It implies that there is a unity and coherence to the development of a life; that a personal history is a gradual unfolding, a continuous and noncontradictory forward movement that "makes sense." Most biographies re-create historical characters by determining the critical influences and experiences that have shaped them. In dramatistic terms, character is established through scene. Key aspects of a candidate's origins, childhood, adolescence, early adulthood, and career are recounted. These moments are the causes of which an identity is an effect. Biographies establish characters who can be recognized; their courses are familiar, predictable, and reassuring to the viewer who relates to the image projected.

The majority of the presidential campaign films that I include in this study are biographies in the traditional sense. However, the resumé and visionary campaign films that focus on the candidate's past accomplishments or future goals are biographies of a sort. These films focus on role rather than identity. They establish character through a depiction of actions and purpose: a person is the sum of his/her deeds. Like the strictly biographical films, they present images of candidates, country, and American people whom they represent.

Challengers to a political office are most likely to use biographical films that identify them to voters, while incumbents frequently use resumé films that stress their accomplishments in office. Challengers typically want to establish credibility, while incumbents want to create positive perceptions of their first term in office. But incumbents who wish to alter their images may do so by producing biographical films. Incumbent Richard Nixon's *Portrait of a President* (1972), broadcast at the convention and again on election eve, combatted perceptions that he was cold and distant by presenting him as personally warm, humorous, and compassionate.

Incumbents' natural advantages over challengers are reflected in their campaign films. Presidents can associate themselves with the aura of power and authority that surrounds the office. They can run as "president" rather than candidate, appearing too busy running the country to actively campaign. Presidents can easily attain media coverage of their activities and have little difficulty staging pseudo-events (Boorstin 1961, 11–12): news planned for the primary purpose of its reproduction by the media. Trips abroad and meetings with foreign heads of state, while easy pseudo-events to produce, convey the impression that the candidate belongs among world leaders.

Most importantly for this study, presidential campaign films offer insight into the processes whereby American myth, or ideology, is created and maintained. Simply stated, American myths are the central beliefs, values, and aspirations that define and unify "The People" (McGee 1975) in a rhetorical community. The films provide comprehensive, structured storehouses of mythic images of the president, the country, and its citizens. Candidates are complex symbols whose projected self-images embody cultural myths and ideals. Denton (1982) discusses the presidential self as a mythic construct that emerges through interactions with the public. Fisher (1980, 122) refers to the president as a rhetorical fiction, "a symbolic construction that exerts persuasion force in the making of persons, community, and the nation." A successful presidential candidate taps into the public zeitgeist and simultaneously articulates and shapes its mythology.

Both the classical and modern films promote mythic images of candidates and country within constructed sociohistorical contexts. They simultaneously reflect and reinforce preexistent norms, values, and understandings, while functioning as advertisements that promote a candidate. But the hybrid films are better able to transform myth; their evocative imagery provides forms for otherwise inchoate desires and aspirations.

## ANALYZING CONTENT: MYTHS OF THE PRESIDENT, COUNTRY, AND PEOPLE

Heale (1982, 161–62) distinguishes three interconnected types of presidential images—archetypal, personal, and party—which encapsulate myths concerning the ideal leader, the country, and its people. Heale uses his categories to discuss political image making in the biographical books of the antebellum period, but they also provide useful starting points for a contemporary analysis of mythic images in presidential campaign films.

### Archetypal Images

Presidential campaign films, like the books that preceded them, convey archetypal images of presidential candidates that remain consistent throughout American history. Their thematic similarities provide a partial description of the ideal (male) American, a prototype that has changed remarkably little.

Presidential campaign films establish a candidates' characters by replaying highlights of their lives and careers. From the biographical books to the films, candidates' personal characteristics and backgrounds are remarkably similar: they love nature, are athletic, religious, honest, sincere, and courageous. Most hail from small towns or farms. Candidates speak of their parents in tones of hushed reverence, and are always able to articulate the different contributions each made to their development. They commonly learn love of duty and country from their fathers, while their mothers instill religious and moral principles. The father is stern, hardworking, and dedicated to community service, while the mother is gentle, moral, and pious. Both parents are self-sacrificing and devoted to their children. For example, George McGovern acquired "a gentle spirit" from his mother, and "the value of Christian principles, hard work, and a love of history" from his father. His father, too, "chose to serve those who were immigrating to America to seek a better life" by becoming a minister. Gerald Ford grew up with a loving family that "taught him the obligation to serve." Richard Nixon's father was self-educated, intelligent, strict, and, according to the candidate, "he perhaps put in the desire for me to enter politics more than anyone else." His mother was firm, but gentle; when disciplining her sons, "she would just sit down and talk very, very quietly, and when you got through you knew you had been through an emotional experience."

Most candidates' parents are self-sacrificing and devoted to their children, and the candidates themselves come from happy families. Nixon also commented, "I would say the reason the family was happy was because of [sic] the mother and father were both deeply devoted to their children and both would do anything for them." Only Bill Clinton, whose birth father died in a car accident before he was born, could not portray such a typical family in his campaign film. Thus, his grandparents took on the traditional role of parents; according to Hillary Clinton in an on-camera interview, "he was able to read at a really young age in part because his grandmother valued it so much and helped so much."

Brown (1960 39) notes that before 1840, little was written about a candidate's early years. From 1840 to 1868 the candidates were presented as model children, although after 1868 they became more mischievous and high-spirited. For the most part, the biographical films concentrate upon candidates' high school years and stress their athleticism (a trend that began with the written biography of Theodore

Roosevelt). The Richard Nixon (1968), Gerald Ford (1976), Walter Mondale (1984), Ronald Reagan (1980), Michael Dukakis (1988), and George Bush (1988) films mention the candidates' football careers, intercut with still-photographs of them in uniform and/or as members of a team. The candidate as athlete becomes a metaphor for the typical American: strong, healthy, and virile. The athlete is both an individual achiever and a member of a team, and thus the image can support either Republican or Democratic versions of the American Dream.

Candidates often come from humble beginnings, but work hard to become successful. Whenever possible, they are described as poor, although hard work, determination, and commitment to education enables them to succeed. The candidates conform to the American ideal of success embodied by the rags-to-riches, Horatio Alger myth. The individual who strives to achieve can overcome economic hardships; persistence, hard work, and determination will be rewarded. Humphrey conveys the moral of this story: "I'm a sentimentalist about this republic, about this country . . . about what it has meant to me, a child of the depression, a man born in the plains of humble parentage, and yet I can stand before you as a candidate for the office of president." Richard Nixon describes doing chores on the family's lemon ranch, then working six days a week at the family store and service station. He states, "And that was what we were then, we were poor. We worked hard, we ate very little, we all used hand-me-down clothes, I wore my brother's shoes." Millionaire Jimmy Carter declares on camera: "Nobody in my family before my generation ever had a chance to finish high school. We've always worked for a living. We know what it means to work." In Reagan's 1980 film, the narrator claims that "young Dutch always had to work for spending money and to help out his family." Similarly, Walter Mondale sold fresh vegetables door-to-door during the Depression and worked his way through college in the farm fields of Minnesota. Even George Bush, born into a wealthy family, describes his early years of marriage: "We lived in a little shotgun house, one room for the three of us."

Both literary and film biographies present the "candidate at home." Since the 1870s, wives have received an increasing amount of attention, and both books and films include a segment on the couple's courtship, marriage, and home life. Barry Goldwater's brief 1964 biographical film shows an anniversary portrait, while the narrator states, "And for 30 years, Peggy Goldwater has been a loyal wife, devoted mother, and the center of a happy home." Betty and Gerald Ford are "a love story." Rosalynn Carter insists that "Jimmy has never had any hint of scandal in his personal or public life." In an infamous scene from the 1984 half-hour Reagan film, the candidate muses, "Nancy. I can't imagine life without her," while a still-photograph of the embracing couple, backed by violin music, appears on screen. In 1992, seeking to dispel public conceptions of the Clintons' troubled marriage, Bill Clinton's mother-in-law asserts, "I think they deeply love and are committed to each other. They have what I like to call synergy. The combination of the two of them makes a third element that is just invincible."

Children and grandchildren have gradually become more visible in the campaign films, occasionally serving as emotional fodder for the candidates. Dwight Eisenhower attends the birth of his granddaughter in his 1952 film, while forty years later, candidate Bill Clinton waxes poetic about the birth of his own daughter. Jacqueline Kennedy sits on a sofa with her young daughter, while husband John reads them a story. In the Humphrey film, the candidate tearfuly recollects the birth of his retarded granddaughter. As film footage depicts the small blond child playing on a swing, he declares that she taught him the meaning of "perfect love." The Richard Nixon, Gerald Ford, George Bush, and Bill Clinton films have segments where their children appear on camera and discuss what wonderful fathers they are. George McGovern walks in the rain with his wife and children, Walter Mondale and George Bush attend outdoor picnics, while Richard Nixon strolls on the beach with his family (the same images appear in his 1968 and 1972 films). Nixon's 1972 election-eve film even included a sequence where the proud father escorts his daughter up the aisle at her White House wedding. Bill Clinton plays softball with his daughter in his 1992 convention film, followed by a shot of the entire family relaxing in a hammock, arms wrapped around one another. In a 1990s twist, he recalls watching an inteview on national television in which the Clintons discussed their past marital problems. "I'm glad you're both my parents," daughter Chelsea allegedly responded when he asked for her opinion. Only Ronald Reagan, estranged from his children, did not include them in his 1980 or 1984 film.

Depictions of the candidate as husband and father have become increasingly crucial in presidential election campaigns, as the Democrats and Republicans battle over which is the party of "family values." As issues become both more complex and less prevalent during campaigns, people judge candidates' characters by the perceived quality of their domestic relationships. Despite burgeoning numbers of nonnuclear families, the candidate as family man represents Americans as they want to perceive themselves. The candidate as traditional family man both maintains America's idealized image of itself and provides a point of identification, reassurance that the candidate is one of the people despite having been called to lead them.

The Cincinnatus image, first applied to Andrew Jackson, fits many presidential candidates: the virtuous, patriotic, self-sacrificing farmer is called away from the soil to serve his country and save "The People" from ruin. Still today, candidates often mention a farming background or closeness to the soil, harkening back to America's preindustrial roots and evoking the agrarian myth that equates virtue with the land (Lee 1993). Although most of the country is urban and industrial, the farmer remains the ideal symbol of the common man: a hardworking, honest, level-headed, independent individual. The farm itself, a symbol of the country's simpler past, is treated nostalgically, with images of wheat fields and farmers tilling a constant visual motif in virtually all of the films.

*The McGovern Story* (1972) provides a classic example of the myth of the president as a man of rural origins. The film stresses that McGovern grew up on a farm on the prairie. His father's immigrant experience establishes McGovern's roots in the heartland. Images of the windswept prairie and archival footage of farmers during the Depression appear on screen, and a longtime friend appears on camera to testify to McGovern's dedication to the land. Similarly, the Carter (1976) film presents the candidate as a small-town peanut farmer who works the family land. Carter wears jeans and a checkered shirt as he wanders through rows of peanuts and vegetables; he scoops handfuls of peanuts spewing out of chutes in his factory. He gets his hands dirty; working the land is in his blood.

The twentieth century films associate candidates with small-town America if the farm is not possible. Typically, old sepia-toned photographs depict the candidate's birthplace, bringing the viewer back to a simpler time. The Humphrey film includes shots of wheat fields and still-photographs of weathered farmhouses and the small town of Dolan, South Dakota, "population four to five hundred, depending on how far you think the town extends." Gerald Ford's film shows old photographs of Omaha, Nebraska back when people were still driving covered wagons. Ronald Reagan "grew up in small towns in Illinois, a midwesterner at heart." Michael Dukakis, who ran an admittedly unsuccessful media campaign, is the only candidate who makes a virtue out of growing up in an eastern suburb out of America's heartland. Most of his film consisted of his cousin Olympia taking viewers on a tour of Brookline, one of Boston's wealthier communities. The image lacks mythic resonance. Four years later, Bill Clinton, having learned the lessons of the failed Dukakis campaign, nostalgically reminisces about Hope, Arkansas. He relates the small town to the myth of the American Dream: "And yet in many ways all I am or ever will be came from there, a place and a time where nobody ever locked their doors at night, everybody showed up for the parade on Main Street, and kids like me could dream of being part of something bigger than themselves."

The biographical films traditionally reiterate candidates' background, parentage, early youth, education, athletic achievements, marriage, commitment to home and family, duty to country, public service record, and experience in foreign affairs. Typically, the presidential campaign films demonstrate candidates' selfless devotion to their country with an account of their wartime service records, simultaneously depicting their willingness to serve their country and evoking patriotic sentiments in viewers. They almost always enlist in the service because they are overcome with patriotic sentiment.

Acts of wartime heroism are often emotional high points of the political campaign films, illustrated by requisite battle footage and on-camera testimony from one of the candidate's subordinates. War footage, familiar to viewers from films and television, excites emotions and evokes patriotic feelings. Candidates' war experiences demonstrate their love of country and ability to lead. In terms of myth, candidates' acts of heroism demonstrate their ability to enter the darkness and emerge transformed, with a new wisdom that enables them to lead the common man. Depictions of heroism fulfill the mythic pattern of the leader who is tested, overcomes challenge, and is the wiser for it (Campbell 1988, 123). In many cases, the archival images bear no relation to the represented event; grainy, black-and-white World War II battle footage, complete with sound effects of exploding bombs and gunfire, document the heroic exploits of Dwight Eisenhower, John Kennedy, George McGovern, Gerald Ford, and George Bush. In the McGovern film, footage is shot so that the viewer appears to be in the airplane with the pilot as the narrator recounts McGovern's daring landing after his plane was hit by a bomb.

When a candidate has no heroic war record, filmmakers may construct heroism out of extraordinary events. In Ronald Reagan's 1984 campaign film, producer Phil Dusenberry presented Reagan's survival of an assassination attempt as a heroic exploit. In a departure from tradition that doubled Reagan's status as a mythic hero, the recuperated president provides his own testimony about the shooting while replayed news footage appeared on screen. In a blatant attempt to appear transformed after the assassination attempt, Reagan asserts his belief, "Whatever time I've got left, it now belongs to someone else," nodding towards heaven as he concludes the sentence.

Candidates' devotion to country is also demonstrated by their public service records. The books and films reiterate the experiences and skills learned in private life that have prepared the candidate to lead. According to Brown (1960, 11), one theme that recurs in biographical books is that "the office seeks the man." This theme remains apparent in political campaign films. Candidates seek office out of responsibility to duty rather than lust for power. Eisenhower, a military war hero asked to run by both parties, fit this figure in the fifties. In 1984, Ronald Reagan echoed the sentiment: "You don't really become president. The presidency is an institution, and you have temporary custody of it."

The resumé films, in particular, illustrate candidates' accomplishments with footage of them at work, whether in the Senate or, if an incumbent, in the White House. Interviews with friends and family members convey candidates' personal attributes, while testimony by established political leaders lend the candidate credibility through association. The narrator frequently recites campaign themes and issues, vividly illustrated with pictures.

Candidates are virtually always associated with past heroes, whether symbolically or actually. The 1980 Carter film opens with symbolic images of presidential heroes: statues of Washington, Jefferson, and Lincoln. The 1972 Nixon election-eve film opens with portraits of past Republican presidents. Bush's 1992 convention film consists almost entirely of pictures and quotations from past presidents. John Kennedy is a particularly popular choice. Barry Goldwater quotes the recently deceased president in 1964, creating a symbolic, if unlikely, association. Both Hubert Humphrey and George McGovern replay old footage where they appear in John Kennedy's company as he commends their achievements. A youthful Bill Clinton shakes hands with Kennedy, in footage that was clearly a coup for the Clinton campaign. Even George Bush cites Kennedy's imagination as a positive attribute for a president in his 1992 convention film.

Candidates often appear "presidential" in documentary footage depicting them meeting with foreign leaders. Nixon's *Ambassador of Friendship* (1960) consisted almost entirely of his trips abroad as spokesperson for the United States, including scenes from his historic meeting with Nikita Khrushchev in the summer of 1959. Both Richard Nixon and Ronald Reagan brought film crews to record their goodwill trips to China during their reelection years. Although they were not officially campaigning, the footage appeared in their campaign films. Footage of then-president Mikhail Gorbachev of the Soviet Union visiting the United States appears in George Bush's 1988 film. Even though there are no shots of Bush and Gorbachev together, his inclusion links the two candidates.

## Personal and Party Images

According to Heale (1982, 170), from the 1830s on, candidates embodied characteristics of the party as their campaign strategists wanted the electorate to perceive them, combined with a presentation of the candidates' personal qualities. These images expressed some aspect of the myth of the American Dream. The myth of the American Dream, central in presidential campaign discourse, articulates the deeply embedded belief that America's purpose and destiny is to achieve liberty, equality, and moral and material prosperity (Fisher 1973, 161–62). Presidential candidates typify different versions of the American Dream by presenting themselves as rugged individuals who shape their own destinies and pursue their own interests, or by presenting themselves as representatives of the common people who must sacrifice themselves to the common good. They are, like George Washington, wise and virtuous leaders whose unique talents enable them to rise above the people, or, like Andrew Jackson, populist men of the people who are merely instruments of their will. Contemporary Democratic and Republican candidates embody the myth of the American Dream that reflects their ideology: they may be leaders above the people, populist men of the people, or attempt to synthesize both qualities.

To some extent, leaders need to show empathy with the common citizen, while populist candidates must demonstrate their capacity to lead, but candidates rarely, if ever, present themselves as solely one or the other. In some instances, Democratic candidates may present themselves as leaders while Republicans may present themselves as populists. The emphasis depends on situational exigencies and party. Democrats, as the former majority party, are frequently men of the people, while Republicans more often image themselves as leaders. Most notably, as the Republican base widened in the seventies and eighties, and candidates learned to use television to be all things to all people, Republican candidates attempted to synthesize both images.

## Images of Country and People

Besides personifying myths about the presidential character, campaign films express candidates' visions, which are myths about the nature of the country and its people. The founding myth of the American Dream elicits hope and optimism in a better future, as well as fear and pessimism that the country's mission will fail. The mythic visions presented in the presidential campaign films follow the pattern of political campaign discourse Nimmo and Combs describe in *Mediated Political Realities*. They write that election campaigns are rituals that enact a drama about an ideal community that has been lost but can be regained, or is yet to be found (1983, 50). The dramas enacted in presidential campaign films fall into two categories: malaise, in which candidates name present problems that they will resolve; and resurgence, in which candidates emphasize all that is right with the country, and promise that if elected, the country will achieve the greatness that is its destiny. Candidates either envision crisis, where collapse is inevitable unless prevailing conditions are remedied, or they envision a country of virtuous citizens, where fulfillment of the American Dream is imminent. In rare cases, such as Barry Goldwater's *Choice* (1964), the entire film is devoted to his vision of a choice between two mythic Americas: one morally degenerate and the other pure and strong.

While there are similarities in the images of the ideal candidate across films, Republican and Democratic candidates tend to stress different visions of the American Dream as they insinuate themselves within the corpus of American mythology. Since the 1960s, Republican candidates have increasingly associated themselves with resurgence, while the Democrats have warned of malaise. Democratic candidates from Hubert Humphrey to Bill Clinton, often in the position of challenging an incumbent, press for change rather than continuity, and thus more often envision malaise. Republican candidates from Barry Goldwater to George Bush have increasingly appropriated the mythic vision of resurgence.

## FORMAL FEATURES OF PRESIDENTIAL CAMPAIGN FILMS

Genres are dynamic as well as static; presidential campaign films change over time, yet both classical and modern films share commonalities of content and a set of formal features and conventions that bind them into a genre and guide viewers' expectations. It is useful to delineate the formal parts of the films without losing sight of their interrelation in an irreducible whole.

### Structure

Bill Nichols, in *Ideology and the Image*, refers to narrative, exposition, and poetic as the three lynchpins of cinema, corresponding to fiction, documentary, and experimental or art films (1981, 70). These categories often overlap; moreover, narrative and exposition share the same underlying structure. The classical campaign films are predominantly expository narratives. They unfold in chronological order, beginning with an initial state of equilibrium where the candidate (or more rarely, the narrator) appears on-screen, to disequilibrium which revolves around the question of the candidate's identity, background, qualifications, and vision of America, to closure as the film, having filled the gaps in the viewer's knowledge with the story of the candidate, brings the viewer up to the present.

Classical presidential campaign films proceed by way of short vignettes which serve as demonstrative proofs of the candidate's life and character. They may include "authentic" still-photographs and archival film footage, or testimony by friends, colleagues, or family. Candidates may give substantive arguments, in the form of segments from earlier speeches or more rarely, they may speak directly into the camera.

These documentary codes signal objectivity and veracity to the majority of viewers. Semiotic signs and codes indicate whether films are perceived as fictional or nonfictional, subjective or objective representations of reality. Presidential campaign films rely primarily upon perceptions of documentary images as representative of historical actuality. They are coded as nonfictional representations of actual people and events, and thus structured by the seemingly impartial frame of documentary that signifies reality to the viewing audience.

As the campaign films evolve, they break away from the strict conventions of narrative-expository films. As the genre transforms from classical documentary to modern hybrid documentary-advertisement, its narrative-expository structure becomes increasingly poetic. Advertising images and strategies structure the modern campaign films. Techniques such as implication, juxtaposition, and association of words, images, and music impress the candidate's virtues upon viewers. Images appear that resonate with American mythology, but bear no logical or actual relation to the candidate. These films incorporate the form as well as function of product advertisements.

The first definitive shift from documentary to hybrid came in both Gerald Ford's and Jimmy Carter's 1976 films; this new hybrid presidential campaign film reached its acme with Ronald Reagan's *A New Beginning* in 1984. The modern films combine the high production values, style, and marketing techniques of television advertisements with "actual" news and documentary footage. Yet, even the latter are psuedo-events, those which exist solely to appeal to an audience. The result blurs the distinctions between fiction and nonfiction, reality and fantasy, as simulations designed to persuade by a complex arrangement of visual, aural, and verbal symbols became framed as reality.

## Narration

Presidential campaign films, rooted in the documentary film tradition, are typically narrated by an off-screen, anonymous, simultaneously reassuring and authoritative male voice which explains and renders the images coherent. The omniscient narrator takes the point of view of the camera, and thus seems to objectively represent reality rather than a single character's point of view. The narrator, in a position of knowledge, becomes the authoritative source of the truth. The discourse often includes linguistic binders such as "you" or "we" that create identification with the members of the viewing audience.

Several campaign films use unidentified though familiar celebrity voices: Jason Robards in Kennedy's *The New Frontier* (1960); Raymond Massey in Goldwater's *Choice* (1964); Richard Basehart in both of Nixon's 1972 films; E. G. Marshall in Carter's *Jimmy Who?*; Gregory Peck in Carter's *This Man, This Office* (1980); and Robert Mitchum in George Bush's 1992 convention film. Joe Garagiola appeared on-camera to introduce Gerald Ford's 1976 election-eve special, a move that signalled a shift from cinematic documentary film to television documentary conventions. Television documentary narrators frequently appear on camera, conveying a sense of liveness and intimacy with viewers. Formerly a professional narrator, Ronald Reagan was the voice behind his own film in 1984. His disembodied voice assumed the omniscience of the narrator, while his on-screen character was imbued with the authority of the presidency. In 1988, both George and Barbara Bush narrated parts of his film, although the traditional anonymous narrator carried most of it. This device maintained perceptions of the narrator's authority, while enabling the Bushs to speak informally and personally to viewers. In the same year, actress Olympia Dukakis became the first female narrator of a presidential campaign film when she narrated her cousin Michael's convention film. Whereas Reagan's double role intensified his imbued authority, Olympia Dukakis's constant on-camera presence diverted attention from the candidate; she reminded viewers of the subjectivity of her point of view and eroded the authority of the anonymous off-screen voice and her cousin the candidate. The most democratic approach to presidential campaign film narration appeared in Bill Clinton's 1992 film, where only the candidate and members of his family told his story, each providing their own point of view on the candidate.

## Testimonials

The use of testimony comes from the tradition of using surrogates to stump for presidential candidates before candidates actively campaigned for themselves. Esteemed political leaders, Cabinet members for incumbents, old friends and colleagues, comrades from military service, celebrities, or family members often appear on-camera to espouse the candidate's virtues. Candidates may also appear on-camera to directly address viewers, in this way offering testimony for themselves.

In 1952, Eisenhower pioneered the use of testimonials by ordinary Americans with a technique borrowed from advertisements. These "people on the street" gave their favorable opinions of the candidate; they appeared to be spontaneous, although generally were prescreened. Often particular representatives of social and economic groups appeared, distinguished by clothes that reflected their occupations or accents that revealed social class.

Construction workers, factory employees, and farmers are typical types who regularly appear in both parties' films—these form the backbone of America; they are the people who make the country work. Women are infrequently located by occupation. Members of ethnic groups or other minorities targeted by campaigns also appear. The point is to get viewers to identify with their on-screen cognates.

## Rhetorical Depictions

Rhetorical depictions are simple, mythic pictures, verbal or nonverbal, that embody common values and goals (Osborn 1986, 79). These resonant images foster identification and create a coherent community of "The People." The images may be original or stock footage. They consist of shots of symbols such as the flag, Statue of Liberty, mountains, rivers, streams, fields, farms, cityscapes. There may be shots of Americans, seemingly unaware of the camera's presence as they go about their business. Sometimes they are borrowed from fiction films, as for example in Richard Nixon's *Ambassador of Friendship* (1960), where shots of "Russian" people reacting to his speech broadcast over Russian television came from a Hollywood movie (see Wyckoff 1968).

Rhetorical depictions provide a handle for assessing the advertising strategies that appear in many campaign films. According to Tony

Schwartz (1974, 24–25), successful ads use familiar visual and aural symbols that resonate with preexisting feelings—they evoke positive or negative experiences that become associated with a product (or candidate). Linguistic, visual, and aural symbols already meaningful to a particular audience provoke an emotional response that can be transferred to the candidate. These "familiar" depictions enable viewers to recognize themselves as members of a community. By using these resonant images, some of which are clichés, stereotypes, and formulas, the political campaign films speak to viewers in familiar ways, and create an illusion of stability. The symbolic images, typical of those used in advertising, occur more frequently in films made from 1976 to the present.

Discussions of "issues" in presidential campaign films serve the same purposes as rhetorical depictions. An analysis of the perennial issues that appear in presidential campaign films supports Murray Edelman's (1988, 12–13) contention that social problems, issues, and crises are not "facts," but constructions provided in specific situations in order to reinforce an ideology. The range of discourse about issues is relatively predictable from campaign to campaign, and what is excluded is as significant as what is included. Specific issues come and go, but statements about the economy, defense, peace, and freedom—all abstract terms without precise meanings—appear in every film. The candidates' positions and the aspects of these terms they address vary across time as much as party. For example, both Nixon and McGovern reproduced images of ghettoes and starving Appalachian children in their 1972 films. In the liberal domestic climate of the 1970s, both candidates advocated social programs and assistance. In 1984, with the conservative Republican revolution firmly in place, there were no images of poverty in the Reagan film. Images of prosperity supplanted those of need. The Republicans constructed one reality while negating another by omission.

Although Edelman concentrates on political news reporting and on linguistic constructions, this analysis of political campaign films extends his work to include analysis of the way that arguments and issues may be presented visually. Not surprisingly, the extent of issue-oriented, substantive argument diminishes as the films become more visual and poetic.

## Stock Footage

Every campaign film uses footage purchased from film libraries, news organizations, or archives to visualize past events or illustrate a point. Stock footage is cheaper than shooting original material and helps to lend authenticity to a claim. *The McGovern Story* (1972), for example, uses stock footage of the depression as the narrator recalls its indelible impression on the candidate. Or Humphrey's *What Manner of Man* (1968) incorporates rare footage of Humphrey leading a walkout at the 1948 convention to remind viewers of Humphrey's commitment to civil rights.

Clips from candidates' speeches often provide substance, although the extended use of speech making decreases as the films become more visually oriented. Footage from conventions, rallies, and incumbents' inaugurations provide condensed renditions of campaign rituals, and shots of past political leaders, preferably with the candidate, lend their credibility. Frequently black-and-white, scratched, and faded archival battle footage, complete with sound effects of artillery and bombs exploding, illustrates the candidate's bravery during war while a fellow soldier, located on-screen in the present, recounts the candidate's heroism. But the generic combat footage may have no relation to the candidate. "Realistic" stock footage accompanying narration serves as an intrinsic sign; it implies a connection that may or may not exist. For instance, Charles Guggenheim's *The McGovern Story* (1972) presents footage of soldiers and Vietnamese people as the narrator describes the candidate's aversion to the war. The narrator states that McGovern witnessed firsthand the horrors and deprivations of the Vietnam War. But the music and images that follow his comment also appear in Guggenheim's earlier film tribute to Robert Kennedy, a transformed presidential campaign film that won an Oscar for Best Documentary in 1968.

## Original Film vs. Video Footage

Presidential campaign films usually combine some original shooting with stock footage from news or government file footage. The amount of original footage shot, typically the most expensive part of production, depends on the campaign budget. Original footage may consist of scenes of the candidates at home or work, interviews, testimonials from people on the street, or the candidate's direct, on-camera address to viewers. Sometimes "natural" events are arranged for the cameras, as when the Humphreys and Muskies go bowling in the presidential lanes, or Ronald Reagan spends time on his ranch, "chopping" wood with a jigsaw.

The classical films, in black and white until 1968, were typically made on grainy, inexpensive 16mm film characteristic of documentaries. Beginning in 1976, many presidential campaign films either combined 16mm film and video, or used videotape exclusively. Both have different qualities and aesthetics. Video is far more mobile, easily edited, and conveys a sense of immediacy. Film, more expensive by far, has a deeper, richer quality and is preferred by most filmmakers. In 1984, 1988, and 1992, the Republicans indicated their commitment to high-quality, high-production value films by eschewing both 16mm film and videotape in favor of professional quality 35mm film—the kind used in advertisements and feature films. The 1984 Reagan campaign film-makers, widely regarded as having raised the presidential campaign film to new aesthetic levels, shot original 35mm film footage of "morning in America": sunrise, people raising flags, going to work, attending pic-nics, moving house. The resulting lush, high-quality images and camera-work portrayed a unified, consistent vision of America and Americans. George Bush emulated this style in 1988, while Bill Clinton appropriated positive images of America with footage of his cross-country bus tour in 1992. Before Clinton, the less well-endowed Democratic candidates typically did not put such effort into their campaign films.

## Music

Orchestral music is commonly used in political campaign films as background to create emotion. This music, readily available from music libraries, is what people are accustomed to hearing in documentary and fiction films. *Jimmy Who?* (1976) innovated the use of rock music featuring guitar and drums, while both candidates in 1976 incorporated original songs into their films. Ronald Reagan's 1984 film included the music video of a popular country song, Lee Greenwood's "God Bless the USA." The filmmakers also hired an orchestra to play an original score composed for the film, as did the makers of Bush's 1988 film. The Reagan and Bush films were also cut to music, creating a rhythm of sound and picture that was not determined by the narrator's words, as was the case with the classical documentaries.

## Special Effects

Special effects are infrequently used in campaign films, for most want to maintain the "documentary" look and feel. Freeze frames before titles or at the conclusion of films are most common. One notable exception is *Jimmy Who?*, which made use of animation, superimpositions, graphic displays, and video outlines of images. No candidates after Carter used such gimmickry, and even Carter returned to conventional techniques in 1980. Some films make subtle use of special effects. In Reagan's 1980 biography film, the candidate was tinted blue to stand out in black-and-white still-photographs. This effect was not obvious at first glance.

## ORGANIZATION OF CHAPTERS

Presidential campaign films instruct us about the ways political communication both maintains and transforms itself over time. This visual form enables us to explore the interaction of verbal, audiovisual, and production codes in the construction of the political image, and helps us to decode the ways candidates use television to project images of self, country, and people. Presidential campaign films speak volumes about the themes and issues that drive a campaign, and the cultural milieu in which it is conducted. In a larger sense, they illustrate the ways that the wider matrix of a society's image of itself is created and maintained through discourse.

Presidential campaign films emerge out of several discursive traditions: campaign oratory, biographical books, newsreels, documentaries, and advertisements. I begin in Chapter 1 by exploring their roots and relating the films to a developing tradition of political discourse.

Next, I trace the evolution of the presidential campaign film from classical documentary to the modern hybrid documentary-advertisement. This transformation reflects technological developments, the symbiotic union of television and politics, and the shifting power struggles between political operatives, advertising experts, and media consultants. Chapters 2, 3, and 4 address the evolving narrative-expository forms, and Chapters 5 and 6 discuss the modern hybrid documentary-advertisement characteristic of modern merchandising campaigns.

Finally, Chapter 7 addresses changes in the 1992 presidential campaign films, in the context of the Democrats' attempt to reappropriate Republican territory by distancing themselves from the vision of crisis that permeated past liberal discourse.

This study shows the way politics has merged with entertainment in contemporary American culture; in order to accomplish this task, it is itself a merger of film and television studies, politics, rhetorical criticism, and cultural analysis. In the end, I can only hope that my method and my subject prove illuminating, and that this study provides an edifying contribution to our knowledge and understanding of mediated political campaign communication.

# I

## THE CLASSICAL FORM: THE EXPOSITORY PRESIDENTIAL CAMPAIGN FILM

# Chapter 1 _____

# Discursive Threads of
# the Presidential
# Campaign Film

Presidential campaign films consist of diverse, interconnecting, and overlapping modes of discourse. The films are technological adaptations of political communication that incorporate earlier campaign forms and practices. Signs and symbols of the live campaign pervade the films, as do the oral traditions of campaign discourse. They are visual versions of the literary biographies that created favorable images of candidates as early as 1824. The genre initially developed from the documentary film and its subgenre, the newsreel, but as campaign films evolved, they came to share characteristics with the commercial advertisements that first appeared on radio and television. In recent years, the films have taken on a shape that is specifically televisual, designed to dazzle and entertain with state-of-the-art techniques. The hybrid documentary-advertisements exemplify the shifting form and content of contemporary political persuasion in a visual culture.

All of the discursive threads that shape presidential campaign films share a common ancestry in propaganda. Broadly defined, propaganda promotes a particular cause or viewpoint by appealing to popular sentiment; it relies upon devices such as simplification, repetition, verbal and visual symbolism to achieve emotive mass persuasion. Ellul (1973) distinguishes between integrative and agitative propaganda: simply put, integrative propaganda evokes culturally conditioned reflexes and myths to explain and justify prevailing cultural values, while agitative propaganda aims to arouse action. The presidential campaign films demonstrate the ways that candidates use integrative propaganda to draw voters in to their platforms before agitatating them to vote against their opponents. The films unify propagandistic image-making traditions of the presidential campaign, the documentary film, and the advertising and public relations fields. Throughout American history, successful presidential candidates have harnessed available communicative forms, whether oratory, spectacle, print, radio, film, or television, to manipulate public attitudes and opinions. These forms and strategies coalesce in the presidential campaign film.

## PROPAGANDISTIC TRADITIONS OF THE PRESIDENTIAL CAMPAIGN: ORATORY AND ADVOCACY

Presidential campaign films have more in common with older American presidential campaign traditions than is commonly supposed. The films often present the character and qualifications of a candidate while avoiding substantive argument or serious discussion of important issues. But throughout much of American political history, presidential candidates were mute tribunes who did not publicly espouse their positions. They eschewed the appearance of actively seeking office. Common wisdom held that the office sought the man; it was undignified for the man to seek the office.

George Washington set the precedent for the mute tribune. He did not seek the office of the presidency, but he dutifully accepted the position when he was called to serve. In the context of a newly formed government founded upon opposition to monarchy and fear of individual power, self-serving and ambitious persons were not considered presidential material; therefore, aspirants made no overt appeals on their own behalf. They did not make speeches or openly solicit votes. They had no need to communicate directly with the people, for in the early years of the republic, electors rather than voting majorities determined candidates.

Yet, despite presidential hopefuls' official postures of indifference, rudimentary campaigning began as early as 1800. When George Washington refused a third term, propaganda in favor of Thomas Jefferson or John Adams abounded. As mute tribunes, Jefferson and Adams did not publicly indicate their desire for the office. But their supporters held rallies, published newspaper articles, and distributed handbills, broadsides, and pamphlets to encourage voters to select presidential electors favorable to one candidate or the other (Jamieson 1984, 5).

Campaigns began to deliberately craft candidates' images in the 1820s, not coincidentally at a time when personal attributes, rather than party, were all that distinguished viable candidates from one another, and reforms that democratized the presidential election process increased candidates' need for popular support. The 1824 election signalled a shift in presidential campaign practices, as the need to court public opinion exacerbated image-making activities on behalf of presidential candidates. Several potential candidates belonged to the same Democratic-Republican party: John Quincy Adams, Andrew Jackson, Henry Clay, John T. Calhoun, and Daniel Webster. For the first time, a presidential aspirant communicated with voters, although in a limited and indirect fashion. Andrew Jackson broke from the tradition of the mute tribune by stating his views in an ostensibly private letter written to a friend, which was subsequently published. Such letters became rote in later presidential campaigns.

The candidates generally maintained low profiles, although they and their supporters attempted to curry favor with local and state leaders. Supporters of particular candidates held local meetings and organized small-scale rallies in the hope of galvanizing popular opinion. Propaganda devices appeared, such as brass campaign buttons depicting Andrew Jackson. Partisan newspapers printed favorable articles, while volunteers distributed torrents of pamphlets, broadsides, and convention addresses.

Esteemed political leaders delivered public speeches to garner popular support for their candidate. In the absence of party as a distinguishing factor, advocates stressed their candidate's personal characteristics. Supporters of John Quincy Adams, Henry Clay, and Andrew Jackson spoke in their own and nearby states, making this the first limited mass-campaign (Trent and Friedenberg, 1983, 77). Surrogates live on in the presidential campaign film, where testimonial interviews with colleagues and important political figures establish a candidate's character and credentials.

Most importantly, the campaign biography first appeared in 1822 in the form of a serialized memoir of candidate John C. Calhoun published in the *Philadelphia Franklin Gazette*. The following year, the *Colombian Observer* of Philadelphia published a series of letters describing Andrew Jackson's character. Jackson's friend and supporter John H. Eaton wrote these under the pseudonym "Wyoming," and they were later published as a 104-page book. Other portraits of Jackson were also published, as was a biographical sketch of John Quincy Adams (Heale 1982, 51).

Both Calhoun's and Adams's biographies presented them as statesmen whose leadership abilities elevated them above the common person. But Jackson's promoters appealed to popular audiences by portraying him in dramatic terms as a heroic man of the people whose opposition to corrupt Washington powers would save the nation. According to Heale, the Jackson image-making campaign had a profound effect on later political culture (1982, 53). Many presidential campaign films still evoke the scenario portrayed by the Jacksonian images of the president and the country.

The manipulation of candidates' images intensified in 1828, when challenger Andrew Jackson opposed incumbent John Quincy Adams. Booklength biographies of candidates were integral to this campaign. Twenty-four biographies were written for presidential candidates, including anti-biographies written to disparage opponents. These books crafted images designed to secure or discourage support of candidates; they were persuasive propaganda rather than unmotivated accounts. Jackson's biography described him as "The Modern Cincinnatus," both a soldier who had served in two wars and a farmer who worked his own land. Adams' supporters, however, rightfully complained that Jackson was only thirteen years old at the time his biography purported that he fought in the first Indian war; moreover, he was a plantation owner and slaveholder who never farmed his own land, despite the books' suggestions to the contrary (Jamieson 1984, 6).

This election marked the first time that a campaign organization was formed to plan an image-making strategy for a candidate. Amos Kendall, a former newspaper editor, was Jackson's media man who shaped campaign plans, arranged for the production and distribution of campaign materials, and founded a partisan newspaper, the *Washington Globe*, as a vehicle to articulate Jackson's policies. Jackson stayed on his farm and made few public appearances, although he did attend two ostensibly nonpolitical ceremonial events where he covertly indicated his willingness to serve the country (Heale 1982, 73).

Organized political parties were just beginning to take shape, and local and state conventions met to affirm their support for candidates. Correspondence committees for both Jackson and Adams foisted an unprecedented barrage of print material upon the public: leaflets, pamphlets, broadsides, handbills, cartoons, and convention addresses. Both Adams's and Jackson's campaign managers organized political celebrations, highlighted with music, military salutes, or public dinners. Jackson's supporters carried his portrait in public processions and waved hickory branches as a symbol of his nickname, "Old Hickory," while Adams's advocates waved oak branches in his processions. Homemade and manufactured paraphenalia proliferated; both campaigns produced buttons, badges, snuff boxes, cloth ribbons, bandanas, glasses, cups, and ceramic pitchers and plates to sway public opinion in favor of Adams or Jackson (Fischer 1988, 1). Influencing popular sentiment was important, for this election marked the first time that people in a majority of states voted for electors who were publicly committed to particular candidates. The new practices prompted John Quincy Adams to remark, "Here is a revolution in the thoughts and habits and manners of the people. Electioneering for the Presidency has spread its contagion to the President himself. . . . Where will it end?"

Torchlight parades began with Jackson's 1832 reelection campaign (Schram 1987, 65). People marched in evening processions, carrying torches attached to the top of hickory branches as patriotic symbols. The entertaining spectacle merged with presidential politics. These events were a useful means to attract the illiterate voters who formed one-third to one-half of the voting population. As with later televisual campaign films, campaigns created images and impressions in the hopes of swaying voters.

Candidates broke further away from the mute tribune tradition during the 1840 contest between Democrat Martin Van Buren and Whig candidate William Henry Harrison. Martin Van Buren published a series of public letters, the first president to make public statements while seeking reelection. But the conservative Whig party, linked to wealthy aristocrats and supporters of John Quincy Adams, illustrated the burgeoning use of image advertising and made extensive innovations in the presidential campaign.

Harrison delivered the first campaign speeches used by a candidate for self-promotion when he took to the stump in 1836 to indirectly refute charges that he was too old and ailing to be president. Harrison's precampaign tour was a harbinger of the artfully arranged pseudo-event in presidential politics. Harrison travelled through Pennsylvania, New Jersey, Maryland, and Ohio and delivered ostensibly apolitical speeches on the glory of America's past. At each stop, a committee arranged for him to be greeted by "welcoming citizens on horseback, carriage processions, brass bands, bonfires, torchlights, clanging church bells, booming cannons, young ladies with flowers" (Jamieson 1984, 13). This carefully designed display engendered popular support for the candidate, who did not publicly acknowledge that he was campaigning.

Harrison's effort is often referred to as the first major image campaign. His managers almost completely invented his biography by associating him with personal symbols of the common man, such as the log cabin and hard cider. Yet Harrison was born in a two-story brick house in Virginia, and lived on a 2000 acre estate. They also portrayed him as a national hero and prolific Indian fighter, assigning him the nickname "Old Tippecanoe." The retired army general once staved off a Shawnee attack in Tippecanoe, but it took place twenty-nine years before, and he lost more men than the Indians did (Jamieson 1984, 11).

The Whigs also orchestrated the first national campaign by sending surrogate speakers for Harrison to twenty-six states. They organized days-long mass political spectacles consisting of up to 100,000 people, animated by fireworks, live animals, and street parades for the candidate. People rolled giant balls bearing campaign slogans from city to city. Men wearing raccoon-skin caps pulled floats with life-size log cabins on them, complete with smoke emanating from the chimneys. Miniature log cabins, cider barrels, and paraphernalia such as bandanas, handkerchiefs, satin ribbons, hand mirrors, shaving soaps, and knives bearing Harrison's image or name were distributed at rallies, along with barrels of hard cider. Campaign songs celebrated his humble origins or repeated catchy campaign slogans (Heale 1982, 106–7).

After Harrison's victory, the Whig party candidates continued to campaign on their own behalf, whether speaking, writing letters for public dissemination, or organizing entertainment. The Whigs, out of power after Harrison, had little to lose by taking risks. From 1840 until 1932, active campaigning was done primarily by candidates belonging to the party out of power. Similarly, Democrat Stephen Douglas overtly broke the taboo against campaigning by travelling throughout the North in 1860, although his Republican opponent, Abraham Lincoln, made no campaign speeches. After Douglas's failed presidential bid and the long-term entrenchment of the Republican party, Democratic candidates strove to get themselves elected by unorthodox means. William Jennings Bryan initiated the whistlestop campaign tour in 1896 by travelling around the country and giving speeches from the rear platform of the observation car of a train. He visited twenty-one states, gave 600 speeches, and was seen by 5 million people during the 1896 campaign (Trent and Friedenberg 1983, 77). Bryan was the first presidential candidate to openly discuss issues in public.

Bryan also broke the tradition that aspiring candidates stay away from the national convention lest they seem too eager. He spoke at the 1896 Democratic convention; his much renowned "Cross of Gold" speech brought the crowd into a frenzy and resulted in his nomination on the fifth ballot. Just as critics today sometimes worry that alluring images may supersede logic, Bryan prompted a *New York Times* comment that his speech proved "oratory is more potent than reason" (Weisbord 1964, 76).

Republicans James Buchanan, in 1856, James A. Garfield, in 1880, and Benjamin Harrison, in 1888 ran "Front Porch" campaigns; William McKinley popularized this form in 1896 (*We the People* 1975, 40). In such a campaign, surrogates toured the country, while the candidates provided rehearsed speeches from the front porches of their homes to invited delegates. These occasions were examples of pseudo-events that enabled candidates to be "above politics" in the mute tribune tradition, and more importantly, to minimize the possibility of errors.

McKinley's campaign manager, Mark Hanna, masterminded a modern-style propaganda campaign; he recruited as many as 20,000 visitors in one day for McKinley to greet from his front porch. Hanna assembled delegations from a range of demographic groups, in many cases paying their train fare with money from campaign contributions. Some wore costumes and marched to the house in a parade, accompanied by a marching band. Hanna asked the visiting chairman of each delegation to prepare a speech, which he showed to McKinley in advance. McKinley would then make revisions and design appropriate responses. McKinley made up to twelve speeches in one day, each directed to a concern of a particular delegation; copies appeared in major newspapers (Weisbord 1964, 75–76).

Hanna channeled all campaign messages to state and local committees through a central office, and he ran crude opinion polls to determine public attitudes. In regions where McKinley's support was weak, he sent a slew of speakers and flooded the area with campaign literature. McKinley's symbol was the American flag, shown on campaign buttons and waved in parades, thus affirmatively associating him with patriotism. In an early critique of this style of political marketing, Theodore Roosevelt complained that Hanna was selling McKinley "like a patent medicine" (Thum and Thum 1972, 108). In the early twentieth century, patent medicine salespersons were known for their slick and often deceptive practices.

Although its vestiges remain, the military model of campaigns initially began to disintegrate when Republican William McKinley's decisive victories over Populist Democrat William Jennings Bryan in 1896 and 1900 realigned voters along North-South lines. Presidential elections were no longer competitive within local communities, so that mustering the troops served little purpose. At the same time, the Populists and then the Progressives initiated election reforms by advocating direct primary elections for political candidates. The reforms debilitated the power of the largely urban political bosses who hand-picked candidates in proverbial smoke-filled rooms, and who provided patronage and, in some cases, protection in exchange for voters' support. By 1917, all but four states had implemented the primary system for state candidates. As a result, parties weakened and partisanship declined.

Social, cultural, and economic changes also contributed to the changing landscape of American political culture throughout the twentieth century. Whereas in the nineteenth century, political parties served as social organizations in between elections, the mass media became vehicles for propaganda that subsumed the political parties' entertainment functions and replaced the political spectacles of the nineteenth century. The advent of film in 1895 and the growth of newspapers and popular magazines created mass audiences. Candidates utilized modern media technologies to reach audiences newly susceptible to mass propaganda. One of the earliest technologies was the documentary film.

## PROPAGANDA AND DOCUMENTARY FILM TRADITIONS

Initially, presidential campaign films were structured according to documentary and newsreel conventions. The documentary originated in France in 1895, when the Lumière brothers developed the cinématographe, a lightweight, portable camera that they used to photograph people engaged in everyday activities. Their films, called *actualities*, represented real events as they occurred. The films were one minute long, the length of a film reel, and they unfolded in one continuous take.

The Lumières trained a cadre of camera operators, who travelled around the world photographing events that were shown to patrons in French theatres. These quickly supplanted the actualities of mundane, everyday events. By 1896, cinématographe operators were fueling the public's appetite for footage of luminaries, public occasions, and foreign places, filming events such as the French Congress, a bullfight in Madrid, the Coronation of Czar Nicholas II in Russia, and the presidential campaign of William McKinley.

Grover Cleveland was the first president to appear on film; he attended William McKinley's inauguration in 1897 and was photographed moments before McKinley was sworn in as the new president (Fielding 1972, 32–33). But Theodore Roosevelt was the first to understand film's propagandistic appeal. Already in 1898, newsreel companies were bringing images of the Spanish-American War to the American people, creating patriotic and nationalistic sentiment. Roosevelt resigned his position as secretary of the navy and joined the first U.S. Volunteer Cavalry, second-in-command to the unit referred to as the Rough Riders.

Roosevelt invited two cameramen from the Vitagraph Newsreel Company to accompany the group to Cuba. During the march up San Juan Hill, Roosevelt halted to pose for the film cameras.

But from the very beginning, the supposed transparency of documentary was tainted by more than preening for the cameras. Many filmmakers believed that documentaries provided impartial reports on significant world events and human interest stories. Documentaries were rooted in the scientific tradition of logical exposition; they presupposed an "actual, photographable, and unfabricated nature as the background against which men inevitably act and from which, in the ethnological sense, men just as inevitably draw some of the meaning of their acts" (Tyler 1971, 271). This presupposition that the camera can render reality without altering it exists to this day. Audiences typically regard documentaries as authentic representations of reality in a way that fiction films are not.

Yet, not only are subjects affected by the presence of the cameras, but subject selection, camera angle, shot composition, and editing style are some of the factors that communicate the filmmaker's point of view rather than the raw material of reality. Even the Lumières' cinématographe operators became unwitting purveyors of government propaganda by accepting official sponsorship in order to gain access to ceremonial functions (Barnouw 1979, 19). Even when outright deception was not involved, filmmakers often "reconstituted" events for dramatic and narrative purposes. During the Spanish-American War, Vitagraph filmmaker Albert J. Smith constructed the visually boring battle scene at Santiago Bay in his bathtub so that it would look more exciting. Fraudulent news films were endemic to early documentary, and about 50% of the later newsreels were made up of "manufactured" news events (Fielding 1971, 32–33).

Documentaries underwent a transformation when Charles Pathè introduced the newsreel in 1910. The newsreel was a weekly or biweekly magazine of news events, in contrast to the brief single subject actuality film. The newsreel had a predictable format, based on a combination of actuality film topics: a royal visit, military maneuver, sports event, funny story, natural disaster, or native festival with people in costume (Barnouw 1979, 26). Parades, conventions, speeches, inaugurations, foreign places, visits from foreign leaders, and other ceremonial events characteristic of newsreels also became incorporated into presidential campaign films.

Although newsreels proliferated after 1910, filmmakers continued to make documentaries. The first presidential campaign film longer than a minute was *The Life of Calvin Coolidge*, a sixteen-minute film produced by William Fox for the Republican candidate in 1923. The silent film with intertitles provided a bridge between the literary biographies and later sound films. Still-photographs, stock footage, and some on-location shots described Coolidge's birthplace, farming background, home in Northhampton, Massachusetts, family life, election as governor of Massachusetts, selection as vice-president, and his role as commander-in-chief of the army and navy. His wife, described by the text as an expert knitter, sits clicking her needles in a sequence where the hand-cranked camera speeds up to amplify her talents.

Republican candidate Herbert Hoover also had two silent campaign films in 1928: *Upbuilding with Prosperity*, a biographical film produced by H. S. Kimberly, and *Master of Emergencies*, an hour long resumé film produced by the Brown brothers. These early films were projected from the back of trucks in small, rural towns cut off from media. They simultaneously provided entertainment and instruction, and often a live orator followed their presentation. The Brown brothers updated *Master of Emergencies* for the 1932 election, principally by converting it to sound. However, they got into a dispute with the Republican National Committee over distribution rights, and proceeded to destroy all copies of the revised film. There are no known prints of the 1932 version in existence.

Woodrow Wilson began governmental use of motion pictures for propaganda purposes, although he was not personally successful at manipulating the media (Schram 1987, 73–74). Although candidates Coolidge and Hoover had campaign films, once installed in office they made little use of film to promote their programs. Hoover did, however, pressure the newsreel companies into remaining silent about the depression. He persuaded them that undermining confidence was a public disservice, and that optimism was a sign of statesmanship (Barnouw 1979, 111). The newsreel companies complied and avoided mention of the depression and other controversial issues, continuing to do so through the 1930s.

After Franklin Delano Roosevelt was elected in 1932, he perceived the value of using film and newsreels as active propaganda for his policies. Newsreel films showed him as a warm, humane, sympathetic figure, in contrast to the cold and distant Hoover. He appeared in scenes arranged by his top two advisors, both of whom were ex-newsreel company executives. Roosevelt's famous fireside chats were filmed and distributed to theatres, in addition to being played on the radio. *The Fighting President*, an unreleased film made in 1933, followed the structure of a campaign film, though it was not used for this purpose. The film footage was typical of campaign films, with depictions of his parents, early childhood, college years, start in politics, the precedent-setting attendance at his acceptance address at the 1932 convention, his first term inauguration, war footage, and of his family.

In the 1936 campaign, the Progressive National Committee sponsored a twenty-eight-minute campaign film, produced by Albert Hubschman. Universal Pictures produced campaign "newsreels" for both Alf Landon and Roosevelt, titled *With the Landons* and *With the Roosevelts*. Both films showed the personal sides of the candidates.

Roosevelt continued to use film throughout his presidency to advocate his policies. He ingratiated himself with the newsreel companies by asking several of them to bid on a contract to produce a series of thirty films on the success of his Works Progress Administration program. Pathè won and agreed to distribute one free film to each contracted theatre as part of the newsreel programming. The Republicans protested that this was an unfair use of federal funds, and the project was disbanded after this one series. But the resettlement administration, an agency whose purpose was to help relocate drought-ridden farmers living in the midwestern dust bowl, decided to publicize their programs through film. Pare Lorenz, a film critic turned filmmaker, convinced the agency that they needed a new kind of dramatic/informational/persuasive movie, what he termed "films of merit" (Ellis 1989, 82). Lorenz made two films: *The Plow that Broke the Plains* (1936) and *The River* (1937). Both are notable for their combination of images, words, and music. Virgil Thomson, a professional composer, wrote the score for each, and the music stands alone as an orchestral suite. The images are dramatic and emotionally riveting as they detail the horrors of rural poverty. *The River*, in particular, is considered a masterpiece. Lorenz's films directly influenced later presidential campaign films; for instance, Charles Guggenheim's biography of George McGovern uses images from *The Plow that Broke the Plains* as stock footage to illustrate the ravages of the depression in the Midwest.

*The Presidential Campaign of Wendell Wilkie*, distributed by Hearst-Metrotone News in 1940, consisted of newsreel footage of important Wilkie speeches, rallies, and parades edited together. From 1948 until the late 1960s, when they went out of business, newsreels produced during presidential campaigns described the life and times of the major candidates. These were presented as public service announcements by the motion picture industry. Universal Pictures, representing the newsreel companies, produced biographies of Truman, Dewey, Eisenhower,

Stevenson, Nixon, Kennedy, Goldwater, and Johnson. *The Dewey Story* was a theatrical newsreel that contained some reenacted events along with assembled footage of the candidate. The other films, all produced later, consisted largely of stock footage.

In an infamous incident described by Jack Redding, then director of public relations for the Democratic party, Louis deRochemont, producer of *The March of Time* series, made the newsreel for Republican candidate Thomas Dewey in 1948. Dewey was favored by the corporate executives in the film industry. Like *The March of Time* films, *The Dewey Story* used enactments. For example, paid actors dressed up as gangsters in a scene that illustrated Dewey's success at controlling crime in New York City. The film cost $35,000 to produce, and the Republican National Committee bought 900 copies at $35 per print. They planned to release the film through the newsreel companies and distribute it to theatres across the country in the two weeks prior to the election. There were 20,000 theatres in the country, with a weekly audience of around 65 million people of all political persuasions, who could not help but see the film. Redding feared the impact of the Dewey film in an election that Truman was supposed to lose anyway. He threatened the theatre owners with picket lines and warned the newsreel companies that unless they made a film for Truman, the Democratic Congress would hold hearings to investigate how arrangements were made to distribute the Dewey film (Jamieson 1984, 33).

With little time remaining in the campaign, the motion picture industry executives, represented by Universal Pictures, succumbed to the pressure. They produced and distributed *The Truman Story*. They showed the ten-minute special feature during the last week of the campaign, after the Dewey film was already shown. Out of necessity, they assembled the film entirely from stock footage that showed the incumbent president in office, meeting world leaders, and acting "presidential." They intercut World War I footage with a 1918 picture of Captain Truman, field artillery in the Allied Expeditionary Force (AEF), thus establishing the candidate's patriotism and linking him to history. When the completed film played in the theatres during the last week of the campaign, the audience saw what appeared to be a factual rather than theatrical newsreel. Whether their perceptions of this film as objective, authentic, and thus "true" accounted for Truman's surprise victory over Dewey is questionable, but Redding wrote, "During the last 6 days of the campaign, no one could go to the movies anywhere without seeing the story of the president. It was probably the most important, most successful publicity break in the entire campaign. The motion picture industry, to this day, is convinced that their film elected Harry S. Truman, President" (Redding 1958, 254).

*The Dewey Story*, sponsored by the Republican National Committee, aired locally on one NBC affiliated television station in New York on 31 October. It was the first campaign film ever to be televised, although it played to an extremely limited audience because so few people owned television sets.

Presidential campaign films after *The Dewey Story* still shared some characteristics with *The March of Time* series produced by Louis deRochemont from 1935 to 1951. *The March of Time* was a cross between the traditional newsreel and the feature-length documentary film. Unlike the newsreels, *The March of Time* dealt with controversial subjects and was overtly partisan. The films typically addressed only one topic in a twenty-minute episode. They used maps, charts, diagrams, and titles as supporting materials. Dramatizations and re-creations appeared quite liberally. Even when actual footage was available, the filmmakers preferred reenactments if they better clarified the narrative. Henry Luce, one of the series' founders, referred to it as "fakery in allegiance to the truth" (Elson 1971, 108).

*The March of Time* is best known for the authoritative voice of its narrator, Westbrook Van Voorhis. His sonorous voice was the inspiration for the term *Voice of God* to describe the omniscient, disembodied narrator who explains events in documentary films. The films used mostly stock footage, heavy-handed, obvious music, and few sound effects. The narrator's words rendered sounds and images coherent, so both music and pictures were cut to illustrate the words. Presidential campaign films also employ graphics, use archival music, combine staged and stock footage, and use anonymous Voice of God narration. Films from the classical period are more likely to give precedence to words over images. Both *The March of Time* and presidential campaign films also have an obvious propagandistic intent.

Even when presidential campaign films were made for television in their classical period from 1960–1972, they retained the conventions of film documentary. Many of the early films were designed for armies of the faithful organized in small settings. Kennedy's *The New Frontier* (1960) and Nixon's *Ambassador of Friendship* (1960) were never aired on national television; Barry Goldwater's *Choice* (1964), while withdrawn by Goldwater himself, played to avid audiences in rented theatres and even storefronts and drive-in theatres across the country. Producer David Wolper made three versions of *The Nixon Years: Change Without Chaos*, two for television and one for local party organizations. These films still presupposed a military model of political campaigns, where it was important to motivate loyal followers who would volunteer for the campaign, or to provide political leaders with information to disseminate about a candidate's program.

A final mode of documentary deserves mention: the poetic documentary. This film emerges out of art rather than science; it aims at representing aesthetic patterns and subjective truths (Ellis 1989, 47). *Manahatta*, an abstract depiction of New York City produced in 1921, was one of the first poetic documentaries. The film made no reference to specific people or places; Lewis Jacobs succinctly describes its style:

Carefully composed angle shots, foreshortened viewpoints, patterns of mass and line, the contrast of sun and shadow defining pyramid like office buildings stretching upward into space . . . silvery smoke rising in plumes to drift across filter dimmed skies; a ferryboat scudding out of a dazzling nay onto a darkened pier; a sudden swarm of commuters radiating into sun-drenched streets in a climax of flowing movement and myriad rhythms (1971, 6).

Although it took many years, the political campaign films of the modern period, from 1976–1988, incorporated many of these stylized and symbolic techniques. They began to convey a feeling, an ambiance, perhaps more so than factual, substantive, historical information about candidates and their ideas. This shift came about through the influence of soft-sell or deep-sell advertising, which has more in common with poetic documentary than other documentary modes.

## THE INFLUENCE OF ADVERTISING
## AND PUBLIC RELATIONS

The contemporary presidential campaign film exemplifies the increasing prevalence of advertising and public relations techniques in electoral politics. Often, campaign films are not differentiated from campaign advertising. Like advertisements, campaign films are one-sided, selective messages about candidates, typically paid for by campaign organizations. But they illustrate the development of political communication throughout the twentieth century. They shift from propagandistic documentaries that function as advertisements, to hybrid documentary-advertisements that share the form and function of advertisements. They also demonstrate the public relations experts' ability to "create" news events, either by incorporating such pseudo-events as scenes within the films, or through publicity proclaiming that the films are themselves "news events."

Both advertising and public relations assumed their modern forms at the turn of the century, developing in response to the needs of business and industry. With factories producing at optimal levels, manufacturers hired advertisers to extoll the virtues of still-unfamiliar manufactured products in the print media. The political use of advertising techniques soon followed. Albert Lasker, one of the early advertising gurus, did publicity for the Republican party, and later supervised publicity and speech writing for Warren G. Harding. As early as 1916, both Democrats and Republicans hired agencies to place advertisements in popular magazines. The Batten Agency worked for Republican Charles E. Hughes, who won in areas where he advertised heavily. Hughes's success prompted *Printer's Ink* magazine to proclaim, "The advertising method has made gains, and greater gains are still to come" (Fox 1985, 306–7). The following year, Congress considered regulations on political advertising for the first time.

From 1920 on, both parties regularly hired advertising experts for presidential campaigns, and the winners were generally those who spent the most on advertising (O'Shaughnessy 1990, 26). In 1926, Calvin Coolidge expressed an almost religious faith in advertising in a speech directed to members of the new profession: "Advertising ministers to the spiritual side of trade. It is a great power that has been entrusted to your keeping which charges you with the highest responsibility of inspiring and ennobling the commerce of the world. It is a part of the greater work of the regeneration and redemption of mankind" (Bush 1991, 3).

When the Great Depression (1919–1929) threatened consumers' faith in commerce, advertisers resorted to new tactics. Early product advertisements used hard-sell persuasion, associating a product with characteristics that gave people reasons to buy; during the depression, products began to symbolize values. Connotation, metaphor, inference, and suggestion were devices that sold products. Advertising agencies hired psychologists, such as behaviorist John B. Watson who worked for the J. Walter Thompson Agency. Watson believed that effective ads evoked basic emotions, declaring, "To make your consumer react it is only necessary to confront him with either fundamental or conditioned emotional stimuli" (Fox 1985, 85). In order to do so, J. Walter Thompson revived the consumer testimonial, an often deceptive ploy used in patent medicine scams in the nineteenth century. They made one innovation, using celebrity endorsements as testimonials. According to J. Walter Thompson president Stanley Resor, these relied upon irrational drives. "The spirit of emulation" Stanley Resor called it. "We want to copy those we deem superior in taste or knowledge or experience" (Fox 1985, 90).

By 1930, the journal *Advertising Age* remarked that a presidential campaign was largely an advertising campaign. Madison Avenue became a campaign issue in 1940 when Democrats protested because a cadre of advertisers and businessmen supported Republican Wendell Wilkie. Yet, both Republican and Democratic candidates were charged with surrendering to Madison Avenue in 1944. The Republicans hired Batten, Barton, Durstine, and Osborne (BBD&O) in what would become a long-standing alliance, while the Democrats hired the less prestigious Warwick and Legler.

From the postwar period to the mid-sixties, presidential candidates became increasingly dependent upon the techniques used in commercial advertising. Advertisements began to focus on the consumer rather than product, a development related to motivational research. Motivational researchers assumed that people were driven more by unconscious motives than by rational thought. Advertisers began to give their products deeper appeal by using soft-sell techniques such as association, fantasy, music, aesthetic imagery, and emotive appeals that became part of a product's meaning. A product's image became "a total set of attitudes, a halo of psychological meanings, associations of feeling, and aesthetic messages over a product's physical qualities" (Martineau 1957, 146). Products became symbols that satisfied people's inner yearnings and desires; product attributes were linked to existing beliefs, values, and desires to strike a "responsive chord" (Schwartz 1974).

Presidential candidates began to adopt these techniques after their establishment in the business world. Their most famous application was with Tony Schwartz's 1964 ads for Lyndon Johnson. Through the 1960s, product ads moved from hard sell to soft sell, as did political commercials. Presidential campaign films, too, initially structured as hard-sell documentaries, gradually incorporated soft-sell techniques. The more contemporary films shifted to the phase of advertising which began in the commercial world in the late sixties. These advertisements made products representative of lifestyle, and they reflected developments in market research, such as VALS—value and lifestyle survey—and more sophisticated computer technologies that located groups of consumers. Political campaigns, too, began to target groups of voters and to design appeals for particular constituencies. The Republicans, more so than the Democrats, embraced these marketing and research techniques and applied them in their campaign films.

Modern campaign films, notably those produced for Republican candidates since 1976, integrate public relations skills with advertising techniques. Like advertising, public relations played an important role in presidential campaigns from the early twentieth century. As industry expanded and rural opportunities declined in the early years of the twentieth century, public reaction turned against business. Popular magazines, newspapers, and novels protested excess and exploitation, prompting a need for industry to hire publicists to promote its virtues. Press agents, long a feature of political campaigns, crafted messages in defense of industry. The first professional public relations men, Ivy Lee and George Parker, were newspaper journalists who served as press agents and publicists in presidential campaigns. Lee worked for Alton Barker, while Parker was Grover Cleveland's press agent. In 1905, Lee and Parker created a press bureau to fight negative public images of business.

Government became involved in public relations activities during World War I. Woodrow Wilson established the Creel Commission on Public Information in April 1917 to create propaganda in favor of the war effort. The commission bombarded people with ads, news, posters, and volunteer speakers who appeared in schools and theatres. War exhibits, films, and mass meetings and rallies were held around the country, continually reinforcing the aims and ideals of the war.

The success of World War I propaganda led to the expansion of public relations in government. Edward Bernays, a Creel committee member, set up his own public relations firm in 1921, becoming the first to call himself a public relations expert. Bernays saw the public relations expert differently than the publicist; the former determined policies and practices to win public support, while the latter was merely concerned with building good will.

By the 1920s, publicity experts were essential in presidential campaigns. After Al Smith lost the 1928 election to Republican Calvin Coolidge, the Democrats set up a full-time publicity bureau, and the Republicans followed suit four years later. But public relations still had a limited impact on presidential politics. Bernays remarked in 1928, "Politics was the first big business in America. Therefore there is a good deal of irony in the fact that business has learned everything that politics has had to teach, but that politics has failed to learn very much from business methods of mass distribution of ideas and products" (Westbrook 1983, 145).

The first professional political consulting firm that merged advertising and public relations skills was established in 1933. Ardent Republicans Clem Whitaker and his wife, Leona Baxter, formed Campaign Associates in California. California's political parties were weak, and its population was largely mobile, suburban, and without long-standing roots or traditions. It thus proved a receptive environment for political image making, one that presaged contemporary campaign practices.

Whitaker and Baxter differentiated their techniques from those typically employed by party bosses, political operatives, and lobbyists. They used commercial advertising campaigns as their model, and they recognized that propaganda was central to campaigns. Like the consultants who came after them, they demanded control of expenditures and determination of issues, and thus began to wrest control from the political operatives.

Whitaker and Baxter's methods were audience-centered; they conceived of political markets, framed issues in appealing ways, delivered ideas directly to voters through selected mass media, and used sophisticated and scientific methods to determine appeals, such as polling, direct mail, and later, computers and television. They articulated strategies that have become commonplace in campaigns, such as the need to distill issues into themes or slogans. In the words of Leona Baxter, " Every minister preaches from a text—and every campaign, if it's a successful campaign, has to have a theme. The theme . . . should have simplicity and clarity. Most of all, it must high-point the major issues of the campaign with great brevity—in language that paints a picture understandable to all people in all circumstances (Kelley 1956, 49).

In addition, Whitaker and Baxter wrote about the need for gimmicks to capture attention, while unidentifiable press releases and pseudo-events allayed public skepticism of political "messages." Moreover, they conceived of "the appeal beyond politics" by making politics into a form of entertainment. According to Whitaker:

There are two ways you can interest him [the average American] in a campaign, and only two that we have ever found successful.

Most every American loves *contest*. He likes a good, hot battle, with no punches pulled. He likes the clash of arms! So *you can interest him if you put on a fight.*

No matter what you fight for, *fight for something*, in our business, and very soon the voters will be turning out to hear you, providing you make the fight interesting.

Then, too, most every American likes to be entertained. He likes the movies; he likes mysteries; he likes fireworks and parades. He likes Jack Benny and Bob Hope and Joe E. Brown!

So if you can't fight PUT ON A SHOW! And if you put on a good show, Mr. and Mrs. America will turn out to see it (Kelley 1956, 50).

Whitaker and Baxter's lessons were well learned throughout the rest of the twentieth century. Especially with the coming of television, the old military model of campaigns increasingly broke down and was replaced with a merchandising model, which explicitly aimed to sell candidates by capturing elusive viewers rather than committed voters. As the history of presidential campaigning practices has shown, the personalization and entertainment function of campaigns is not new. Only the commercialization of campaigns, made possible by social, geographic, and technological changes, has led to a qualitatively different kind of campaign.

# Chapter 2

# Instatement of a Genre: The Classical Presidential Campaign Film, 1952–1960

Throughout the twentieth century, as the military model of political campaigns has broken down, propaganda techniques drawn from the world of commerce have created a merchandising model of presidential campaigns. The decades following World War II marked a qualitative shift in American politics and culture, where membership in political parties and partisanship continued the decline that began at the beginning of the century. Party patronage and protection benefited the waves of immigrants in the early twentieth century, but the postwar generation of native-born Americans found jobs and opportunities without the help of party bosses. Increasing numbers of geographically and socially mobile voters did not necessarily vote as their parents did. Suburbanization produced communities without histories, and identities were not shaped by party preferences. Both the decline of party loyalties and increase in television viewing facilitated the rise of image-politics, where voters made judgments based upon their perceptions of a candidate's character rather than party ties. With the coming of television in 1948, commercial marketing techniques began to become more visible in presidential campaigns. Television and the merchandising of presidential candidates evolved together, and television facilitated the modern shift from a military to merchandising model of political campaigns. With television, candidates needed knowledgeable experts to help them appeal to heterogeneous viewing audiences. Old-time political operatives, many with backgrounds in law, did not know how to use the television medium. But advertisers did.

## TELEVISION AND THE 1952
## PRESIDENTIAL CAMPAIGN

The 1952 presidential campaign first exploited television's potential as an instrument of mass persuasion. Although both major party candidates used television in limited fashion in 1948, few people owned sets and there were no national networks. Four years later, 19 million homes had televisions, transcontinental cables made coast-to-coast transmissions possible, and both Republican and Democratic party conventions were broadcast nationally for the first time. Both the Eisenhower and Stevenson campaigns hired television advisers, and public appearances were orchestrated for the benefit of the television cameras. When Eisenhower opened his general election campaign in Philadelphia with a speech simulcast on television and radio, workers had thirty-nine pages of guidelines for the event. They distributed 25,000 roses, 300 noisemakers, 500 flags, and 25,000 programs to the crowd. Eisenhower's "handlers" instructed him to position himself for photographs with his right hand resting on the Liberty Bell (Bloom 1973, 56).

The Eisenhower campaign introduced the presidential spot commercial to television in 1952. Eisenhower was the first presidential candidate to hire a special advertising unit independent of the party agency. Rosser Reeves, an advertising executive from the Ted Bates Agency, headed the unit and produced the first televised spot commercials. Reeves proposed the idea to Thomas Dewey in 1948, but Dewey declined in the belief that it was not dignified (Diamond and Bates 1984, 41). Eisenhower accepted.

Reeves' research found that most people did not remember the content of a political speech, and they could remember only one idea or concept from an ad. So spot commercials with a single theme had high "penetration": they were quick, efficient, and easily remembered. They could be shown repeatedly and avoided the vicissitudes of live programming. Reeves brought hard-sell advertising principles to television politics, based on the philosophy that ads should give people reasons to vote for a candidate. According to Reeves:

I think of a man in a voting booth who hesitates between two levers as if he were pausing between competing tubes of toothpaste in a drugstore. . . . The brand that has made the highest penetration in his brain will win his choice and the nature of the human brain is such that a one-minute or 30-second spot, expertly crystallized, gets a maximum penetration on its content (Cotler 1952, 8).

He consulted George Gallup, whose polls revealed that most Americans were concerned with cost-of-living increases, government corruption, and the Korean War. These became the campaign themes, addressed in simple, brief, easily recognizable terms, and hammered home by repeating them in speeches and print material and on television.

Reeves made forty 20-second commercials, each dealing with one theme, aired in a series called *Eisenhower Answers America*. Ordinary Americans asked questions that the candidate answered. Reeves's staff recruited American tourists from outside Radio City Music Hall in New York City. They held over 150 interviews with middle-class citizens to "get the vernacular," and they used volunteers with regional accents for the final filming (Diamond and Bates 1984, 57). Both the choice of "typical" Americans and the selection of Eisenhower's lighting, make-up, and clothing demonstrated the Republicans' attention to television as a visual medium. They even arranged for people to gaze upward as they asked questions, which were later cut together with shots of Eisenhower glancing down as he provided answers. The resulting images nonverbally connoted authority and leadership while also giving the impression of simultaneity. Although Eisenhower acceded, he was not enthusiastic. During the recording, he remarked ruefully, "To think an old general should come to this" (Jamieson 1984, 85).

The Democrats responded rancorously with a charge that they have continued to make against Republican candidates. George Ball, a Stevenson staffer, complained, "They have invented a new kind of campaign—conceived not by men who want us to face the crucial issues of this crucial day, but by the high-powered hucksters of Madison Avenue" (Fox 1985, 309). The Democrats protested to the FCC that the networks were unfairly making time available to the Republicans. When their cries went unheeded, the Democrats produced spots of their own. But the media-resistant Stevenson did not appear in them. As has been the case throughout the twentieth century, Republican presidential candidates have been first to embrace the new media technologies and tactics that characterize the merchandising campaign.

Despite the Republicans' continuing edge, most presidential candidates after Eisenhower and Stevenson gradually moved away from the military model and shifted to a merchandising model of campaigns that employed the services of advertising experts. The prosperous fifties led to an advertising boom, and advertisers began to expand their services to include market research, merchandising, technologically sophisticated media, and refined polling and sampling techniques. Through the late sixties, advertisers developed consumer marketing techniques to "sell" candidates like products. In a context where parties were weak and many voters were uninvolved, disaffected, or had no strong loyalties, modern television-based campaigns aimed to attract the undecided rather than to mobilize the faithful. A conception of the voter-as-consumer replaced the voter-as-soldier.

As the merchandising model came to dominate American politics, conceptions of the nature, purpose, and audiences of political campaign discourse changed accordingly. The evolution of the televised documentary films produced for presidential candidates articulates these changes. Initially, these films exemplified the military model; the classical films made from 1952 to 1960 were primarily conventional expository documentaries produced to educate and activate private gatherings of supporters. They retained this form through the early years of television as the films developed from 1964 to 1972. Even as advertisers' and consultants' importance increased, professional documentary filmmakers with little background in politics commonly produced presidential campaign films throughout this period.

Yet, beginning with Eisenhower's 1952 election-eve *Report to Ike*, the films bear signs of change. They reflect the tensions between the military and merchandising models of campaigns, manifest in the power struggles between political operatives, advertisers, and the emergence of the professional media consultant, who combined advertising and public relations skills. They also demonstrate Republican and Democratic presidential candidates' different approaches to televisual communication: in general, the Republican candidates embrace the image-politics characteristic of the merchandising model, while the Democrats, less well funded or well-connected to Madison Avenue, express ambivalence.

## THE EISENHOWER CAMPAIGN

Madison Avenue advertising experts and public relations professionals brought commercial marketing tools and production techniques to Dwight D. Eisenhower's 1952 presidential campaign. Members of Batten, Barton, Durstine, and Osborne (BBD&O), Young and Rubicam, the Kudner Agency, and the Ted Bates Agency contributed their expertise. Despite the reliance on television and advertising techniques, only Ben Duffy, president of BBD&O and stalwart Republican, served as part of Eisenhower's inner circle of advisers; the old-time party politicians still largely determined strategy.

Publicity director Robert Humphreys, head of the media division of the Republican National Committee, drafted a campaign blueprint modeled after commercial advertising and public relations plans. Humphreys's plan named two target groups: traditional conservatives loyal to failed Republican aspirant Senator Robert Taft, and "stay-at-homes" who rarely voted unless they were sufficiently dissatisfied with prevailing conditions. Reaching this latter group was less a matter of "motivating the troops," than one of swaying the uncommitted with no strong political loyalties. Thus Eisenhower's campaign depended on heavy use of television, whose strengths were its capacity to convey personal qualities and to attract uninvolved voters. Personalized television appeals allowed people to see and hear the candidate, close-up and intimate, in the comfort of their own homes. Humphreys recommended, "informal, intimate television presentations, addressed directly to individual Americans and their families, their problems and their hopes," and a departure from televised speeches, "which, by their very nature, cannot impart the real warmth of character with which both candidates [Eisenhower and Nixon] are endowed" (Jamieson 1984, 52).

Eisenhower, a military hero wooed by both Democratic and Republican parties, ran as a candidate who was "above politics." The avuncular Eisenhower, whom polls indicated was the most admired living American, was an ideal nonpartisan candidate. One scholar wrote: "While most politicians pretended to be for peace, home, mother, God, and country, Eisenhower really was. He had no political, social, or economic program to trade for votes. He had only his transcendent goodness" (Weisbord 1964, 151).

The Eisenhower campaign staff pioneered the use of the documentary format for creating public support (Mickelson 1989, 72). They modified the traditional form of the political speech by preceding televised Eisenhower speeches with filmed "documentary" footage of the candidate, accompanied by his wife Mamie, in the midst of crowds of enthusiastic supporters. The campaign also produced two television documentaries in which the candidate did not appear. Instead, Clare Boothe Luce used testimony and visuals such as maps, graphs, and diagrams to discuss the problems of corruption and communist infiltration in government.

### Report to Ike

For the campaign finale, Eisenhower's election-eve special, *Report to Ike*, used state-of-the-art television techniques to combine live and filmed, documentary and enacted images in a sixty-minute extravaganza. Designed explicitly for television, it is a somewhat aberrant example of the classical documentary campaign film. Produced by Arthur Pryor of BBDO, it appears to be a nonpartisan report to Eisenhower on the state of the Citizens for Eisenhower Committee's "crusade" to elect the general. An on-camera announcer mediates the segments of live, filmed, fictional, posed, and archival footage that comprise the film. All in all, there were eighty-one switches from live television to film and from city to city. The program, simulcast on radio and four television networks from 11:00 P.M. to midnight, cost about $280,000 to produce and air, and its combined Nielson rating over all the networks gave it an extraordinary 53.7% market share (Craig 1954, 65, 136).

*Report to Ike* attempts to present the campaign as a crusade of the disaffected while also demonstrating Eisenhower's natural leadership and universal appeal. He fits the image of the presidential candidate patterned after George Washington throughout American history: the heroic, uniquely talented leader rises above the ordinary through the challenges of battle. Like Washington, Eisenhower was called to lead, and reluctantly accepted. The program also contains other conventions of the presidential campaign film: biographical material on Eisenhower's home in Abilene, still-photographs of his parents, stock newsreel footage of Eisenhower with soldiers in Korea and appearing with Winston Churchill, and attending the birth of his grandchild. As in later films, the biographical "newsreel" footage of Eisenhower's early life and military service in Korea replicates material that also aired in sixty-second spot commercials.

*Report to Ike* mimics the live form and reflexive techniques characteristic of other fifties television shows. It opens with a close-up of Eisenhower. The camera pans back to reveal Eisenhower, Mamie, Richard and Pat Nixon gathered in a living room in front of a television set. The living room is a television studio, where a hidden camera records the foursome as they watch themselves watching themselves on television. An announcer's voice introduces the program to viewers; then Eisenhower briefly breaks out of the television "frame." He directly faces the camera and instructs viewers on how to interpret the experience:

All we know about it [the program] is that it's in the nature of a report to Pat and Dick, Mamie and me. The point of the show is that you share it with us. As we look on, you share it with us, as we sit here to take a look at what they're going to do, you look also. So in that way we'll all get to be together, all in your living room. So let's all sit together and find out.

Throughout the hour, the camera periodically cuts back to the studio, where Eisenhower or Nixon, still planted in front of the television, comment on the proceedings. The film attempts to unify Eisenhower and his audience in the shared experience of watching television, while "live" reports from Eisenhower supporters gathered across the United States unify Americans from different segments of the population in their support for Ike. The actuality, immediacy, and supposed spontaneity of the testimonials help create perceptions of a countrywide, shared media experience.

The Republicans were already audience-centered in 1952, relying upon polls to determine their campaign themes. A Gallup Poll revealed three dominant issues in the minds of most Americans: the cost-of-living, the Korean War, and corruption in government. These themes, reinforced throughout the campaign, recur in the film. It begins with an excerpt from Eisenhower's nomination acceptance speech, where he mentions these issues. The following scene then provides visual illustrations. The narrator mentions inflation, and an image appears where prices on a supermarket cash register change from forty-nine to ninety-four cents. He refers to corruption, and the image (implicitly referring to income tax scandals) depicts a man taking the Fifth Amendment in court. Mention of communism is accompanied by a shot of alleged Communist sympathizer Alger Hiss in handcuffs, as well as Julius and Ethel Rosenberg. Footage of the Korean War appears next. These images also contrast the virtuous Eisenhower with the Democrats who were in the White House during these events.

As the film progresses, the people who voice their support for Eisenhower also mention these themes. Interviewers in Los Angeles, San Francisco, Seattle, Baltimore, Cleveland, and Philadelphia solicit testimony from celebrities, political figures, and ordinary Americans shot on location in their own milieus. Celebrities such as John Wayne, Darryl Zanuck, and ballet dancer Maria Gambarelli, sports figures such as black San Francisco fullback Joe Perry, and political leaders such as Governor Earl Warren and Senator Huey Long endorse Eisenhower. Blacks, farmers, a factory worker, a secretary, a Korean War veteran, and an Italian-American appear on-camera to announce their support for the candidate. In addition, representatives speak from various groups organized around the country: Coffee Hour for Eisenhower in L.A., Nisei for Ike in Seattle, Kids for Ike in Minneapolis, and Democrats for Eisenhower in New York. The film also uses testimony to emphasize that traditional Democrats are voting for Eisenhower. John Roosevelt, son of FDR; Sarah Roosevelt, his granddaughter; Mrs. John Warner, daughter of Al Smith; and a secretary and representatives of Democrats for Eisenhower announce their intentions to vote on the Republican ticket.

Banners, posters, and cheering crowds across the country convey excitement and popular support, as does a staged scene of campaign workers canvassing door-to-door. A woman answers her doorbell and accepts an Eisenhower poster, which she promptly displays in her window. One of the final scenes depicts the Eisenhower bandwagon as it rolls down a city street, intercut with "live" images of the Eisenhowers and Nixons watching it on television. The "We Like Ike" wagon was itself an artful campaign fabrication that paved the way for the candidate's campaign appearances. The wagon arrived in a city prior to an Eisenhower speaking engagement. Workers distributed buttons, confetti, and posters, while an "I Like Ike" coterie of young women wearing Eisenhower uniforms danced from the wagon's platform to the tune of a marching band. The wagon was an extremely effective device to attract enthusiastic crowds, especially desirable if the campaign appearance was broadcast on television. The use of the bandwagon at the end of *Report to Ike* was a metaphoric last appeal for the viewing audience to get on board.

*Report to Ike* is primarily devoted to exposition and to presenting its "actuality" in a convincing way. Supporters, narrators, and even Eisenhower himself state rather than imply most claims. People declare that Eisenhower is honest and trustworthy; the images do not carry the argument. Few images appear without narration to explain their significance. It primarily attempts to create identification with the viewing audience, as both ordinary and esteemed Americans voice their support on camera, simultaneously reminding viewers of the issues on the Republican agenda.

The use of "live" testimony from ordinary and famous Americans across the country and multiple levels of narration distinguishes *Report to Ike* from later presidential campaign films. Whereas later films portrayed stereotypical characters without identifying them as such, *Report to Ike* is intent upon defining characters, socially and geographically. By travelling to different cities across the United States, and by airing the voices of a plurality of different races, classes, and ethnic groups, the film conveys the impression of a unified, on-going celebration all across the land.

However, *Report to Ike* was fiction. The *New York Post* printed the text of the supposedly "spontaneous" presentation eight hours before it was broadcast. The paper described the seemingly randomly chosen speakers as "masses of carefully drilled and prompted crusaders" (quoted in Craig 1954, 64). There were also paid actors and staged scenes in the "documentary," although production notes said that the film was unplanned. Yet even critics acknowledged that the film was adeptly done.

Saul Carson, writing for the *Nation*, asserted, "With great skill, the 'people' had been written into a masterful script. . . . It was a mammoth production. It was done with vast skill. It was a monstrous patent fraud. It was excellent propaganda" (1952, 449). Thus began a great tradition of Republican presidential campaign films.

## THE STEVENSON CAMPAIGN

In contrast to the Republicans, the Democrats did not use television inventively in 1952, despite early boasts that their party would use television "in a more exciting, more dramatic way than any political party had ever dreamed of" (quoted in Mortenson 1967, 84). This was partly because of lack of funds and partly because of the disposition of the party and their candidate. The Democrats saw Madison Avenue as Republican territory and were wary of advertising. The Democratic National Committee hired a middle-sized advertising agency, the Joseph Katz Company, and the Volunteers for Stevenson Association hired Erwin Wasey. However, Stevenson's publicists generally came from news and government information services rather than the commercial world of product merchandising, and the campaign considered the advertising agency workers as technicians rather than strategists (Kelley 1956, 158–160).

For the most part, Stevenson used television as an extension of radio, and purchased time for thirty-minute fireside chats, which were actually lectures addressed to 500,000, not a home audience of two or three (Seldes 1952, 19). Even worse, the campaign bought economy time slots, from 10:30 to 11:00 P.M. on Tuesdays and Thursdays from 2 November until election day; they reasoned that as the speeches continued, a regular audience would build. The Republicans, on the other hand, preempted popular programs with their own, and benefited from the larger numbers who had tuned in to watch something else. Stevenson was preaching to the converted, while the Republicans were converting the uncommitted.

### Campaigning with Stevenson

The Democrats produced one documentary film, *Campaigning with Stevenson*, an expository form structured around the campaign speeches delivered by the candidate. The film cost only $75,000 and it aired on NBC-TV and played on MBS radio on 15 September from 10:30 to 11:00 P.M. (*New York Times* 16 September 1952, 26). Compared to the

Republican's *Report to Ike*, fewer people saw *Campaigning with Stevenson*, its audience was 2,700,000, and its Nielson rating was only 6.2 (Craig 1954, 136).

*Campaigning with Stevenson* opens with shots of Stevenson appearing at the Democratic National Convention. After establishing the candidate's background by showing him at home in Illinois, at work with his colleagues in the governor's office, on vacation in Wisconsin, driving up to his campaign headquarters, and then boarding a plane on the campaign trail, the film follows the candidate's itinerary as he speaks in New York, New York; Detroit, Michigan; Dallas, Texas; Portland, Oregon; Seattle, Washington; Kasson, Minnesota; and San Francisco, California.

The film follows a single chronological narrative, and no stylized editing techniques juxtapose otherwise unrelated images. The images are subordinate to the narration track; they merely illustrate verbal points, and convey little meaning independently of words. The narrator, for instance, informs viewers that Stevenson's address to an audience in Seattle climaxed his campaign tour; no formal devices indicate that this is the high point of the film. There is no rousing music, no fast cuts, no shift in pace. The final scene is structured much like all of the others, with the candidate speaking from behind a podium, intercut with reaction shots from the crowd. The sequence concludes with the audience's applause, and a cut to Stevenson and his campaign workers on the plane, en route to San Francisco.

Like virtually all campaign documentaries, *Campaigning with Stevenson*'s anonymous narrator explains sequences to the viewers and provides the film's coherence. Excerpts from actual campaign speeches delivered around the country contribute to perceptions of its reality, as do images of Stevenson's personal and public life that were designed for the camera. In one clip, Stevenson chops wood during his vacation; the narrator informs viewers that he did this for the press, but even so, "he did an expert job." The mythic implications of the candidate chopping wood are obvious; yet in other sequences, the filmmakers chose images designed to show Stevenson as a man of the people, but with little positive symbolic resonance. He reads the newspaper at home and then drives himself to his campaign headquarters—just an ordinary American having an average day. When Stevenson walks in the woods and cooks eggs at a campfire with his sons, the camera provides a puzzling close-up of two eggs frying in a pan. In another shot, viewers are treated to an undignified close-up of Stevenson's face covered with shaving cream as he grooms himself on the campaign plane. He blows kisses to women at a rodeo. Even at this early stage, Republican filmmakers selected more strategic images of the candidate.

Unlike *Report to Ike*, *Campaigning with Stevenson* was not produced with particular segments of the viewing population in mind. Rather, it assumes an undifferentiated mass of viewers. Both films try to demonstrate their candidate's widespread appeal in different geographic locations across the United States. However, *Report to Ike*, shot on location, shows cable cars to identify San Francisco, and supporters who are visually identified with a particular occupation or place. In *Campaigning with Stevenson*, the narrator informs the audience about whom Stevenson is addressing in his speeches. However, this verbal ploy is less effective than having a Korean veteran or former Democrats testify that they are voting Republican, as was the case in *Report to Ike*. For the most part, Stevenson's on-screen audiences consist of homogeneous people all over the country. He typically speaks at banquets or conventions whose geographic location is indecipherable. His audiences dress in evening wear, making them seem more elite than the ordinary Americans who supported Eisenhower.

The film's narration, too, does little to draw in the viewing audience. Whereas Eisenhower and his narrator refer to viewers as "we" or "you," thus creating a feeling of intimacy, *Campaigning with Stevenson*'s narrator does not acknowledge the presence of the home audience, and the narration appeared to come from nowhere. With the exception of *Report to Ike*, which differed from later films primarily in its narrative techniques, campaign films typically use this omniscient, voice-of-God narration. The technique works as a means of convincing viewers of the authority behind the words and images that construct the films, yet does little to take advantage of television's perceived capacity to replicate a conversation, where individual viewers can be addressed and recognize themselves as subjects of the discourse.

## THE 1956 CAMPAIGN: A TIME
## FOR EXPERIMENTATION

At the beginning of the 1956 campaign, Republican spokesperson L. Richard Guylay remarked that the day of the thirty-minute political speech was past (Diamond and Bates 1984, 20). The speech, which worked on the stump and for a time on the radio, was no longer a campaign centerpiece. Once again, the Republicans hired BBD&O to do advertising in 1956. The Democrats, despite Stevenson's publicly expressed disdain, tried to hire a Madison Avenue advertising agency. However, none of the agencies wanted to risk alienating their primarily Republican business clients by working for a Democrat. Stevenson settled for a less prestigious firm, Norman Craig Kummel.

The Republicans continued to use television inventively. Eisenhower had one campaign film where he appeared for sixty seconds, then the rest was film and spokespersons (Diamond and Bates 1984, 83). Other films combined excerpts from his speeches with filmed scenes, music, and narration. The Republicans also experimented with other formats. They aired Eisenhower's sixty-sixth birthday party on national television, and Republicans organized gatherings around the country where people were treated to a slice of birthday cake. One half-hour show entailed ordinary Americans asking "spontaneous" questions that were answered by the president. Although it appeared that he was present, they used a split screen and he saw his interrogators only on a monitor. In another case, seven women "chatted" with Eisenhower and his wife Mamie; this aired during the daytime to attract the women in the viewing audience. Eisenhower's campaign managers planned another election-eve special like *Report to Ike*, but the president opted to stay in Washington; instead, they televised a rally that he addressed via closed-circuit television, and later he gave a final campaign speech.

The Democrats made one significant innovation with regard to campaign documentaries at their convention in Chicago. A Democratic party film narrated by John F. Kennedy, *The Pursuit of Happiness*, followed the keynote speech. They wanted the networks to broadcast the film as part of their convention coverage, despite its obvious propagandistic intent. The CBS network protested what amounted to free media coverage, and showed the conventioneers in the darkened hall rather than the film; however, the other networks accepted the film and set a precedent that a convention documentary was a legitimate news event. In later years the networks aired both party and campaign films, until they truncated their convention coverage in 1968 and the decision once again became controversial. Beginning with Richard Nixon in 1972, candidate's campaign films preceded their acceptance speeches, a trend that has continued to the present.

The 1956 campaign saw the continuation of the thirty- and sixty-second spot commercials, as well as the development of the five-minute hitchhike—a lengthier advertisement used by both parties that preempted the end of regularly scheduled programs. The Stevenson campaign made one significant innovation with the negative spot commercial, where they disparaged Eisenhower with clips from his own advertising. Otherwise, the Democrats were reluctant or unable to exploit television. One party official stated, "While we are not indifferent to the risk of boring [the public], we are not willing to sacrifice substance and content to up our presentations. We are not above these things; we just think the old way of sticking to issues is better" (*Business Week* 30 June 1956, 95). Stevenson continued to rely primarily on the televised speech, despite mounting evidence of its negligent effect. He had no televised documentary films. Filmmaker Charles Guggenheim, who worked on Stevenson's campaign and later produced a number of biographical campaign films, proposed a televised political campaign film to Stevenson, but the candidate refused.

Despite Stevenson's reluctance to accept television, and Eisenhower's decision to rely on the traditional rally and speech for the campaign climax in 1956, the ground was broken for televisual campaign films. The Eisenhower campaign, in particular, developed the techniques that ultimately shaped the modern merchandising campaign and led to the hybrid documentary-advertisement. Eisenhower's campaign strategists translated poll data into simple issues and put them in emotional terms that would appeal to a mass audience. They developed a sophisticated sense of audience, and paid attention to the style and mode of viewing unique to television. Although political operatives remained in control of strategy, television became increasingly central in presidential campaigns.

## THE 1960 CAMPAIGN

The period from 1956 to 1960 was marked by further experimentation and innovation with television as a campaign tool. Both Kennedy and Nixon relied extensively on television to get their messages across to the voters in 1960. This campaign is best remembered for the Great Debates between the two candidates—the first such events in American presidential history. The FCC suspended article 315, which required equal time for all candidates, and thus allowed the networks to make time available to the two major presidential and vice-presidential candidates only. Although the professional politicians in the Nixon campaign opposed the idea on the grounds that the debates would give the lesser-known Kennedy much needed exposure, the public relations specialists believed that an effective showing on Nixon's part would secure his victory (Chester 1969, 119). Both men agreed to debate. As history has shown, the debates were the deciding factor in the election, and they underscored the importance of the television image. Those who watched the tanned, youthful Kennedy, as opposed to the more sallow-skinned Nixon (who was recuperating from an illness), perceived that Kennedy won the first debate, although radio listeners believed the opposite. Nixon never recovered from the boost that Kennedy received after the first debate.

Kennedy and Nixon made use of documentary films in the primary and general election campaigns. Both the Nixon and Kennedy campaigns approached filmmaker Jack DeNove, a Republican who had worked for BBD&O and a Catholic who had worked with Jean Kennedy Smith on *The Christopher Hour*, a religious television program. DeNove decided that his Catholic ties outweighed his Republican ties and went to work as advertising manager for the Kennedy campaign.

Kennedy preferred DeNove to the Democratic National Committee's contracted agency, Guild, Buscom and Bonfigli. As a result, there was no centralized control of media. Both DeNove and the ad agency duplicated each other's efforts, and DeNove did not approve the ad agency's proposals, no matter how worthy. Their competition created financial and organizational problems for the campaign, none of which were ever surmounted.

### The New Frontier

DeNove's *The New Frontier* was a thirty-minute biographical film that also depicted the high points of the Kennedy campaign. More so than the Eisenhower or Stevenson films, *The New Frontier* emulated the biographical newsreel films that audiences were accustomed to seeing in the theatres, and it became emblematic of the classical expository campaign film. It corresponded to a military campaign model that aimed to inspire volunteers, motivate supporters, and inform local party leaders of Kennedy's platform, rather than to attract uncommitted television viewers. In fact, it was never shown on television, but only at local party meetings or after hours in workplaces sympathetic to the Democrats. It was also shown to groups of supporters gathered on election eve.

Kennedy initially appears on-screen delivering the "New Frontier" speech that provided the focal point of his campaign. Kennedy relied quite heavily on filmed excerpts of his important speeches throughout his political career. Besides being a remnant of pretelevision campaign practices, political candidates' heavy reliance upon filmed speeches had a technological component. Cumbersome, immobile synchronized sound and image cameras made it difficult for camerapersons to follow spontaneous action or to shoot uncontrolled on-location footage. The development of lighter cameras and the portable one-quarter-inch tape recorder in the late fifties enabled filmmakers to move along with their subjects and to film a greater variety of material. Although *The New Frontier* was still very much tied to the speech-making tradition, in several shots Kennedy was wearing or holding a microphone as he strolled among his constituents—a technically impossible achievement not long before. The image also had a symbolic appeal: the candidate who promised to "get America moving" was himself mobile.

Like all of the early presidential campaign films, *The New Frontier* makes use of the documentary codes and conventions that signal veracity to the viewing audience. *The New Frontier* shares the form and techniques of television news and public affairs programs that viewers associate with objectivity, neutrality, and veracity. Despite the fact that Kennedy is often described as the first television president (largely as a result of his perceived victory over Nixon in the first of their television debates), *The New Frontier* is a substantive, more verbally than visually oriented film. It is an expository text that proceeds in chronological order as it introduces the candidate, defines the major campaign issues, and offers evidential support for his leadership qualities and qualifications to be president. Actor Jason Robards's unidentified, off-screen narrator's voice, with its deep, resonant tones, betrays no uncertainty, and guides the viewer through the sequences of images. The film primarily consists of stock footage. There is a compilation of speech excerpts, with some biographical material, archival material, one dramatization, and graphics tied together by music and narration. The film reiterates events that actually happened, such as clips from the definitive speeches of Kennedy's campaign: the famous "New Frontier" speech, his 8 May speech in West Virginia clarifying his position on the separation of church and state, the announcement of his candidacy, and his acceptance address at the Democratic National Convention after he received his party's nomination for the presidency. It also reconstructs past events, so that stock World War II battle footage appears as a sailor recounts Kennedy's heroism as a navy lieutenant. In another case, Kennedy appears in a domestic scene where he enters his Boston home, then sits on the sofa with his wife and daughter. This sequence is borrowed from *The Kennedy Story*, a film produced for his 1958 senatorial campaign. As with most such documentaries, the selection and inclusion of representative events, the editing together of otherwise disparate events, and the repetition of images simulate reality while appearing to simply transmit it.

At the same time, *The New Frontier* is a powerful conduit of myth that helps to account for Kennedy's charismatic hold over the American people. *The New Frontier* is the only Democratic candidate's film in the age of television that evokes the image of the candidate as leader without ambivalence. Kennedy is depicted as a strong, heroic character who will ensure a safe passage to the new frontier. In a speech clip included in the film, Kennedy clearly associates himself with the myth of the American Dream: "For there is a new world to be won, a world of hope and abundance, and I want America to lead the way to that world." The narrator reminds viewers that Kennedy received a medal for his "courage, endurance, and leadership"—qualities any president should have. The film stresses his strength, training, and experience as much as possible. Kennedy, running on the theme of forward-moving change, needed to inspire confidence in his vision. More practically, the youthful candidate needed to assure Americans that he was qualified for the presidency.

Kennedy himself appears strong and vigorous, despite the fact that he was almost constantly in pain and used crutches to walk when in private (Berry 1987, 87). He wears only a suit jacket and tie on the campaign trail, although in one scene snow flurries dance around him. His style is subdued; he gives no evidence of discomfort before the cameras. When speaking to the people, he uses no notes. On all occasions, his gestures are well suited for the intimate television screen.

His privileged background that did not accord with the American rags-to-riches myth is tactfully ignored; the narrative omits mention of his prodigious family and early upbringing altogether. In other cases, the film overtly addresses Kennedy's perceived weaknesses. Kennedy's lack of experience was an issue in the campaign, especially in contrast to Richard Nixon, whose main strength was his experience as vice-president for eight years. At forty-two, Kennedy was thought to be too young for the presidency. Not only does the film's narrator address this issue as an opening gambit, but the film proceeds to reiterate his accomplishments as a scholar who wrote a Pulitzer Prize winning book, *Profiles in Courage*, World War II hero, and state senator. The film mentions Kennedy's work on the Senate Foreign Relations Committee. A clip of John and Robert Kennedy interrogating labor leader Jimmy Hoffa also appears, as does part of a strongly worded speech on U.S.-Soviet relations. This latter speech is accompanied by images of the USSR which, in juxtaposition with Kennedy's words, seem to imply that he had been there. There were not, however, any specific images of Kennedy in Russia.

Kennedy's religion was another problem, for a Catholic had never been elected president. To address this issue, the film includes a clip from Kennedy's speech to coal miners in West Virginia prior to the primary there, where he attested to his belief in the separation of church and state.

West Virginia was 95% Protestant, and Kennedy's subsequent primary victory there made him a viable candidate for the presidency. A film of this speech was shown regionally throughout the general election in addition to being included in *The New Frontier*.

*The New Frontier* speaks to a society on the cusp of change, one where the ethic of pleasure and consumption threatens to overtake the Puritan work ethic. In the midst of the postwar technological boom fuelled by Cold War hostilities, and the resultant affluence of the (new) largely white suburban middle class, Kennedy celebrates the consumer society as an aspect of progress at the same time that he warns against its excesses. "The insidious challenge of luxury," the narrator proclaims, while a woman at a gambling table lifts a champagne glass to her lips in apparent abandon. In a world of rapidly proliferating goods, services, leisure time, and "modern" conveniences, Kennedy assures Americans of the morality of certain kinds of consumption and the value of progress. He equates progress with other undefinable terms such as freedom, choice, and opportunity, all of which shape the "good" America which he represents and the "new frontier" where he will lead his followers. The image of the new frontier is invoked by clichéd images of the familiar American landscape. Fields of wheat, rushing streams, leafy trees, and expansive mountains open the film, reminders of the good, pure, lush, new American land of song and story. These images are not, however, placed in opposition to images of progress such as urbanization and industrialization. Rather, the narration and music track joins them with other resonant American symbols: farmers, workers, children, soldiers, and portraits of venerated presidents such as George Washington and Abraham Lincoln. The narrator states that America is "good" because of the sacrifices of the past, and throughout the film Kennedy reiterates the need for sacrifice, but the only film images remotely related to sacrifice are brief shots of soldiers who died during World War II.

Kennedy's vision, according to campaign chronicler Theodore White, was developed in the first ten days of the campaign, as he spoke in public to live audiences and sensed their reactions to his comments. Even without benefit of sophisticated polling techniques, Kennedy was able to intuit the voters' moods and attitudes and to fashion his message accordingly. (Kennedy also had pollster Louis Harris on his staff.) White refers to Kennedy's grand theme: America cannot stand still; her prestige fails in the world; this is a time of burden and sacrifice; we must move (White 1961, 256). This grand theme, exemplified in *The New Frontier*, may be characterized as malaise, perhaps surprising in a period of peace and prosperity. However, Kennedy warns of the spread of communism and America's loss of prestige abroad, a rousing alarm meant to heighten Cold War insecurities. He also complains of the stagnating domestic economy, as he calls for an unexplicated "sacrifice" for the higher good. Kennedy promises future revitalization, progress, movement; he consciously invokes American mythology as he delineates a new frontier to be conquered by science and technology, a myth whose ecological repercussions are only now beginning to be realized.

Contemporary malaise is both described and depicted by images of empty food troughs followed by a surfeit of wheat, unemployment lines, crowded schools, men sleeping on park benches, trash-strewn buildings, riots in city streets, gambling, and newspaper headlines reporting the television quiz show scandals. Ironically, these are not presented as problems resulting from progress, but as problems that will be alleviated by it. The film's emphasis is upon future glory that exists in opposition to present malaise, as Kennedy promises a new world of "peace and good will, of hope and abundance." He supports these abstractions with proposals to alleviate the internal crises in American society: improvement in education, more plentiful housing, medical care for the elderly, and aid to farmers and to impoverished areas.

The language in the film is a mixture of strong and inspirational—strong when confronting threats to the American way of life, inspirational when invoking the new frontier. At one point Kennedy quotes scripture as he promises to lead Americans to the Promised Land, the New Frontier: "But I believe that the times require imagination, and courage, and perseverance. I'm asking each of you to be pioneers for that new frontier. I'm calling for the young at heart, regardless of age, to the strong in spirit, regardless of party, to all who respond to the scriptural call, be strong and courageous, be not afraid neither. . . ." Implicit in Kennedy's statement is his tough stance against the external threat of communism. More often than not, references to challenges and threats to "freedom" are codes for communism in *The New Frontier*. At the height of the Cold War, Kennedy was a committed anti-Communist.

The film indicates that Kennedy attempts to appeal to particular constituencies as well as to a homogeneous middle-class audience. He talks with students about improvements in education, the elderly about better health care, and farmers and coal miners in West Virginia about economic improvements. These were interested parties rather than generic Americans, and these domestic concerns were the domain of Democratic candidates. Thus, *The New Frontier* blended New Deal democracy with hard-line anti-communism, focusing on present crises that would resolve into future glory. Kennedy appeared as a strong leader who was prepared to deliver the American Dream, but only if the people showed that they deserved it.

## Ambassador of Friendship

Nixon employed advertising executive Carroll Newton, vice-president of BBD&O, as director of television operations, and Ted Rogers, one of the most experienced political television producers available, as his personal television consultant. Newton and Rogers envisioned one of the most imaginative uses of the medium ever in a national campaign, and they assembled a group of volunteers from top Madison Avenue advertising agencies to make their vision reality. They proposed a number of innovative programs that would foster an image of the candidate through visual means. In *Khrushchev As I Know Him*, film and videotape footage would contrast the "villainous" Khrushchev with the peace-loving Nixon. *For You and Your Family* would show Nixon at home, talking about typical problems faced by ordinary families such as his own.

Despite his advisers' visual acumen, Nixon was not yet committed to the electronic media. He shied away from their proposals, fearing the criticism that he was a packaged candidate. He followed his own intuitions regarding television, and the volunteers were relegated to a back room on Vanderbilt Avenue—away from Madison Avenue—with little influence on the ensuing campaign (White 1961, 312–13).

Nixon's thirty-minute documentary, *Ambassador of Friendship*, was a resumé film that aired several times in California prior to the primary election. It was well received, prompting Carroll Newton to hold off airing it until the end of the general election, when it would provide a "final emotional jolt" (Wyckoff 1968, 28). Newton went as far as to preempt the General Electric Theatre at 9:00 P.M. on 6 November, the Sunday evening before the election. However, Nixon decided that he wanted one last chance to speak to the people, and vetoed airing the film altogether. Perhaps inspired by the success of his 1952 "Checkers" speech, Nixon preferred to use television to give informal talks (against the advice of his advisors) rather than filmed productions. Thus, *Ambassador of Friendship*, Nixon's only campaign documentary in 1960, was not aired on national television during the general election campaign.

*Ambassador of Friendship* stressed Nixon's foreign policy experience—providing an implicit contrast with Kennedy, who lacked experience in foreign affairs. Yet, as a representative anecdote of the Nixon campaign, it exemplifies the campaign's limits. It deals solely with

Nixon's experience in foreign affairs, a one-sided portrayal that down-played Nixon's knowledge of domestic affairs. It portrays him as a leader, with little effort to create identification or to show him relating to the American people. Nixon was riding on the crest of the Eisenhower wave: Eisenhower provided leadership, and Nixon would continue to do so. Whereas Kennedy complained of economic stagnation, Nixon boasted of economic progress during the Eisenhower presidency. In the midst of the Cold War, Nixon's campaign slogan, devised by Carroll Newton, was "The man who understands what peace demands." As evidenced by his campaign film, Nixon was vigorously anti-Communist and advocated peace without surrender of principle. The lesser known Kennedy, however, offered that and more. The film may have high-lighted Nixon's superior experience in foreign affairs, but his views were not noticeably different from Kennedy's.

The opening of *Ambassador of Friendship* quotes from one of the most famous propaganda films ever made, *The Triumph of the Will*. Wyckoff hints that he used images of clouds, followed by the sound of a motor, and then the wing of a plane glistening in the sun, to achieve the same effect as the similar opening of *The Triumph of the Will*, "to detach the audience from all reality beyond that of the screen." Despite this bold attempt, *Ambassador of Friendship* does not compare with the older masterpiece. The Nixon film is a primarily verbal, substantive piece of political film that uses little visual language apart from Wyckoff's machinations. It is difficult to impart drama into what is essentially a sequence of travel vignettes, although Wyckoff asserts that both Democrats and Republicans who saw the film afterwards professed their admiration for Richard Nixon.

Wyckoff's account of the making of *Ambassador of Friendship* reveals a great deal about the way that all documentaries produce rather than represent reality. Producer Wyckoff, in *The Image Candidates*, gives a straightforward account of the making of the film. He explains that the film was originally produced as a favor by Paramount Pictures, whose president, Barney Balabar, was an ardent Nixon supporter. It arrived in his hands as a compilation of stock footage of Nixon flying to different countries to meet with world leaders. The film had all of the shortcomings that Wyckoff attributed to bad political documentaries: it lacked visual continuity, had no reaction shots, and there was too much talking by the candidate. There was nothing to tie the various sequences together. The film was unusable, a "dull, illustrated lecture" that they had to recut to make more visually dramatic and exciting (1968, 23).

Some political campaign films use music and/or narration to accomplish such a task; however, Wyckoff believed that a visual leitmotif would help to unify the film. Given the subject of the film, shots of an air force transport plane would be ideal for this purpose. Paramount Pictures had no such footage in their stock footage files. But a fiction film starring Jerry Lewis, *Geisha Boy*, had outtake shots of an air force C–54 plane. Although the shots were in Cinemascope, the center portion of each frame was rephotographed in an optical lab, and then the rephotographed plane was used as a transitional shot as Nixon flew from country to country. In addition, Wyckoff obtained close-up shots of each country's flag from the United Nations; titles were superimposed and traditional ethnic music that represented each country accompanied Nixon's arrival so that different locations could be easily recognized.

After Nixon arrived in each country, he was photographed giving an address or traveling in a motorcade. According to Wyckoff, *Ambassador of Friendship* included too much footage of Nixon giving speeches without any cutaways or reaction shots to heighten visual interest. Cutaways and reaction shots, Wyckoff noted, translate spectacles, such as the motorcades in which Nixon traveled, into human terms that add to the dramatic impact of the film. The filmmakers allayed this problem by obtaining shots after the fact, a common strategy used to salvage poorly made documentary films. In this case, Wyckoff found them in *Radio Patrol*, an old B-picture. Thus, in a scene where Nixon addresses the Russian people from a television studio, the film cuts to an outdoor antenna—as Wyckoff notes, it *could* have been Russian. They added reverberation to the soundtrack so that it seemed that Nixon's voice was coming out of a loudspeaker. Then they cut in close-ups of people listening to him, also taken from *Radio Patrol*. The artificiality of the resulting scene is not apparent to the naive viewer.

The narration assumes America's cultural and political supremacy, and people from foreign countries are largely shown as "other," entertaining the bemused Americans with traditional songs and dances or expressing their profound thanks for the benefits of American technology. Asians express "overwhelming gratitude" for farm equipment as the accompanying image shows an admiring crowd surrounding a man with a hand-held tractor. The Chinese are "expressing ambition to catch up with the western industrialized world," and the Central American countries "want our help." Africa is the "dark continent," and Russia is clearly depicted as the enemy as Nixon takes on Khrushchev in their famous television debate about the benefits of capitalism versus communism, where Nixon had the last word.

*Ambassador of Friendship*, while indisputably showing Nixon as an experienced world leader, remains tied to the word, despite Wyckoff's efforts to the contrary. Many of its images are not clearly related to the narration track, or even of discernible content. There is little attempt to mythologize the candidate as a man of the people. Despite attempts to transform the film, there is not much of a dramatic storyline. The narration warns of the dangers of communism, but there is little sense of a Nixon plan of action; he lacks the inspirational, if vague, language of his opponent. Overall, not much is done to attract viewers not already committed to the candidate—the Nixon film regresses to the military model, as did his 1960 campaign, where he pledged to travel to all fifty states and meet directly with the people.

## SUMMARY

The 1952 campaign was the first in which campaign events began to be arranged with attention to the television medium, and the use of the campaign "documentary" marked an adaptation to television as a visual form. All of the early televisual campaign films were framed as nonfictional documentaries, though *Report to Ike* also embodied the "live" television typical of the time. By intercutting oratory with filmed sequences, the Stevenson, Kennedy, and Nixon films showed some attempt to accommodate television as a medium that differed from radio or a live appearance. Yet Stevenson ended his campaign on election eve with a thirty-minute program of speeches by Truman, vice-president Barkley, running mate Sparkman, and himself. (Stevenson ran out of time, and last-minute arrangements had to be made to allow the candidate to return to the airwaves to finish later that evening.) Kennedy's *The New Frontier* was not deemed important enough to air on national television, and Nixon himself opted to use speech instead of film.

All of the films relied heavily on speech; only the exceptional *Report to Ike* used ordinary citizens and celebrities rather than the candidate. The Eisenhower film alone demonstrated awareness of television as distinct from other media, and attempted to use television's perceived immediacy, intimacy, and ability to personalize the candidate. The Eisenhower campaign began to merchandise the candidate, while the others resisted the inevitable. When Stevenson was renominated to oppose Eisenhower in 1956, he professed disdain for the union of politics and television advertising: "The idea that you can merchandise candidates for high office like breakfast cereal, and that you can gather votes like boxtops is, I think, the ultimate indignity for the Democratic process" (Jamieson 1984, 95).

But television, bolstered by the success of the Eisenhower campaign's use of marketing techniques and public opinion polls, had indelibly altered presidential campaigns. Professionals convinced of the efficacy of television, skilled in its production techniques, and willing to embrace its entertainment values began to overshadow the expertise of party advisers and even the candidates themselves. Media experts were becoming strategists rather than mere technicians. Through the mid-sixties, the presidential campaign films continued to evolve along with television.

# Chapter 3

# Growth and Development of the Classical Presidential Campaign Film, 1964–1972

By 1964, 95% of American homes had at least one television set, and they were watching an average of six hours per day (Gilbert 1972, 193). With the country still in emotional shock following the assassination of President Kennedy, conservative Barry Goldwater opposed the acting-president, Lyndon Johnson, in the 1964 presidential campaign. Both candidates took advantage of television's increased cultural dominance and experimented with televisual communication.

The time was the height of the Cold War. The country was becoming more entangled in Vietnam, and the threat of nuclear war—primarily Goldwater's alleged propensity to engage in one—loomed over this election. At home, the nation was in the throes of change. Industry and technology were expanding and creating more prosperous lifestyles, while blacks were pressing for civil rights. American society was at a crossroads: rising rates of syphilis, crime in cities, riots in cities and resort communities, and more permissive attitudes toward gays led to the conservative claim that morals were in decline. Yet some of these statistics were misleading: while rising high school dropout rates were creating a school crisis, more people were going to college; while hard liquor purchases were increasing, per-capita consumption was not. This translated into a debate about the quality of life—in Goldwater's terms, morality; in Johnson's the Great Society (White 1965, 304–6). Goldwater ran on a platform that denounced the new immorality and the excesses of big government and federal bureaucracy, although his proposal to modify Social Security proved part of his downfall. Johnson, stressing the theme of continuity with the path hewn by the martyred president, had little fear of losing the election. He offered to carry out the promises of John Kennedy: a compassionate welfare state, a strong posture in defense of the "free world," a belief in economic growth and progress, and increased opportunities for all Americans, black or white.

## THE 1964 GOLDWATER CAMPAIGN

Early on, Richard Guyluy, director of public relations and advertising for the Republican National Committee, stated that candidate Barry Goldwater would rely heavily on television, "We think it is his medium; we think it isn't Johnson's" (Chester 1969, 117). Almost 40% of Goldwater's campaign budget went into broadcasting (Gilbert 1972, 206). Despite the increasing popularity of spot advertisements, the Goldwater campaign made extensive use of thirty-minute television time slots to include documentary films, speeches, interviews, and discussion programs. The lengthy formats were produced on the advice of Goldwater's inner circle of professional party politicians, rather than the campaign's advertising agency—Erwin, Wasey, Ruthrauff, and Ryan—who recommended spots. Goldwater's political advisors believed that lengthy programs were necessary to get his message across to the voters, although none of the Goldwater presentations received particularly high ratings. In fact, they preempted the 9:30 to 10:00 P.M. slot on NBC three times in October, and NBC president Robert Kintner suggested that it was during this period that "Peyton Place," run on a rival network, acquired its huge following (1965, 126). One adman following the election remarked that members of national committees "generally do not understand the nature or purpose of advertising," and he complained, "You couldn't convince them that voters' favorite entertainment shows— like Petticoat Junction—shouldn't be preempted" (Nuccio 1964, 64). Throughout the early years of the union of politics and television, advertisers and political operatives remained at odds with one another: common lore was that the advertisers knew nothing about politics, and the political operatives knew nothing about television. The Goldwater campaign was no exception.

Goldwater's first half-hour show, produced by the Citizens for Goldwater-Miller Committee, aired nationally on the CBS network, from 9:30 to 10:00 P.M. on 18 September. A ten-minute biographical film ended with a speech by the candidate, thus initiating the trend to use campaign "documentaries," particularly biographical ones, to kick off the general election campaign. The short biography used little original footage; the narrator's points were illustrated by Goldwater family tintypes and photographs of Arizona taken by the candidate himself, who was an amateur photographer.

## Choice

Goldwater's first half-hour program made little impact, but his "documentary" *Choice* was one of the most controversial—and prescient—presidential campaign films ever made. *Choice* first articulated the Republican vision of a return to traditional America that eventually came to dominate American politics. *Choice* was a visionary film that built upon the premises established by Kennedy's *The New Frontier*. The film's final sequence even tried to link the two men in a segment where Goldwater quoted the deceased president. Overall, *Choice* expanded upon Kennedy's vision of impending malaise, but linked it to liberal policies. *Choice* opposed a currently corrupt America with the virtuous land of bygone days that was free from "sin," used both literally and figuratively. Russ Walton, publicity director for the Citizens for Goldwater-Miller Committee, conceived of the film; Walton was himself a fundamentalist Christian. Thus, the film had overtly religious overtones, although it concentrated far more on contemporary malaise than future deliverance. *The New Frontier* used vaguely religious language to direct the nation toward the future; *Choice* overtly embraced religion as it turned back to the pure, innocent, nostalgic America of an earlier time.

The film was produced by Raymond H. Morgan and Henry Ludwin from the Los Angeles advertising agency, Anderson, Morgan, DeSantis and Ball, for about $50,000 (Irwin 1964, 25). *Choice* resulted from dissension in the Goldwater campaign between Goldwater's Arizona advisers, campaign director Denison Kitchel and Republican National Party Chairman Dean Burch, and consultant F. Clifton White, who ran Goldwater's preconvention campaign. Kitchel and Burch prevented White from becoming director of the National Citizens for Goldwater Committee during the general election; they secured Erwin Wasey, Ruthrauff, and Ryan as the national committee's advertising agency. Erwin Wasey proposed "bland, homey fare," while White, who rebounded by heading the state-run Citizens for Goldwater Committee, wanted "hard-hitting television with punch (Evans and Novak 1964, E7). The result was *Choice*, made with Goldwater's approval but not his active participation.

*Choice* was a compilation documentary composed of images taken from news stories and outtakes from Hollywood films, cut together in a seamless presentation of so-called contemporary American society. The film responded to the schizophrenia of a culture split between the ordered familiarity of tradition and the novelty of change and innovation. It contrasted the corrupt, overly permissive, morally bankrupt America prevailing under the Johnson administration with the good, traditional America represented by Barry Goldwater. The film simplified the complex as it juxtaposed images of rioting, gambling, pornography, and sexual permissiveness with images of an innocent, virtuous land of patriotic, hardworking people. Blacks rioting in city streets were intercut with well-scrubbed white children reciting the pledge of allegiance in a classroom. Images of striptease joints and teenagers dancing the twist in licentious fashion cut to Main Street America, picnics, and children saluting the flag. Narrator Raymond Massey ruefully asks, "What has happened to America?" as images of modern excess appear, while the cutbacks to simpler times include photographs of the Pilgrims landing, Valley Forge, Western settlers, the Constitution, and the Declaration of Independence. The film closes with actor John Wayne (who also appeared in Eisenhower's 1952 election-eve program) reminding Americans that the choice to alter events is in their hands.

*Choice* was scheduled to air on NBC on 22 October at 2:00 P.M., when a majority of viewers were women. According to Russ Walton, fear of an increasingly turbulent society was rampant and, "We find this fear in the minds of everyone, particularly in the minds of women" (quoted by Robertson 1964, 35). But the problem was that the images of liberal decadence were themselves decadent. Shots of a topless woman dancer, a male Mardi Gras parader wearing only a fig leaf, and a magazine cover reading "Jazz Me Baby" were most ironic and controversial. John M. Bailey, the chairman of the Democratic National Committee, asked the Fair Campaign Practices Committee to evaluate the film. He referred to it as "the sickest political program to be conceived since television became a factor in national politics. It appeals to the prurient and the prejudiced in a fashion which makes a mockery of its pretension to be speaking for moral conduct" (Robertson 1964, 35). NBC reviewed the film, and wanted some of the more offensive material deleted. However, neither Goldwater nor Dean Burch, chairman of the Republican National Committee, had seen the film; nor had they been involved in its production. Upon screening *Choice*, Goldwater ordered it withdrawn, stating, "It's nothing but a racist film" (Thomson 1966, 126).

*Choice* never aired on television, although parts of it were excerpted and aired as spot advertisements, and it was shown in rented spaces and even drive-in movie theatres around the country. Two hundred copies were sent to state organizations before the television screening, and many of these were shown at private screenings even when the film was recalled. Walton surmised that more people saw the film after it was censored than would have if it aired. Its themes continued to define the Goldwater campaign, and set the tone for subsequent Republican discourse.

*Choice* was the first presidential campaign "documentary" where sound and image predominated over the word. More images appeared in the film than words to explain them, and arguments were often implicit, relying upon previous cultural knowledge. Black people primarily demonstrated American immorality in scenes of violence, looting, and rioting, hence Goldwater's own charge of racism. There were also unexplained shots of Billie Sol Estes, the Texas financier and friend of the president who illegally made $14 million while on the government payroll, and Robert G. Baker, a former Senate Democratic secretary and Johnson protégé forced to resign his position after the Senate Rules Committee charged him with conflict of interest. Neither Estes nor Baker were explicitly linked with the Johnson administration, nor were their crimes mentioned. Estes's photograph was shown alone, while a montage of newspaper headlines followed by a still-photograph shot from a number of camera angles indicted Baker, the latter a filmic device placing him under a magnifying glass for viewers' perusal.

The Republicans claimed that there was only one staged scene in the film, in which a black Lincoln Continental is shown alternately speeding then braking across the screen, while beer cans are occasionally tossed from the driver's window. Although Johnson was not mentioned by name, this alluded to a widely reported and editorialized incident where the president, taking reporters on a tour of his Texas ranch on the previous 28 and 29 March, drove ninety miles per hour in his Lincoln Continental, drinking beer, and graphically describing the sex life of a bull to the four reporters, three of whom were female (Evans and Novak 1964, 429–31). Despite the Republicans' claims of authenticity, Walton, who had contacts in the film industry from his previous tenure as executive director of the Conservative United Republicans of California, obtained footage from Hollywood films previously shown on television to make his film (Bloom 1973, 147). (Walton himself, in an interview over twenty years later, maintained that all of the footage was taken from the evening news—impossible in the case of the speeding car shots). At the very least, the music that underscored the film's images was familiar from Hollywood films. Viewers were thus preconditioned to respond in a particular way. For example, the pulsating, sexually suggestive rhythms of Afro-Cuban jazz accompanied images of the problematic America, while orchestral arrangements of hymns, marches, or "The Battle Hymn of the Republic" accompanied the good America. The film used subliminal techniques: the word *choice* was faintly superimposed whenever Goldwater's photograph appeared. In other cases, a black background with white letters indicating *choice* introduced scenes of the liberal America, while the conservative, moral America was introduced by black letters against a white background. Visual rather than logical continuity often linked shots, as for example when the camera pans up a tree trunk, then cuts to a pan up a stone pillar. Throughout the film, rapid cuts and montages from more than one camera angle created a feeling of confusion; these techniques only depicted the morally corrupt America. For the virtuous America represented by Barry Goldwater, shots were slower paced and from a single point of view. As the film progressed, the "good" images disappeared and the film took on a darker tone. Narrator Raymond Massey warned in an apocalyptic tone that both Americas are possible, but people must choose one.

According to transcripts of the story-planning conference circulated to the press, Walton remarked: "Therefore the purpose of this film is to portray and remind the people of something they already know exists, and that is the moral crisis in America. . . . We just wanted to make them mad, make their stomachs turn." He also announced that the film should arouse "raw, naked emotions," and when describing a "built-in" prejudice people in small towns and rural areas have against the big city, he said, "This film will obviously and frankly play on their prejudices" (Robertson 1964, 35).

Whereas many of Goldwater's speeches and spot commercials were defensive attempts to articulate Goldwater's positions, *Choice* went on the offense against Johnson and the decadent America that he purportedly represented. This was the first negative political campaign film, where as much time was spent disparaging the opposition as espousing the virtues of Barry Goldwater. *Choice* sought viewers who were not committed to the liberal Great Society, whose values were rooted in tradition rather than faith in progress. It addressed white middle class voters who yearned for a mythic America. Black people were not part of this myth; they were part of the evil city. Subtle racism, which would become part of Nixon's and later the Republicans' successful "southern strategy," had its roots here. Moreover, liberal consumption and the ethic of consumption were openly attacked as sources of current crisis. The film defined the current state of affairs as a moral crisis, thus disassociating it from its economic and political contexts. It articulated the otherwise inchoate, if in simplistic fashion, and it provided a position from which those addressed by the film could understand profound cultural transformation.

No matter how objectionable, *Choice* was an innovative and visually engrossing work of fiction. It elaborated upon Kennedy's vision of malaise, and took his notion of two opposing worlds very seriously. *Choice*'s images appeared in subsequent Republican films, it set the terms for later Republican discourse, it presaged the marketing strategies that eventually were used to organize the New Right, and it demonstrated awareness of visual techniques upon which future campaigns could expand. Years later, Ronald Reagan achieved great success by expanding upon *Choice*'s nostalgic images of the "good" America and its attention-getting visual style, as Reagan claimed Goldwater's vision of a moral America as his own.

## THE 1964 JOHNSON CAMPAIGN

Lyndon Johnson had no political campaign films made for the general election in 1964. With television in mind, he did request that political films be shown each night of the Democratic National Convention: *Quest for Peace*, which was about America's military strength and preparedness; *The Road to Leadership*, a paean to Johnson; and *A Thousand Days*, a tribute to Kennedy produced by filmmaker David Wolper and rescheduled by Johnson to air after his nomination. During the general election, Johnson had a few televised, thirty-minute speeches and one interview program format, *We the People*, where people on the street appeared on camera and voiced their support for the president. The Democrats didn't want to jeopardize Johnson's huge lead in the polls, so they decided to let the news primarily carry his message. His advisors also believed that the audience for longer films consisted primarily of partisan viewers, and spot advertisements were more likely to reach indifferent or opposed viewers (Gilbert 1972, 210).

Johnson was the first and last Democratic presidential candidate to make use of the services of a large Madison Avenue advertising agency. The campaign hired Doyle, Dane, and Bernbach, with whom Kennedy had already engaged in preliminary discussions. Despite their lengthy rationale for taking the campaign (on account of their fear of a Goldwater presidency), they also, in all likelihood, accepted it because of the virtual certainty that Johnson would win. Johnson had a substantial lead in the polls even before the campaign started, and it did not subside as the campaign progressed. According to consultant Joe Napolitan who worked on the Johnson campaign, "We walked through that campaign.

Don't forget. Kennedy was assassinated only 11 months before. There was no way that Johnson was going to lose."

Johnson's campaign is most renowned for producing the first national spot campaign advertisements, several of which gained long-lasting notoriety, but are mild by today's standards. The Daisy commercial, for instance, was a soft-sell ad produced by Tony Schwartz that attacked Goldwater by implication and innuendo. Throughout the campaign, the Johnson strategists made nuclear responsibility (or lack of it) one of the central issues. Goldwater was widely perceived as dangerously hawkish, largely because of his advocacy of nuclear testing and his suggestion that tactical nuclear weapons could be used in Vietnam. Although Goldwater was never mentioned by name, the Daisy commercial implicitly associated him with people's fears of a nuclear war. A small girl counts the petals of a daisy as she plucks them off; the camera cuts to a close-up of her pupil as a male voice overrides hers and counts backwards in what is apparently a countdown for a nuclear explosion. The final image depicts a mushroom-shaped cloud, and Johnson's voice closes with the admonition, "We cannot afford to fight another nuclear war." The ad aired only once, and was pulled after protests by the Republicans. It goes down in history, however, as one of the first ads to work by bringing to the surface feelings—in this case, fears—that people already had, and to associate them with a candidate entirely by implication. In fact, Tony Schwartz noted that years later people still remembered the feelings evoked by the ad, rather than its content (Schwartz 1974, 93–94).

## THE 1968 CAMPAIGN

The 1964 campaign was tame in comparison to 1968, which was one of the most tumultuous in American presidential history. Civil rights activist Martin Luther King was shot in April, Democratic contender Robert Kennedy was assassinated two months later, Alabama Governor George Wallace ran as a third party candidate, and the incumbent, President Johnson, was challenged for the nomination from within his own party. Initially, Johnson was the obvious choice for the Democratic party candidate, but inner city strife and public dissension about the Vietnam War were reaching a crescendo as the election drew near. After being informed by his advisers that he was sure to lose, the exhausted Johnson withdrew from the race on 31 March. His vice-president, Hubert Humphrey, entered the race on 27 April. Johnson had already scheduled the convention for late August to coincide with his birthday, a ploy that would have worked well for the incumbent, but which proved to be one of the events that contributed to the undoing of the eventual Democratic nominee, Humphrey.

The majority of the population perceived television as the most credible communications medium: 65% relied primarily on television for information about presidential candidates, and for the first time, television surpassed newspapers as the information medium preferred by the majority of college-educated Americans (Gilbert 1972, 228). The information they received came largely in the form of images: the Vietnam War, massive civil rights and antiwar demonstrations, and riots in the cities. Movement organizers realized that television could shape perceptions of reality. Pseudo-events created with the primary intention of attracting the television cameras became common communication strategies.

Pseudo-events dominated political campaigns, too, as political consulting agencies and media specialists increasingly usurped the function of advertising agencies and old-time political operatives. Although advertising experts had the skills to sell products, consultants were adept at planning strategies as well as producing commercials. Most importantly, the consultants knew how to get the candidate free media exposure by staging "newsworthy" events that would play well on television. The Nixon campaign, in particular, began the practice of arranging the candidate's daily appearances with an eye to television coverage. His advisers scheduled events early in the day to leave time for the television crews to process and edit the material for the evening news. He would speak to enthusiastic audiences of schoolchildren, for example, whose audible cheers and visible excitement deflected attention from their older siblings, the college students who were more apt to harangue the candidate in protest of the Vietnam War. Television was an indispensable campaign tool; used with skill and savvy, it could manufacture perceptions of reality.

Many of the technological changes that initially appeared in the early 1960s became conventional uses of the medium in 1968. The 1968 Republican National Convention was the first to be broadcast entirely in color, and the Miami convention hall was the first to be designed specifically for television (Gilbert 1972, 228). Air-conditioning compensated for the uncomfortably hot television lights and cameras, lights were hung from the ceiling, and the television commentators' booths were also suspended from the ceiling to give them an aerial view of the convention. Despite this attempt to accommodate television, 1968 was the first time that all three networks did not provide gavel-to-gavel coverage at either the Democratic or Republican convention. ABC provided only ninety minute summaries of each day's proceedings. To some extent their decision was due to financial problems; it was also likely based on the fact that each election year after 1952, the conventions received increasingly low ratings.

The long political speech aired on television was relegated to the historical dustbin, and the spot commercial became the most prevalent form of campaign advertising. Yet campaigns continued to produce documentary films. Their disadvantages were the expense and the increasing difficulty of having good availability for the most effective time buys. In 1968, both Humphrey's *What Manner of Man* and Nixon's *Richard Nixon: A Self-Portrait* were replayed as often as time and money allowed. Although the ratings for political documentaries were not particularly high, and cynics claimed that only those converted would tune in to the shows, the genre continued to develop and grow. Al Gardner, who had handled Robert Kennedy's senatorial campaign years before, predicted, "Half hour shows will continue to be used by candidates because the quality of impression in a half hour is more intense. You can see a lot more of the candidate, expect more detail (Spencer 1972, 87).

Both Hubert Humphrey's and Richard Nixon's campaign films were in color for the first time. Portable equipment, synchronized sound, and new types of camera lenses opened the possibilities for new kinds of shots and locations. Sound and image could be recorded separately, so that filmmakers were better able to manipulate sound.

The new information technologies became more important in 1968 than in any previous campaign. Polls, attitudinal surveys, focus groups, and computers controlled the course of the campaigns to an unprecedented extent. Campaign pollsters checked the public pulse as often as time and money would afford, and themes and issues were created in response to poll data. The Nixon campaign was so reliant upon the new technologies that campaign manager John Mitchell declared that his job was to "program the candidate" (Chester, Hodgson, and Page 1969, 612).

The candidates' images were designed to give the public what it wanted. Strategists in both campaigns made frantic efforts to establish their candidates as warm, human, ordinary Americans who represented all that was good about the American way of life, especially as the race grew closer. Personality took on heightened import in this race; likability became a "substantive" issue. Both the Humphrey and Nixon campaign films were as much concerned with touching the audience's emotions and creating rapport as they were with espousing positions or establishing credentials.

The Democrats produced two documentary films for their convention. Both shared characteristics with campaign films, although due to circumstances they necessarily became "tribute" films. First, the Democrats planned to air *The Democratic Faith: The Johnson Years*, a film that had all of the generic features of a campaign film except that it had footage relating the Johnson presidency to past glories of the Democratic party tacked onto the beginning. When Johnson decided not to attend the 1968 convention, he ordered members of the Secret Service to collect prints of the film, and it was never shown. Its production remains something of a mystery; the Johnson Library lists David Wolper as its producer, but Wolper has no recollection of making the film.

The second film was *Robert Kennedy Remembered*, a memorial to Robert Kennedy produced by documentary filmmaker Charles Guggenheim. This film aired during the convention and again on 2 November on NBC. An update of the 1964 biographical campaign film made by Guggenheim and used for Kennedy's senatorial campaign in New York, it was also shown in the presidential primaries, with revisions made for each state in which it was shown. After Kennedy's assassination the morning after the California primary, Guggenheim recut it as a tribute film. This was one of the few political "documentaries" ever to gain widespread recognition, winning an Academy Award for Best Documentary in 1968.

When turning the campaign film into a tribute, Guggenheim treated the inherently emotional subject with restraint and respect. Its final scene indicates the power of film to churn emotions: Kennedy romps in the backyard with his children and dog, while his own voice, choking with tears, delivers the eulogy at his brother's funeral. The film closes with Joan Baez singing the classic sixties song "Blowin' in the Wind"; Kennedy's solitary figure strolls along the water's edge at the beach, and eventually he disappears into the mist at the horizon. The image of the lone, contemplative figure, walking along the beach until he disappears into the horizon recurs at the end of later presidential campaign films, such as Humphrey's (1968), Nixon's (1972), and McGovern's (1972).

Delegates broke into tears at the conclusion of *Robert Kennedy Remembered*. But the film also contributed to the calamity at the convention. The pro-Kennedy delegates spontaneously and defiantly began singing "The Battle Hymn of the Republic" as the convention chair banged his gavel in a futile call to order. This image, too, was conveyed to the viewing public.

## What Manner of Man

Hubert Humphrey, who had not campaigned during the primaries, emerged as the Democratic party candidate at the convention. Yet his campaign was doomed from the start, due to conditions prevailing in the country, perceptions of the disruptive Democratic convention, and the late date of the convention which left little planning time for the newly anointed candidate. The convention ended two days before Labor Day, typically the start of the general election campaign.

Humphrey had no media plan and little money, and was tired and demoralized after Chicago. However, he quickly acquired a cadre of advisers and consultants. Humphrey's campaign manager was Lawrence O'Brien, a political consultant who had conducted Kennedy's 1960 effort. His associate, Joe Napolitan, also a consultant, became media director; this was his first presidential campaign. With no time to waste, Napolitan designed the media plan before Labor Day. He hired Sidney Aronson and Shelby Storck to make campaign films, and Tony Schwartz to do some of the spot commercials. Napolitan also wanted Guggenheim, who had collaborated with Storck on a well-received 1966 film for Milton Shapp in the Democratic primary race for governor of Pennsylvania. Guggenheim pleaded exhaustion and declined, although he produced some television shows towards the end of the campaign (Napolitan 1972, 37).

Initially, Humphrey hired Doyle, Dane, and Bernbach, the Madison Avenue advertising agency that had run Johnson's campaign, to do advertising. However, a rift soon developed between the political consultants and the advertising agency. Napolitan thought Doyle, Dane and Bernbach's ads were too expensive, emotionless, and contrived. Napolitan won the battle, and midway through the campaign a smaller agency, Lennon and Newell, replaced the Madison Avenue agency and Napolitan maintained media control. No Democratic presidential candidate used a Madison Avenue advertising agency again.

Napolitan planned spot commercials, question-and-answer sessions, and a two-hour election-eve telethon, although the campaign lacked the funds needed to produce these materials. Napolitan also wanted to make two documentary films—one Democratic party film, *Because It's Right*, that linked Humphrey to the Democratic tradition, and a biography, *What Manner of Man*. Napolitan conceived of these films; Sidney Aronson produced the Democratic party film, and Shelby Storck, known for his work with Guggenheim on Milton Shapp's gubernatorial campaign film, produced, directed, narrated, and wrote *What Manner of Man*.

*Because It's Right* was less than successful. Polling surveys indicated than many Democrats were defecting to the Republican party, so one of the campaign strategies was to reinforce the image of the Democratic party by associating Humphrey with former Democratic heroes. The film used overly simplistic symbolism, with Democrats such as Franklin Roosevelt, John Kennedy, Eugene McCarthy, and George McGovern wearing white hats, and Richard Nixon, George Wallace, Hitler, and Mussolini wearing black hats. Campaign advisers questioned panels of people who saw the film. Based on their responses, the film was shown only a few times (Gilbert 1972, 246). According to Napolitan, the film lacked an upbeat ending; it left viewers feeling that there were too many problems left to be solved. But there was no time to change it, so it was shelved.

In contrast to the failure of the first film, Napolitan, while not exactly a disinterested observer, refers to *What Manner of Man* as a "masterpiece," and "one of the two or three best political films ever made." It was conceived, written, shot, edited, and put on the air in six weeks. The film was relatively expensive for the campaign; it cost about $150,000 to make, primarily because producing the film in such a short time was so labor-intensive. Even Joe McGinnis, who did not share Napolitan's high regard for the work, grudgingly admitted it was one of the most effective political commercials of the campaign (McGinnis 1970, 141). Kathleen Jamieson noted that an appeal for funds at the end of the film raised $320,000 at one showing (1984, 255–56). In a lone voice of dissent, Theodore White wrote that the biography "made Humphrey seem a man thrust forward only by issues" (1969, 448).

*What Manner of Man* aired repeatedly during the last weeks of the Humphrey campaign, culminating with a showing on election eve. It was shown both nationally and regionally, although Napolitan notes that the campaign had difficulty making the most effective time buys due to lack of time and money. Humphrey surged in the polls during this time: the bereft campaign received a large influx of contributions during the last weeks and benefited when Johnson announced that he had stopped the bombing of Hanoi. Whether Humphrey's last minute surge can be attributed to more cash flow, hopes that the war would end, the repeated airing of the film, or a combination of these factors, is impossible to determine. Napolitan, who states that the film was shown seven times on network television stations and another 200 times in selected markets, believes that it accounted for more vote switching than any other single thing done in the campaign (Diamond and Bates 1984, 180).

*What Manner of Man* stands at the crossroads of the shift from a military to a merchandising model of campaigns in presidential politics. *What Manner of Man* is a biographical film that consists of actual footage depicting both high and low moments in Humphrey's life and career, as well as original footage shot for the film of Humphrey at home and with his family. There is an emphasis on the personal. Still-photographs illustrate his early life in Dolan, South Dakota, and Storck shot original footage of Humphrey relaxing at his home in Waverly, Minnesota, spending time with his grandchildren, including his retarded granddaughter, and ruminating in front of the camera. Napolitan subscribed to Tony Schwartz's resonance theory and wanted the film to be emotional, to strike a "responsive chord" with the preexisting attitudes and experiences of its audience.

According to Napolitan, because *What Manner of Man* was assembled so rapidly, its audience was not specifically targeted. However, an important campaign tactic was to keep undecided Democrats from straying too far away from the party. Polls indicated that defections to the Republican party were hurting Humphrey's candidacy. To allay this problem, the film placed Humphrey within the traditions of the Democratic party, both by its choice of accomplishments to laud, and its use of venerable party figures. George McGovern, representing the party's left (and opposition to the Vietnam War), described Humphrey as a compassionate man, while the more centrist Ted Kennedy reminded viewers that Humphrey was a loyal supporter of his brother John. The unpopular Johnson was not mentioned in the film.

An expository documentary, the film was an American version of cinema verité. At times, camera movements were undisciplined and chaotic, with the cameraperson relinquishing control over the events that just "happened" to occur. The resulting immediacy and spontaneity conveyed an impression of authenticity, of unstaged actuality captured on film rather than precipitated by the filmmaker (although the latter may indeed have been the case). Cinema verité films often have no narrator, although *What Manner of Man* retained the anonymous voice-of-God narrator used in traditional documentaries. The film's three opening scenes, filmed in cinema verité style with voice-over narration, engaged the viewer in a kind of meta-discourse about the difficulties faced by the modern day candidate.

First, Jimmy Durante sings "Young at Heart," and then introduces Humphrey by almost referring to him as Herbert. The narrator then intervenes, and suggests that Durante's mistake was symbolic of a campaign that was "moving slowly in September." The narrator then goes on to complain about costs; the Humphrey campaign was indeed debilitated from the start by lack of funds. The scene then shifts to a reflexive, cinema verité moment, as Humphrey primps before the cameras, obviously ill at ease, in preparation for a television appearance. Wires, lights, and equipment are in full view; viewers can hear Humphrey's discussions with the television cameraperson, although the film cameraperson's presence remains invisible. The narrator (Shelby Storck) here explains that Humphrey's sensitivity to quartz-iodine lights sometimes forced him to look fierce on television.

*What Manner of Man* provides an early example of the attempt to portray the candidate as simultaneously a man of the people and a leader. The film softens Humphrey's image while maintaining his credibility as a leader. According to Napolitan, the film had a twofold purpose: to depict Humphrey as both a gentle, benevolent, "ordinary" fellow and a firm, decisive leader with a proven track record. The style is deliberately unslick, and it shows the human side of the candidate as well as the aggressive man of action. He is a man of peace and a man willing to fight for his principles; a man of sentiment and a man of substance.

As a man of the people, Humphrey is placed within the corpus of American mythology: he grew up poor in America's heartland in the midst of the depression. He declares on-camera, "I'm a sentimentalist about this republic, about this country. About what it has meant to me, a child of the Depression, a man born in the plains of humble parentage, and yet I can stand before you as a candidate for the office of president." Amidst this recitation of the American Dream, idyllic still-photographs of wheat fields, a farmhouse, and Dolan, his sparsely populated hometown, accompany his words. These rhetorical depictions invite nostalgia for a simpler America of bygone days. They contrasted markedly with the world outside of the film.

Yet, in order to construct him as a man of the people, Humphrey is cast in a less than heroic role. Durante almost mispronounces his name. He is obviously uncomfortable as he prepares for a television interview. The narrator reminds the viewer that he had almost no money in September. In an enacted scene where Humphrey and Muskie go bowling, the pin machine breaks, and the two men must reset their own pins. The camera accompanies them into the bowels of the bowling alley as the film's title appears on screen. "Thank God there's one problem we've solved today," Muskie declares. "Who says the age of automation has got us stymied?" Humphrey responds.

Other parts of the film try to present Humphrey as a leader through a reiteration of his accomplishments and his stands on issues deemed important to his candidacy. The issues mentioned, however, were noncontroversial and often from the past rather than present. Humphrey was introduced as a man of action whose past public service record illustrated his "tough-minded, practical approach" to solving problems. Contemporary difficulties were not specifically mentioned. In the context of the Vietnam War and vice-president Humphrey's link to the unpopular Lyndon Johnson, voters were reminded of Humphrey's senate record of dedication to liberal causes. There was rare footage of Humphrey's civil rights speech at the 1948 Democratic National Convention, which at the time prompted a massive walkout in support of equal opportunity for all. This scene implicitly aligned him with the civil rights activists, without having to remind viewers of the violence dividing the country in the present. Hecklers interrupt his presidential nomination acceptance speech, and he feistily fights back, and the film visualizes his experience as a senator and vice-president with still-photographs and stock footage. Humphrey also appears alongside John Kennedy at the signing ceremony for the nuclear test ban treaty. The image associates him both with an antiwar position and with an ex-president perceived as a hero by many Americans. The most pressing issue in 1968, the Vietnam War, was not specifically mentioned until near the film's conclusion, when Humphrey vowed his commitment to peace. In an attempt at final synthesis, the narrator also assures viewers that the troubles plaguing the campaign have ended. Humphrey's affirmation of peace dovetails with the rejuvenation of his campaign and the answer to the question of *What Manner of Man.*

*What Manner of Man* attempts to integrate these opposing sides of Hubert Humphrey—leader and man of the people. In a larger sense, his divided self symbolizes the conflicts that marked the social and political context. But Humphrey was humanized by emphasizing his fallibility. He began a long tradition of Democratic candidates attempting to endear themselves to the American public through self-deprecation.

### Richard Nixon: A Self-Portrait

In the Republican camp, the resurrected Richard Nixon defeated attempts by Ronald Reagan and Nelson Rockefeller to gain the Republican nomination. Nixon had been steadily building his bases of support after Goldwater's defeat in 1964. He was a centrist who could potentially unify the party, and he demonstrated that he had voter support by winning in the primaries. He was endorsed by the Republican power brokers, was generally better organized than his opponents, and thus won a narrow victory as the Republican party's nominee.

Nixon's general election campaign has been well documented in Joe McGinnis's *The Selling of the President 1968*, where the author, who traveled with the campaign, revealed the slick merchandising techniques used to package the candidate. (As time has shown, these were not significantly different from those used in other presidential campaigns.) The Nixon campaign hired an advertising agency, Fuller, Smith, and Ross, to do commercials. However, Nixon's media and advertising team wielded the real power. It was headed by lawyer Len Garment who was creative director of advertising, Harry Treleaven, who had been with J. Walter Thompson advertising agency for eighteen years, and Frank Shakespeare, a CBS television executive. They believed that television could refashion Richard Nixon, although they often conflicted with Nixon's long-term advisers, campaign manager John Mitchell and chief of staff H. R. Haldeman. Roger Ailes, who later masterminded Reagan's 1984 and Bush's 1988 campaigns, came on board as a television producer in his first presidential campaign.

The campaign made extensive use of spot advertisements, held a two-hour election-eve telethon, and innovated with televised regional hour-long question-and-answer sessions called *The Man in the Arena*. Nixon had one biographical film, *Richard Nixon: A Self-Portrait*, a mixture of film and still-photographs. *Richard Nixon: A Self-Portrait* aired frequently towards the end of the campaign, when the Republicans bought as much regional and national time as they could to air the film. It was aimed at a female audience, because polls showed that Nixon was losing strength among women voters (Gilbert 1972, 259). Thus, it was shown frequently in the daytime; it aired nationally on 30 October from 3:30 to 4:00 P.M., twice on the afternoon before the election, and once more on election day. The film was also shown in the evening, from 10:00 to 10:30 P.M. on 27 October, and 8:00 to 8:30 P.M. on 2 November, and it was included as part of Nixon's election-eve telethon. Its purpose was similar to that of the Humphrey film—to show the warm, sensitive, sentimental (i.e. human) side of the candidate.

In contrast to the attention accorded the Humphrey film in many published works, *Richard Nixon: A Self-Portrait* barely gets mentioned in most chronicles of the 1968 campaign. The film did not stringently conform to the genre; it was principally an interview with Richard Nixon, who answered questions addressed to him by reporter Warren Wallace. Nixon's dialogue was conversational; although Wallace remained off-camera, Nixon sat facing him, and thus the viewer, as he discussed his personal life history. Still-photographs were intercut, both to animate the otherwise visually dull talking head interview, and to add authenticity to Nixon's account of his history. The interview frame had several ramifications: Nixon could appear relaxed and casual, speaking off-the-cuff; close-ups of his face enabled viewers to scrutinize him, to feel that they were getting to know him; and more so than the documentary, the interview, which simulated a conversation, created a feeling of intimacy. According to Harry Treleaven's memos, the objectives of the 1968 campaign were to show Nixon the man in ways that would dispel negative feelings about his personality and sincerity. He also wanted to avoid gimmicks that proclaimed "Madison Avenue"; the aim was to make his candor and seriousness apparent (McGinnis 1970, 255).

Treleaven also advised the campaign to "make messages meaningful; make sure the groups they're directed to are where the votes are. Youth and the Negro, no matter how tempting, are not where the game will be won" (255). Because the Republican party was still the minority party, they needed to win over Independents and Democrats, and women of such leanings were apparently deemed an easy group to target. The film's intimate, conversational format, use of extensive close-ups of Richard Nixon, and the use of anecdote more than argument were indicative of strategies meant to appeal to women. Nixon spoke in generalities more than specifics, and he presented sanitized, idealized versions of himself, his family, and his country. The film's simple images and settings did not detract from the man baring his soul on-camera.

The film took place in four simple settings. Two were in a "masculine" study, with wood, hard lines, and leather chairs. Nixon, strongly lit, was dressed formally in a suit and tie. The latter two settings were casual and serene. One was a naturalistic, outdoor setting on the porch of Nixon's summer home. He sat relaxed in a deck chair, wearing a blue short-sleeved shirt, with the wind and the periodic cries of seagulls the only ambient sound. The final setting was in front of a glass window overlooking Mission Bay, California, with sailboats drifting by beneath him. These settings were not explicitly identified; the focal point was Richard Nixon as narrator of his own experiences. The film evidenced the campaign strategy that made this the first campaign ever designed almost exclusively for television. The questions and settings left nothing to chance. There was no spontaneity or uncontrolled camera movement; no trace of direct cinema or cinema verité.

Still-photographs intercut as Nixon recalled his past, and dramatic music to set a mood mimicked the advertising strategies of director Eugene Jones, who produced advertisements that made use of still-images and music without the candidate needing to appear "live." The stills, besides having the advantage of economy, were shot with an animation camera so that zooms and pans created a feeling of motion. They serve as evidence that an event "really" happened, that the past can be reappropriated and represented. Partly they are necessary to tell the story of one's past, the mementos of which are the family photographs. Yet, their use is also a code; the photographs frame the film as reality rather than fiction. The use of still-, black-and-white, or even sepia-toned photographs if they are very old, serve as demonstrative proofs that certify the narrator's words. For example, Richard Nixon implies his compassion for the disenfranchised as he discusses his grandmother on-camera: "It was often said that her house, her house was only about 2 miles from ours, that no tramp ever came to the door and got turned away." After the first clause, there is a cut to a black-and-white photograph of a house with a horse-drawn carriage in front. The viewer surmises from the signs—black-and-white photograph, horse-drawn carriage—that this is a picture of his grandmother's house. There is no photograph of her helping a tramp, of course, which is the more salient point that he is making.

Often, the connection between the narration, photograph, and reality is only implied, as for example when Nixon mentions his family's store and service station, and there is a cut to a black-and-white photograph of a grocery store, laden with rows of fruits and vegetables. The casual viewer does not question this relationship; the assumption is that this is a picture of the Nixon family store. Yet, because Nixon is seemingly unaware of the pictures that accompany his narration, he makes no claim for the verity of this photograph. Quite often, in all of these films, there may be a tenuous relation between the word and image, and their relation is virtually always implied rather than stated. The narration, or less often, the music, provides the connection.

Nixon, like Humphrey, is firmly rooted in American mythology. He also epitomizes the rags-to-riches myth where a poor boy from a humble background makes good through hard work and perseverance. In this myth, anyone who tries hard enough and has the support of a loving family can become president. Nixon describes his parents in accord with this myth: he learned drive, zest for competition, and the value of hard work from his self-educated father; his mother, who never raised her voice, inspired the respect of the Nixon boys. His Quaker parents were deeply religious, and he spent his childhood doing chores and working in the family store. The family was poor but close-knit, and Nixon delivers several anecdotes that reveal their ability to enjoy the good times despite hardships. Even tragedy is placed in a positive context. His mother spent three years away from the family, nursing a brother who later died of tuberculosis; however, Nixon contends that her absence taught him independence and the value of challenge. He insists that he had a happy childhood.

The film proceeds chronologically as it traces Nixon's early life and career. Like most presidential candidates, he was both studious (with a special love of geography and history) and an athlete. He performed military service in the navy, after which he entered politics. The film concludes with a statement of his present philosophy. Sitting in his wood-paneled study, dressed formally, he impresses his leadership qualities upon viewers and presents himself as an emblem of America. His personal credo translates into his political ideology. Early on, he mentions competition as a value in his personal life; here he notes that competition is the American way of life:

As I look at this nation, and I look at its people, what's made America a great people, and this nation a great people in the broadest sense of the word, is that we have been competitive. We're a very proud people. You look to the history of nations, and those nations that have reached the heights of greatness have had people that were competitive. Go, go back to the early people who founded America. We look to our Europeans who came to these shores, and there were the Spanish and the French, and the British, all competing among themselves and between each other, to see who could find a new world. And that competitive drive determined which became the great people of that time.

Competition, for Nixon, is univocally positive; early in the film, he commends both his father and high school football coach for teaching him the value of competition. Here he uses it as a synonym for freedom and democracy, and he decries other (i.e., Communist) countries where competition does not exist: "Whenever you take the competitive spirit out of a people, or run to take it out of an individual, you lose something in a country." Nixon's comments suggest that his anti-Communist positions had a psychological component; his hatred of communism was fear of the other, of that noncompetitive spirit so alien to his personal identity.

Nixon also reaffirms the paternalistic myth of American destiny and links it with his own as he gives his reason for running for president:

I have to bear in mind the challenge, the fact that this time in history the United States faced a responsibility that it never had before, and will never have again. And that is, to lead the world. This responsibility comes to nations only once, and if they fail to live up to it, they will have missed their destiny. And that responsibility comes to a man only once.

He identifies his fate with his country's. He has risen from humble beginnings to become a success; hard work, challenges, and competition have made him strong. He now has a responsibility to lead his country, or, in his words, "to submit my qualifications to the people." Nixon's vision of America, similarly, is that of a strong country, formed by people who overcame hardships and learned the value of competition, with a subsequent responsibility to lead the rest of the world. There is no mention of malaise, or the dissent and disunity that was sundering the nation. "What the United States does and the United States does alone will determine whether peace and freedom survive," he asserts. Nixon presents himself as the best possible choice because he is the embodiment of all that his idealized America represents.

## SUMMARY

As in 1964, both 1968 films demonstrated a growing awareness of television as a medium suited to arguing by implication rather than facts or reasoned argument. At the same time, both remained linked to the documentary impulse, and their tendency was to logical argument and exposition. *What Manner of Man* was committed to informing voters on their candidate's public record while creating a portrait of the private man. The film simulated the warm, lovable side of Hubert Humphrey. No doubt Humphrey often went bowling and fishing, and romped with his grandchildren. Selecting and presenting these activities as representative of his person—whether his own or the filmmaker's decision—was necessarily a simulation, neither true nor false. Similarly, *Richard Nixon: A Self-Portrait* simulated a conversation, with Richard Nixon presenting an idealized, mythic view of his life. The image Nixon presented was not necessarily a mask that disguised his true self. Human beings are complex, and at different moments they can be kind and cruel, generous and niggardly, sensitive and crass. A childhood can be recalled as happy or miserable, depending on the circumstances. Nixon simply conjured a one-sided self through his reminiscences.

The Nixon campaign exhibited the greater awareness of images and their power to construct a reality. According to Harry Treleaven: "Television elected Richard Nixon to the presidency. If the medium did not exist, he simply would not have won" (Gilbert 1972, 260). Whereas in 1960 the candidate refused to succumb to the lure of television, eight years later he seemed far more willing. Humphrey, on the other hand, had a lesser understanding of the importance of the visual medium. Napolitan cites a case where Humphrey cancelled a much needed film session to deliver a talk to the AFL-CIO in Minnesota—yet, if ever there was a group whose support Humphrey could already count on, it was them. He was still convinced of the virtues of pressing the flesh despite the fact that times had changed.

# Chapter 4

# The End of Exposition, 1972

As early as 1969, a congressional house report stated that "broadcasting, and television in particular, has become indispensable to the political processes of our nation. . . . (T)he medium—for whatever reason—has become the public's prime source of information. It is this fact that determines its influence" (*Congressional Quarterly*, 29 January 1972, 204). By the time of the 1972 presidential election, a hefty 96% of American families owned at least one television; a Roper Poll found that 64% of the population got most of their news from television, and people trusted television as the most credible medium by a 2–1 margin (White 1973, 251). The tenor of the 1972 campaign was influenced by television's growing role as an information medium.

Television became a prime player in the contest between incumbent Richard Nixon and challenger George McGovern. Both the Nixon and McGovern campaigns made extensive use of marketing techniques to promote their candidates. Computerized data banks targeted particular demographic groups. Computer technology allowed both campaigns to pinpoint demographic groups and tailor television messages accordingly, while polls correlated the viewing preferences of specific constituencies so that time slots could be selected with likely audiences in mind.

Richard Nixon relied primarily on news coverage of presidential activities, while the challenger McGovern was unable to benefit as much from free media attention. Procedural changes in election practices contributed to the Nixon campaign's strategy to take advantage of his incumbency and the public's faith in news. The Federal Election Campaign Act, signed into law early in 1972, aimed to democratize political campaigns by limiting individual campaign contributions and requiring full disclosure of campaign expenditures and contributions over $100. The law also put a ceiling on the amount candidates could spend on communications media and broadcast advertising. Both Nixon and McGovern were limited to $8.4 million on expenditures for broadcast time. Yet, neither candidate reached this limit. The incumbent Nixon managed to circumvent the law by creating "news" events, while McGovern simply didn't have the funds. This aspect of the law was repealed in 1974.

Campaign strategies were influenced by events other than changes in technology and electoral law. The publication of Joe McGinnis's *The Selling of the President 1968* and other such "exposés" led to increased public skepticism of slick political packaging. As a result, media advisers for both Nixon and McGovern made a point of presenting the candidates as "naturally" as possible. Although television and marketing techniques remained at the forefront of the presidential campaign, both groups of media strategists professed their "abhorrence for antiseptic presentations," and said that they hoped to present the candidates "in a low key manner that maintains their credibility" (*Newsweek*, 31 July 1972, 55B). Patterson and McClure's subsequent content analysis of 1972 political advertisements, *The Unseeing Eye*, concluded that spot commercials were designed to give voters information about the candidate's position on issues, and that advertisements were more informative than news in this regard. The presidential campaign films, too, were substantive expository documentaries during this election campaign. This was the last presidential campaign in which this was the case.

## THE MCGOVERN CAMPAIGN

Despite the somewhat substantive nature of presidential campaign films, values dominated this campaign. George McGovern was the antiwar, antiestablishment candidate who won the Democratic nomination on the strength of his grassroots campaign run outside of the party power structure. At the height of opposition to the Vietnam War, troubled race relations, growing concern about the economy, and widespread sentiment that government officials deceived the American people, McGovern ran as the atypical, open, honest politician. He aimed to convey an image of righteousness, sincerity, honesty, and goodness against the forces of evil represented by Richard Nixon and the political establishment (Bloom 1973, 278).

McGovern's opposition to the Vietnam war was the rallying point around which predominantly young activist supporters gathered. His ardent supporters catapulted him through the primaries and secured him the nomination at the Democratic National Convention. However, the momentum did not carry through the general election campaign. According to his media adviser Charles Guggenheim, Democratic voters who participate in the primaries are typically more liberal and activist than the general electorate. This problem has continued to plague the Democratic party, but was particularly acute in the context of dissent over the Vietnam War. Although McGovern won his party's nomination, traditional Democrats perceived him as too far out of the mainstream. In fact, polls suggested that trends toward conservatism predominated over the general electorate, and although a sizable middle constituency believed that the American system could be improved, they feared the economic and social upheavals McGovern seemingly advocated (Frankel 1972, 35).

In addition, McGovern did not have the unified support of his party or traditional members of the Democratic party coalition. He won his party's nomination amidst conflicts and confrontations at the Democratic National Convention that left the party fragmented. Labor refused to endorse him and AFL-CIO President George Meany referred to him as "an apologist for Communist aggression" (Bell 1972, 180). The state and inner-city party machines were typical of the entrenched power structures that the McGovern candidacy opposed, and therefore they did little to help him. Many Democratic senate candidates ran on local issues rather than risk association with McGovern's leftist positions.

McGovern's own actions also provided fodder for critics who charged that he was too indecisive and incompetent to be president. Most damaging was the Eagleton affair. Two reporters discovered that McGovern's initial choice for vice-presidential running mate, Thomas Eagleton, had been hospitalized for "mental exhaustion." McGovern initially expressed his support of Eagleton, then demanded his resignation from the ticket. Not only did this reflect poorly on McGovern's thoroughness in investigating potential running mates, but his decision to drop Eagleton suggested an uncertainty and lack of candidness that undercut his "presidential" image. Moreover, after the convention, Larry O'Brien was brought on as McGovern's campaign chair to assuage the traditional party coalition members. O'Brien quickly complained that the campaign was disorganized, and contributed to perceptions that McGovern was not entirely in control of his own campaign by publicly demanding that they "put things in order" if he was to stay on (Apple 1972, 1).

McGovern further distanced himself from the Democratic power structure by assembling an in-house organization, Charles Guggenheim

Productions, to handle media. Hall and Levine, the Democratic National Committee's advertising agency, bought broadcast time but produced no campaign material. Guggenheim, a staunch Democrat, was primarily a documentary filmmaker with political campaign experience. He had worked on fifty-four campaigns in twenty-two states, including Adlai Stevenson's 1956 campaign, Hubert Humphrey's 1968 campaign, and Robert Kennedy's 1964 senatorial campaign and 1968 presidential primary campaign. Guggenheim extended his services during this campaign to assist McGovern, who was a personal friend. Guggenheim Productions produced a variety of material: spots, panel discussions, a televised fireside chat, statewide telethons, and a biographical documentary film, *The McGovern Story*.

## The McGovern Story

*The McGovern Story* was a newer version of the films Guggenheim made in 1962 and 1968 for McGovern's senatorial campaigns. Guggenheim asserted that the 1962 film was largely responsible for getting McGovern elected, for he was in the hospital throughout the campaign and made no appearances at all. They updated the film for the presidential primaries, and edited it slightly for each state in which it was shown, in order to address regional issues. *The McGovern Story* was shown to Democratic gatherings throughout the general campaign, and aired on national television on 1 October at 8:30 P.M., and then again on election eve at 8:30 P.M. According to Guggenheim, the film was tremendously effective during the presidential primaries, where dramatizing the positions McGovern represented added to the grassroots campaign's momentum. The film grew less effective as the campaign wore on, for by mirroring McGovern's positions in a forthright manner, it contributed to the Democratic majority's perception that he was too far to the left.

*The McGovern Story* was an expository documentary, one of the clearest examples of the classical campaign film ever made. The film advances in chronological order, with still-photographs, archival footage, and reenacted scenes to depict McGovern's early life and later career. The film, which both begins and ends with clips from McGovern's acceptance speech, documents his ascension from a little-known candidate who was not taken seriously, to the successful candidate in the public eye. *The McGovern Story*'s producer, Charles Guggenheim, was a documentarian whose primary concern was filmmaking rather than politics, and the film, while technically proficient, was almost too straightforward in its portrayal of the candidate and campaign. It did not aim to fashion an image so much as to convey one, even though re-created scenes were used freely in the service of the film.

Although the film seemed to be a straightforward documentary, in several cases the images needed to illustrate McGovern's life and career simply did not exist, so Guggenheim used the tools of the documentarian's trade. He used footage from *The Plow that Broke the Plains*, a famous government propaganda film about the dust bowl during the depression, in order to illustrate South Dakota-born McGovern's compassion for the disadvantaged. Guggenheim takes desolate images from the film, such as a close-up of a spider treading along the cracked earth, as the narrator recalls McGovern's early years during the depression. In another case, archival footage from a World War II battle scene is shot from the point of view of the airplane pilot, making the experience seem vivid, but hardly authentic. Another scene shows McGovern's home during his university days. Although the camera crew photographed the actual building he lived in at the time, symbols of domesticity such as an upright iron on an ironing board, or a child's doll strewn across an easy chair, obviously belonged to the current occupants rather than the candidate. In yet another sequence, shots of anguished Vietnamese women and children followed images of a wounded American soldier in Vietnam. These visual portrayals of pain and suffering served implicitly to undercut Nixon's position on continuing involvement in Vietnam by showing the human consequences of his decision. But the pictures also suggested that McGovern had some link with these people, that he had been there and seen them. Yet, the same music and images appeared in a scene of Guggenheim's 1968 tribute film for Robert Kennedy.

As a representative anecdote, the film most notably displayed the weaknesses of the candidate that ultimately doomed the McGovern campaign. The opening scene illustrates this point. Like most biographical films, *The McGovern Story* begins in the recent past. Inclusive images of America—country and city—introduce a shot of McGovern, deep in thought as he sits on an airplane. Dissolve to documentary footage of the Democratic convention, where McGovern is nominated. Viewers see McGovern as he watches himself being nominated on the television in his hotel room—an image that unintentionally reinforces perceptions of passivity, of a man who *received* rather than *achieved* the nomination.

Throughout the film, McGovern is presented in accord with the myth of the president as a man of the people, to the exclusion of images that would portray him as a credible leader. According to Guggenheim, the film emphasized the qualities that would make McGovern attractive to voters: "He was a man who came out of the heartland in a difficult time and place, a man with fortitude, energy, and individualism, a man who came from very modest means who became well educated, and a man who showed great bravery during the war." He is placed into the corpus of American mythology: he grew up on a farm in the prairie, and the narrator states that he learned the lessons of a gentle spirit from his mother, and the value of Christian principles, hard work, and a love of history from his immigrant father. McGovern's friend, historian Leonard Chenoweth, testifies that McGovern is a man who is close to the soil, who identifies with the hardworking, virtuous American people. Chenoweth states: "If you have worked with your hands, with the people who have gone through the problems that the people went through in the middle border, if you are at all a sensitive person, and George is a sensitive person, then you develop a feeling for this heritage." The candidate is compassionate and sensitive, but not authoritative or dynamic.

In the tradition of presidential candidates, he is also a dedicated family man who married his high school sweetheart. In one scene, the family is clothed in raingear, tromping through the autumn leaves with their dog, as the narrator recounts, "Those were good times, Eleanor would remember. The children were old enough to share the excitement of our life. We were happy and together." The wives of presidential candidates are often invisible; in most campaign films, they are mentioned but remain behind the scenes. In this case, Eleanor does not speak for herself; although she ostensibly knows the candidate better than anyone, her testimony is not solicited. Though McGovern was the progressive candidate, the film techniques were not.

In a later scene designed to show McGovern's identification with the people, images and narration describe his grassroots organizers at work. McGovern himself reminds viewers that he has succeeded through lots of little donations from working people. There is an implicit contrast with Nixon's well-publicized refusal to reveal the names of contributors, as viewers are reminded, "In a time when elections depended on the secret contributions of a few, his campaign would be financed in a different way. We don't have special interests contributing to the McGovern campaign."

McGovern establishes that he is one of the people and that he cares about their interests. On the positive side, McGovern refuses to indulge in fantasy; he spends time with real people in the real world of factories and housing complexes. He enters the environments of specific social groups: the elderly, laborers, students, and blue-collar workers, and listens to their complaints. An elderly woman complains about not getting retirement benefits, a young student protests that there are no jobs, a middle-aged man complains about drugs and crime, several people decry high taxes and corporate profits attained at the expense of workers, farmers report getting squeezed by the government, a middle-aged woman insists that although she's not a feminist, she wants to be treated fairly, and finally, a young man protests the futility of a life spent working in a factory until retirement. This is the disgruntled underbelly of America—they exist. However, he is primarily shown listening to their comments, there are many close-ups of him nodding in agreement; but he offers no plan or advice. He ingests but does not gesture. The McGovern film mirrors McGovern's positions without tempering them; it provides a life history that offers George McGovern as a man of the generalized middle, an ordinary American par excellence.

There are attempts to present the candidate as a leader. The film links McGovern to past Democratic heroes by including clips where John and Robert Kennedy commend him, while the narrator reminds viewers that McGovern is respected by his colleagues in the Senate. Stock footage shows the recently deceased Robert Kennedy endorsing McGovern in his senatorial campaign, and the point is proffered that McGovern is now carrying on Kennedy's work. McGovern's campaign for Democratic congressman from South Dakota is illustrated, as well as the Food for Peace program he initiated in the Senate, accompanied by images of malnourished people. But the attempt to mythologize the candidate as a hero backfires. There is archival battle footage of an air force unit during World War II; one of McGovern's men, waist gunner Bill McEvoy, recounts the tale of McGovern's heroism in which he successfully landed his B–24 bomber plane after its engine was hit, a feat that earned him a Distinguished Flying Cross. This single demonstration of heroic leadership, however, is undercut by the narrator's claim that McGovern remained "haunted" by the war.

The entire film portrays both a feeling and a vision of malaise. Instead of depicting problems and then offering the candidate and his vision as the means to resolution, the film dwells on the past and its problems; no solutions are offered. Even the narration is entirely in the past tense. Its structure is regressive rather than forward-moving, its message nostalgic rather than celebratory. As McGovern states in a segment from his acceptance speech at the Democratic National Convention: "Join with me in this campaign, and together we will call America home to the ideals that nourished us from the very beginning. Come home to the affirmation that we have a dream. Come home to the conviction that we can move our country forward. Come home to the belief that we can seek a newer land." *Come home* was a code term for ending the Vietnam War, yet McGovern does not propose any specific ideas; rather, like the minister that he was, he asks for a renewal of faith. This semi-apocalyptic tone permeates the film.

Shadows and silhouettes predominate, and shots are linked primarily through dissolves that give the film a "soft" feel. But the visual technique works against the candidate. Richard Nixon, perceived as cold and distant, could have benefited from such a technique. Similarly, McGovern could have benefited from fast cuts and action shots that reinforced perceptions of the candidate as a strong, decisive man who was in control of events. Instead, the slow, meditative film technique prevents viewers from perceiving the candidate as a dynamic leader. The style does reinforce the narrator's verbal assertions that McGovern is a man of peace, but it does nothing to allay perceptions that the candidate is not strong or decisive enough to be president.

The biography evidences the problems that plagued the campaign. McGovern is accorded none of the distance that befits a leader. He rides buses rather than airplanes; he solicits donations a dollar at a time; he talks with disgruntled groups of Americans in stark, dimly lit factories and auditoriums. Guggenheim's technique was deliberately unslick. At times, the sound quality of the film is so poor that parts of McGovern's conversations with the people are indecipherable. These scenes were accurate depictions of his presidential campaign, but they were not "presidential."

Even the language of the film's narration doubles what Jamieson refers to as McGovern's tentative, low-status style (1984, 323). Typically, anonymous narrators project certainty and knowledge. However, here at the film's climax, the narrator states: "Perhaps they would find, in the memory of their path, a way out of the wilderness for us all." Perhaps yes, perhaps no—notwithstanding the fact that McGovern's solution to the country's woes lies in the semantically obscure "memory of their path."

There are few images of power or optimism in the film. The film expresses McGovern's vision of malaise, but there is little in the way of form or content to suggest that he will lead the country to a better future. The film is full of images without hope, from the depression to World War II to Vietnam. The weather is dry, windy, or rainy; the sun sets but does not rise. McGovern asserts his opposition to the Vietnam War, supported by footage of soldiers fighting and the Vietnamese people's poverty and deprivation. Scenes of domestic hunger and poverty accompany McGovern's assertion that he also sees wounds in our own country, followed by clips of conversations with ordinary Americans who complain about the quality of life. Towards the film's conclusion, the candidate trudges down the senate corridor enmeshed in shadows, his footsteps echoing dramatically as he recedes into the distance. Only a janitor's mop and pail leaning against the wall disturb the quiet serenity of the shot. In all likelihood, the shot is meant to suggest that the candidate works hard and late into the night, but its associations fail to edify the candidate's image.

The film offers little hope to those who would identify with McGovern's America. His America is a wounded country that needs to be healed; identifying with McGovern or his constituencies is, in effect, to side with losers rather than winners, the powerless rather than the powerful. But for the majority of middle class voters, the American Dream of upward mobility was not dead; as Richard Nixon so aptly demonstrated, it was ready to be revived.

## THE NIXON CAMPAIGN

While the inexperienced McGovern campaign developed strategy along the way, Nixon's Committee to Re-elect the President (CREEP) was organized in May 1971 and had 275 members who spent more than a year preparing for the Nixon campaign. Nixon's campaign manager, Clark MacGregor, headed CREEP and oversaw the advertising strategy. White House advisers Robert H. Finch, John Erlichman, Robert Haldeman, and Charles Colson were informal consultants, although the project had no official ties to the White House; all except Colson appeared in the Nixon campaign films to endorse the candidate.

Early in 1972, McGregor assembled an ad hoc, in-house committee, referred to as the November Group, to handle paid media. This was less expensive than hiring a commercial agency, and more importantly, it avoided overt associations with Madison Avenue. However, November Group was headed by Los Angeles advertising executive Peter Dailey, who hired a number of people from top Madison Avenue advertising agencies, all of whom were reimbursed for their employees' absences. They ran background checks on all members to assure their loyalty to Nixon, and the resulting team was well organized, well financed, and experienced. Made up of Nixon supporters from top advertising agencies who ordinarily competed against one another, the November Group had the creativity and expertise, but not the label of Madison Avenue. The selection of a cadre of Madison Avenue's best and brightest has continued to characterize Republican presidential campaigns.

Nixon's campaign pioneered the now commonplace strategy of coordinating the messages that appeared on paid and free media. Throughout the campaign, Nixon sequestered himself in the White House and relied upon the news media to convey favorable, carefully orchestrated images of him appearing "presidential"; he appeared in no uncontrolled situations where he might deviate from this role. According to Sig Mickelson, "The practice of encasing the candidate in an airtight cocoon began in 1972, and the art of candidate packaging has developed ever since" (1989, 161).

In effect, Nixon reinstated the tradition of the mute tribune. He declined to campaign in 1972. Nixon ran as president, not candidate. He refused to debate McGovern on the grounds that it was unseemly for a president to discuss national policy matters on television, and he relied on surrogates to travel around the country to promote his candidacy. At the same time, he controlled the airwaves with special announcements or contrived public appearances that counted as news. The Nixon campaign's main forms of paid media, the spot commercial and documentary film, supplemented and often recycled images that played on the news. Filmed documentaries, and commercials excerpted from them, supplanted campaign appearances by the candidate.

### Richard Nixon: Portrait of a President and The Nixon Years: Change Without Chaos

The Nixon campaign made extensive use of documentary film rather than slick spot advertisements. According to one source, the staff did not produce many advertisements because they were confident that McGovern's far left position isolated him from the majority, and that he would self-destruct on his own. Nixon had seen and liked filmmaker David Wolper's documentary, *The Selling of the President 1960*, and wanted Wolper to make his campaign films. Like Guggenheim, Wolper was an award-winning documentarian; he had made political films for both Democrats and Republicans, including *One Thousand Days*, the tribute to John Kennedy; *Quest for Peace*, a 1964 tribute to Lyndon Johnson; a biography for George Romney, Republican governor of New York; and one for Paul Shaffer, incumbent Republican candidate for governor of Pennsylvania in 1966. The latter campaign pitted Wolper against both Guggenheim and Shelby Storck, who made a highly regarded biographical film for Shaffer's opponent, Democrat Milton

Shapp, although the longshot candidate failed to unseat the incumbent governor.

Although the Nixon White House was initially concerned about Wolper's political leanings, he told them that he would have a problem making the films only if Nixon stopped supporting Israel. Haldeman assured him that the president was pro-Israel, so Wolper came on board to make three documentary films for Nixon: a personal biography, *Richard Nixon: Portrait of a President*; a resumé film, *The Nixon Years: Change Without Chaos*; and a short piece about Pat Nixon for the Republican convention. Wolper worked independently of the November Group and reported directly to Nixon's White House advisers Haldeman and Erlichman. They told Wolper what to include in the films, and he relayed this information to his directors, Ed Spiegel (*Portrait of a President*), and Alex Grasshoff (*Change Without Chaos*).

The documentaries aired as free media at the convention and paid political programs during the campaign. *Portrait of a President* played as part of the networks' television coverage at the Republican convention; it aired again as paid media on election eve, both preceding and following a brief "live" Nixon speech. A fifteen-minute version of *Change Without Chaos* showed at the Republican convention, and CBS televised a thirty-minute version as a paid political program on 14 October. The Republicans also showed both films to private gatherings of supporters and volunteers across the country. Despite the Nixon campaign's obvious development of the merchandising model of campaigns in their overall strategy, the documentary films were still designed to motivate the troops rather than attract the uncommitted.

Even so, *Portrait of a President* and *Change Without Chaos* reflected the Nixon campaign's tight organization and well-planned strategy. Throughout the 1972 presidential campaign, the Republicans made little reference to their party in an attempt to secure the growing numbers of ticket splitters: uncommitted voters who relied more upon a candidate's personal attributes and perceived competency than party loyalty. They also hoped to appeal to growing numbers of conservative Independent and Democratic voters—primarily from the south—for whom McGovern was too radical. Nixon ran as president, not candidate, and the emphasis was on presenting him as a firm, decisive leader who singlehandedly rescued the country from crisis. Neither of his campaign films made political pleas apart from the closing line, "This is why we need President Nixon more than ever."

In terms of style, both films demonstrate the successful interweaving of news footage—real and manufactured—and fabricated images produced specifically for the film. *Change Without Chaos* opens with a quick-cut montage of news footage depicting various instances of social discord: riots, looting, antiwar demonstrations, picket lines. This is the America of the past, the result of liberal permissiveness, that the Nixon administration is putting to rest. The fast-paced, uncomposed, grainy black-and-white images cut to a serene, static, high-quality color image of the White House, in which Richard Nixon is firmly ensconced. In another scene, Richard Nixon marches through a police station with reporters in tow, a replay of a publicly staged demonstration of his commitment to law and order. Moreover, Nixon's trip to China and Russia in late February and early March was arranged for its image appeal as much as for practical foreign policy. The trip was both news event and material for the campaign films and advertisements; Nixon hired Wolper as the official navy file photographer and footage from the trip later appeared in spot advertisements and in scenes in Wolper's films.

The campaign relied to a great extent on poll data, demographics, and pretesting of its themes to construct a positive image of the candidate. Before the 1972 election campaign even began, Nixon's permanent White House pollster Robert Teeter conducted surveys to determine voters' attitudes. Teeter's polls revealed that Nixon was respected but not well liked. He was perceived as experienced, competent, sage, trained, and honest, but not warm, open-minded, or relaxed (Diamond and Bates 1984, 25). He was considered decisive and willing to promote change, but not compassionate. As a result, the biographical *Portrait of a President* (first shown at the Republican convention as *Nixon the Man*) and the resumé film *Change Without Chaos* present Nixon as a warm, relaxed man with a sense of humor, rather than the cold and distant figure perceived by much of the public. In scenes repeated across the two films, Nixon spontaneously plays "Happy Birthday" on the piano for Duke Ellington at a formal White House occasion, he thanks his Chinese interpreter and jokes that she "got every word right" during his visit to Communist China, and he strolls on the beach with his family in still-photographs that also appeared in his 1968 film, *Richard Nixon: A Self Portrait*. In another instance, both films portray Nixon's compassion in a scene where he visits the grave of Tanya, an innocent Russian child who was killed during the siege of Leningrad in World War II.

In the more personal *Portrait of a President*, Nixon's daughters testify with regard to his character. Julie states that he is sensitive, Tricia that he is shy, and even Henry Kissinger reports that he is "quite gentle" in his manner. Nixon's White House advisors, Leonard Garment, Robert Finch, John Erlichman, and his physician, Dr. Walter Tkach, also offer testimony about his character. Erlichman appears to be responsible for mythologizing Richard Nixon as a virtuous man of the people. He recounts Nixon's impoverished youth, where through his mother's "almost puritanical" conviction about what was moral and right, he learned the value of working hard, saving money, and living a clean life. These are presumably the people who know the "real" Richard Nixon, and by directly addressing viewers, they simulate an intimate conversation.

In addition to poor perceptions of Nixon's character, the November Group's early research also showed that Nixon was in a poor position with regard to the issues, and that people felt a general dissatisfaction with the direction in which the country was headed. More extensive research revealed that dissatisfaction was aimed more at intangible aspects of government and bureaucracy than at the president himself. According to Dailey, "Everything we developed from then on in the positive advertising done under the banner of the Committee to Re-Elect the President embodied in it the concept that the President is working for responsible change" (May and Fraser 1973, 196–97).

*Change Without Chaos* made use of the November Group's research findings and showed Nixon achieving responsible change. The film emphasized Nixon's leadership qualities, experience, and performance in office, and presented him as a political professional in control of the office and the country. It fulfilled the five general objectives outlined in a campaign memo: present the president as an activist, a man with a long-range vision, a man who inherited a mess, a man of courage, decisiveness and dedication, and an issue-oriented candidate (Jamieson, 1984, 195–97).

The masculine language of the film constructed Richard Nixon as a dynamic man of action. Narrator Richard Basehart uses strong verbs and war metaphors to portray Nixon as a fighter; and sentences are structured in the active tense so that Nixon appears to be the sole initiator of events. For example, he *attacked* the problems of poverty, he *insisted* that welfare be replaced, he marshalled the forces of government, he conducts an *assault* on crime, he *launches* urgent research on sickle cell anemia. Singlehandedly, "he reverses the basic priorities of the United States government." He *explores* every path toward peace with honor, *probes* private channels, and begins a *penetrating* investigation of economic concepts. His opponents were not the Democrats or George McGovern, but the impersonal federal bureaucracy, where red tape rather than individuals provided "frustrating roadblocks" to his proposals; the Vietnamese, who refused to negotiate seriously to end the war; and the Congress, who delayed Nixon's initiatives until agreements were "hammered" out. (No mention was made that the Congress had a Democratic majority.)

Nixon contrasts with the indecisive, peace-mongering McGovern without deigning to mention him by name. Under the guise of a simple reiteration of Nixon's accomplishments, the film advocates his positions on the issues where McGovern was most vulnerable, such as Vietnam. While McGovern called for unconditional withdrawal from Vietnam, Nixon held out for "peace with honor." The narrator reminds viewers that the troops have been decreased by over 90%, draft calls have been reduced, and no more draftees are being sent to Vietnam. Then Nixon provides emotional justification for continuing American involvement. In a cut from a televised speech, Nixon states, "Abandoning our commitment . . . would mean turning 17 million South Vietnamese over to Communist terror. It would mean leaving hundreds of American prisoners in Communist hands." Film footage of prisoners of war apparently being brainwashed appears on screen, followed by Nixon meeting with their relatives. These images make the prisoners' plights vivid and heighten the emotional pull of Nixon's argument. Nixon's words assume that all Americans have made a "commitment," and evoke the cultural value of keeping one's word, fear of communism, and empathy for others, particularly other Americans. Without making a direct assertion, McGovern's proposed unconditional withdrawal is made to appear un-American and inhumane. Nixon has done all he can, but his "generous offer" of settlement has been rebuffed by the intransigent North Vietnamese who "refuse to negotiate." Moreover, at the close of the film, narrator Basehart refers to Nixon's "master plan" to replace confrontation with negotiation. Although this is in reference to his dealings with the Communist Chinese and Russians, it reassures voters that Nixon's accomplishments are part of a long-term plan to achieve change.

Both *Portrait of a President* and *Change Without Chaos* highlight accomplishments that will attract defecting Democrats: ending the mandatory draft, reduction of voting age from twenty-one to eighteen, stopping inflation, decreasing the military budget, and increasing Social Security benefits. The latter was mandated by the Democratic Congress, another fact not mentioned. Several issues typically associated with liberals are mentioned, such as environmental protection, support for the arts, and medical research. The conservative issues mentioned are those most palatable to the public-at-large: decreasing crime, stopping the flow of drugs, and using wage-and-price controls to stop inflation. Viewers are reminded of Nixon's proposed welfare and tax reforms, implicitly contrasting him with McGovern. McGovern's plan for these reforms, announced during the primary, was roundly criticized for being too expensive and ill-informed. After several unsuccessful attempts to defend the plan, McGovern capitulated and tabled it, providing yet another indication of his indecisiveness.

Both *Portrait of a President* and *Change Without Chaos* end with Nixon, man of peace, making allies out of adversaries in Communist China and the Soviet Republic. The films position Nixon, and the people of the United States, as a unified group of well-meaning benefactors who are striving to attain global peace and understanding. Partisan appeals have no place in such a world.

The Nixon films attempt to construct a unified group of "ordinary" Americans positioned slightly to the right of center. Separate divisions within the Committee to Re-elect the President were assigned for significant voting groups: youths, blacks, ethnics, Spanish-speaking citizens, farmers, women, Jewish-Americans, lawyers, teachers, businesspeople, and the elderly. *Portrait of a President* and *Change Without Chaos* include appeals to many of these groups, in addition to addressing the generic conservative Republican. The films offer a range of positions that allow them to be read favorably by this wide variety of viewers from different, even oppositional, social formations. For example, *Change Without Chaos* nods to minorities in a segment that describes Nixon's entrepreneurship program for small businesses. Black, Mexican-American, and Native American businessmen appear on camera to acknowledge the benefits they have received from the program. While this segment highlights positive figures of identification for minority viewers, the film also reinforces stereotypes and preconceptions held by the dominant white culture. Social discord is associated with blacks, who loot and riot in the opening scene. In 1964, Barry Goldwater declared that his own film, *Choice*, was racist because blacks were predominantly shown rioting. Yet, no such considerations were involved here. In another scene, Nixon's voice announces that welfare was a "disastrous mess," as he shakes hands with a black woman. The shot implies that blacks are the primary recipients of welfare. When Nixon asserts that his welfare reform plan would make sure that every American had basic needs met, two poor white children in a rural slum are photographed. In this way, the target blocs of voters who resent welfare as a "handout" to minorities are not alienated. In addition, Nixon's averred opposition to busing, repeated in both films, reassures the conservative white constituency that his programs may get blacks off welfare, but they don't provide for racial integration.

Both films speak to diverse demographic groups and construct a number of potential positions—from the conservative mainstream working class American, to the newly empowered eighteen- to twenty-one-year-old voters, to the elderly, to minorities, to women. In *Change Without Chaos*, Nixon's presidential staff assistant Barbara Franklevey asserts that the administration has tripled the number of women in "top" jobs, and moved another thousand into middle management. As she speaks, there are images of Nixon with women in military uniforms, as well as women civilians. The nature of a "top" job remains ambiguous, and the inclusion of the military as part of the Nixon administration certainly skews the statistics.

When inflation is mentioned, along with wage and price controls, increased taxes on imports, and Nixon's proposed cuts in federal bureaucracy, Nixon addresses white working class Americans. These are the ordinary Americans who can be moved by promises to improve the quality of life. They are the "homeowners and wage earners" whom narrator Basehart intimates will "escape" from higher property and sales taxes if there are cuts in federal bureaucracy. As he speaks, representative images of Americans at work appear on screen: farmers, construction workers, mechanics, and office workers. This is the primary audience addressed by the film, those at the core rather than the margins of American society, the rightful heirs to the fruits of peace and prosperity. These are the images of Americans appropriated by the Republican party.

Although the Republican party has traditionally been the party of big business (which truly benefited from reductions in federal bureaucracy), at one point Nixon appears to criticize the auto industry. In an attempt to appeal to more liberal voters, Nixon reiterates his implementation of the environmental protection program, and claims that he bucked the big auto industries who wanted to delay implementation of the exhaust emission rules. Incongruously, Nixon cruises in a motorboat that spews gasoline as he recites poetry regarding the earth's natural beauty that surrounds him.

## SUMMARY

The 1972 campaign marked the last hurrah of the military model, which relied heavily upon the expository techniques associated with traditional documentaries in order to inform and educate viewers. The classical films, shot on 16mm film, used the conventions of cinema verité to convey authenticity. These classical "slice-of-life" documentaries provided chronological narratives of the candidate's life and career, or thematically ordered accounts of an incumbent's accomplishments. Illustrative "proofs" such as still-photographs, archival footage, or newly filmed footage of the candidate support the narrator's verbal assertions.

Both Wolper and Guggenheim were documentarians; as such, their styles and strategies embraced codes of realism, and they eschewed film techniques associated with commercial advertising and emotion-based appeals for their own sake. To some extent, these filmmakers felt some conflict about making political campaign films. Wolper referred to his work as "the creative interpretation of reality," but regarded himself as simply the mediator of the Republicans' thoughts. Director Ed Spiegel claimed, "I justified it to myself by simply allowing them to tell their story, without any manipulation on my part. I approached the film much as a lawyer would advocate a case in court."

These documentarians were concerned that their films presented an "accurate" representation of reality, albeit one-sided. Obviously, filmmakers know the purpose of the campaign film and censor themselves by only shooting and using material that is beneficial to the candidate. Recuts cost filmmakers money, so it is to their advantage to get it right the first time. While acknowledging the limits of representation, documentary filmmakers attempt to maintain some link, however tenuous, between image and reality. Nixon's trips to China and Russia, for example, were faithfully rendered, but they were pseudo-events, arranged for their favorable publicity in the first place. Spiegel noted, too, the impossibility of using cinema verité film techniques with consummate political actors. Even when the filmmakers tried not to tamper with the scene they were shooting, their subjects were influenced by the presence of the cameras. At a cabinet meeting where the filmmakers instructed Nixon to "act naturally," he performed for the camera. He presided over the meeting, telling cabinet members information they already knew and orating rather than conversing. As a result, they had to carefully edit the final film so that Nixon did not seem to be acting.

Even when the filmmakers believe they are capturing "reality," their subjects are typically primed on what to say and how to behave. For instance, *Portrait of a President* includes brief interviews with members of the Nixon White House and his two daughters. Spiegel's method was to allow those close to the president to speak for him, but he provided no script or direction about what to say. However, Tricia sits in the Queen's bedroom and recalls her father's note to her on her wedding night. The moral of her story suggests that he was too shy to speak his thoughts, so he had to write instead. Her deliberate mention of her father's shyness, in light of the campaign's aim to depict him as shy rather than cold, was an unlikely coincidence.

The Nixon films, in particular, moved toward the hybrid documentary-advertisement by blurring the distinctions between factual "news" and constructed images. The recycled news images integrated into the films reinforced popular memory of the orchestrated events that took place in lieu of a campaign and demonstrated the value of repetition. *Change Without Chaos* was particularly successful in this regard. Jamieson notes, "A test of the impact of the film on over 300 voters found that the film increased approval of the president's handling of his job among all segments of voters, increased the feelings of voters that Nixon had accomplished 'quite a lot,' contained no claims that voters found hard to believe, and increased the perception of 'the President's handling of major vote-determining issues, and is especially effective on the issues of taxes, Vietnam, and drugs'" (1984, 296).

Richard Nixon won one of the most sweeping landslides in American electoral history, despite the fact that reports on the Watergate incident had begun to appear in newspapers as early as August 1972. McGovern did not exploit the issue, but Richard Nixon was eventually called to task and suffered the humiliation of resigning from the presidency. An institutional crisis, defined by lack of trust in the office of the presidency, came to accompany the social, economic, and moral crises addressed by McGovern. As Gerald Ford faced Jimmy Carter in 1976, and then Ronald Reagan vied against the incumbent Carter in 1980, McGovern's vision of malaise dominated the political climate. Ford and then Reagan adopted Nixon's strategy of projecting hope and optimism, with crisis relegated to the past, while by 1980, Democrat Carter wallowed in despair. From 1972 on, the Republicans appropriated the positive symbols and values that defined the American people, leaving the Democrats bereft. Barry Goldwater first posed the choice, and the Republican candidates after him opted for the traditional, nostalgic, unified America of myth and fantasy—a place far more palatable to the majority of voters than the gritty, chaotic reality of the disgruntled and disenfranchised.

# II

# THE MODERN FORM: THE HYBRID DOCUMENTARY-ADVERTISEMENT

*Chapter 5* _____

# The Modern Period, 1976–1980

The 1976 presidential campaign marked significant changes in American politics. "Incumbent" Gerald Ford, who assumed the office upon Nixon's resignation in 1974, opposed Jimmy Carter, former governor of Georgia, who emerged as a dark horse Democratic candidate. Neither candidate was a strong contender. Ford won his party's nomination despite a chastening primary challenge by Ronald Reagan, and Carter won the Democratic nomination while running as a party outsider.

A depressed economy and massive disillusionment with American society and government created a political climate amenable to transformation. The country was in the midst of an economic recession, and although inflation was lessening by the time of the presidential election, unemployment remained high. Scarce resources led many people to question the precepts and values of the liberal democratic welfare state that had informed both Democratic and Republican platforms since Roosevelt's New Deal. The country's unconditional withdrawal from Vietnam during Richard Nixon's tenure created fears that American military world dominance was on the wane. Government officials' inability to justify American involvement in Vietnam, coupled with Richard Nixon's ignominious departure from office after the Watergate debacle fostered widespread distrust of government and cynicism toward the presidency. Public involvement in politics and allegiances to a particular political party neared their nadir.

Within this context of social, economic, and institutional crisis, factors aimed at remedying the ills of the political system altered the form and shape of political communication. Changes in electoral rules and procedures, adopted mainly by the Democrats in response to the debacle at their 1968 convention, went into effect in 1976. New delegate selection rules democratized the presidential candidate nomination process by encouraging states to hold primary elections instead of convention caucuses to determine delegates for a candidate. With candidates endorsed by popular vote rather than chosen from within the party ranks, aspiring nominees could use media to circumvent party and appeal directly to voters.

Reforms in campaign spending laws, instigated by Watergate, also intensified television's role in elections. Amendments to the 1971 Federal Election Campaign Act (also amended in 1974) made 1976 the first federally funded presidential election campaign. The government provided matching grants to candidates who raised $5000 in amounts of $250 or less in at least twenty states, while the law limited individual campaign contributions to $1000 and determined a set amount of $25 million for all general election campaign expenditures. As a result, purchasing national television time became more economically and pragmatically feasible than making personal appearances, funding local organizations of volunteers, or distributing campaign paraphernalia. Both the Ford and Carter campaigns spent almost half of their funds on advertising, devising strategies to keep production costs down while making the best use of broadcast time.

Television's renewed importance heightened the status of campaign professionals such as pollsters and media consultants. Beginning in 1976, consultants who were also members of the candidate's inner circle of advisers helmed the presidential media campaigns and determined themes, strategies, and tactics. Versed in politics and skilled at attracting and motivating consumers, they took for granted that well-constructed television images, rather than an emphasis upon party identity or the candidate's stand on issues, could potentially shake voter apathy and even encourage swing voters. Messages designed for television audiences could both reinforce committed supporters and attract the ever-increasing numbers of uninvolved or undecided voters. By the mid-1970s, Americans actively watched over three hours of television per day, about half claimed to rely on television whenever there were conflicting reports in different media, and media information was at the top of voters' lists of causal factors explaining their voting decisions (Sabato 1981, 117).

Armed with an array of pollsters, market researchers, and computer experts, the professional media consultants instituted audience-oriented communications in the presidential campaign. Although polls and commercial marketing techniques were hardly new to presidential campaigns, in the past, polls and other market research techniques measured preexistent public attitudes toward a candidate or issue to help determine themes or plan strategy. But in contrast to advertisers who used research to test their completed themes and products, or documentary filmmakers who loved to make films but had little conception of audience, the new merchandising campaign used polls and research to establish which themes would work for targeted groups in the first place. More sophisticated polling techniques allowed campaigns to specifically identify constituencies and elicit their unspoken hopes and fears as material for themes and issues, while the application of marketing techniques enabled campaigns to pre- and posttest their messages.

As a result of the above changes, the 1976 campaign provided a model of the modern media-orchestrated merchandising campaign entirely crafted for television (see O'Shaughnessy 1990, 50). Carter adviser Gerald Rafshoon, following Democratic consultant Tony Schwartz, wrote that both political and commercial advertising were matters of "striking a dramatic chord and knowing your *customers* [italics mine] and their motives" (Donath 1976, 115). Soft-sell advertising aesthetics translated poll data and pervaded the campaigns. Soft-sell advertisements make few direct assertions, but merely associate a product with feelings or events that target audience values. Political messages consisted of image-based appeals aimed at articulating the public's unspoken hopes or fears, or arousing pleasurable feelings towards the candidate-as-product.

Technological innovations also influenced presidential campaign communication. Both advertisements and documentaries combined film and videotape, taking advantage of film's superior, deep, rich image quality and perceptions of its "objectivity," and videotape's greater flexibility and perceptions of its "liveness" and "immediacy." Electronic video editing equipment allowed for graphics, superimpositions, split screens, animation, and other such "gimmicks" to hold viewers' attention; videotape was also more portable, cheaper, and easier to edit than film. The use of videotape also helped to create perceptions of reality. According to media consultant Bob Squier, "Videotape is more real. It's like the reality of television. Your eyes are attuned to tape images. It gives you a sense of immediacy, action. The viewer thinks he's [*sic*] watching the news" (quoted by Navasky 1972, 90).

Both candidates Ford and Carter had campaign films that exemplified the shifting form and content of political messages. They were hybrid documentary-advertisements geared to mass television audiences, rather than documentaries aimed at enthusing supporters. The (untitled) Ford film and *Jimmy Who?* introduced the candidates prior to their nomination acceptance addresses at their respective conventions, were cut into spot advertisements, and were reedited into lengthier postconvention films. Ford's film also provided a final election-eve punctuation mark.

The hybrid documentary-advertisements attempted to secure the viewer's attention, then affection by adopting television's entertainment values and making no specific claims that might alienate blocs of voters. Designed for an audience of viewers rather than voters, these modern films followed televisual rather than cinematic conventions. Short vignettes edited together provided a portrait of the candidate, facilitating the films' supplementary use as spot advertisements during the campaign. The modern hybrid films juxtaposed visually excessive images, signified by graphics, special effects, musical spectacle, animation, and symbolic images of America, with the more spare conventional representations of the documentary film: direct address, testimonials, still-photographs, archival and news footage, and seemingly unorchestrated live action shots. They combined fantasy images typical of soft-sell advertising with television's perceived authenticity and film's "objectivity," ultimately rendering the different modes of discourse indistinguishable. Symbolic visual images unanchored to concrete historical events—farmlands, picnics and parades, even the Statue of Liberty, were intercut with more substantive, representational images in order to associate the candidates with pleasurable representations of their country. Music supplanted the once-dominant narration; both Ford and Carter's 1976 films incorporated campaign songs, with image montages representing "America" accompanying the lyrics. *Jimmy Who?* even had an extended animation sequence and special effects. These films initiated the modern era of the presidential campaign film.

## THE FORD CAMPAIGN

At first, Gerald Ford followed Nixon's example in choosing his campaign team. Republican campaign veteran Stuart Spencer directed (he was later replaced by James Baker III, but remained in an advisory role), while Bob Teeter was pollster. Peter Dailey, head of Nixon's November Group, was in charge of Campaign '76, a similar ad hoc group of advertising experts on leave from their agencies. But Ford's political team was not impressed with Dailey's primary campaign ads, and convinced Ford to fire him. Ford briefly shifted to Jim Jordan, president of BBD&O, before following Teeter and Spencer's recommendation to hire Bailey-Deardourff, a newly established Republican consulting firm.

Bailey-Deardourff joined the campaign as "volunteers" a few weeks prior to the Republican National Convention; they were officially hired after Ford's nomination, when they could be paid with federal funds. Although many media consultants lacked political knowledge, both were graduates of the Fletcher School of Government at Harvard, and had increasingly found their attention focused on the supervision of advertising when they moved into consulting. Despite the fact that this was their first national political campaign, they demonstrated the consultant's growing power by insisting upon, and receiving, complete control of advertising throughout the campaign. Both were in charge of planning and implementing the advertising campaign, while also serving on the executive committee that advised Ford on overall campaign strategy.

Teeter's polls suggested that the majority of the country was in a conservative though optimistic mood. Social rather than economic issues and people's feelings about the candidates' personal traits rather than issues were most important; people yearned for honest leadership and felt deeply about traditional American values such as work, faith, and family. Early on, Deardourff clarified the media plan:

We want to strengthen the personal dimension of the President. People have to know more about him—his roots, his family. He is an unelected President; he did not campaign. There are large gaps in the people's knowledge about him.

We want to strengthen the leadership dimension—to explain the record of the last two and a half years, to compare where we are with where we were when he was thrust into the presidency. We want to explain what his concept of the presidency is.

We have to demonstrate to voters where the president wants to go. He is not simply running on his record. He has a vision of where he wants the country to move.

We want to make clear the contrast between the President's experience and general competence, the differences in approaches to the nation's problems (*Broadcasting*, 6 September 1976, 28).

The candidate's image was clearly the most important "issue" in this campaign. The campaign wanted to convey information about Ford's personal and family life, his democratic concept of the presidency, and his accomplishments since taking office. They wanted to portray him as personally warm, with integrity and leadership skills (Donath 1976, 1). For Ford's specific plan of action, Spencer and Teeter put together a book that surmised, "One positive thing is that we are not working against a hard, anti-President Ford feeling. Even the disapproval in the Gallup Poll [although high] is not firm. . . . It is just that not enough voters have a strong, positive feeling about the Ford personality and character" (Drew 1977, 531). They added that in order to win, "we must persuade over 15 per cent (or about 10 million people) to change their opinions. This will require very aggressive media-oriented efforts" (533).

In response, Bailey and Deardourff came up with a media plan that had five aims: to show Ford's human dimension; leadership abilities; accomplishments; compassion for those less fortunate; and to change perceptions of Carter from positive to negative (MacDougall 1977, 74). Spot advertisements tailored to different demographic and geographic groups dealt with each of these themes, and several of the advertisements were incorporated into a convention film that later became the election-eve film that recapped the campaign.

### The Ford Film

Ford's convention film was planned only two weeks before the Republican National Convention, when the Ford campaign realized that they should have a film to compete with Carter's, which aired at the Democratic National Convention. They hired Ed Spiegel, director of Nixon's *Portrait of a President* (1972), to work on the film. Spiegel quickly gathered preexistent biographical material from primary spot advertisements, and shot new footage of the Ford family and colleagues, which became a source for spot commercials during the general election campaign. They made the ten-minute convention videotape in five days; Spiegel spent two days taping Ford and his family at Camp David, two days interviewing cabinet members in the White House, and another day taping the president at work. It cost the Ford primary campaign its last $120,000, and they sent the finished product to the networks a few hours before it aired at 11:30 P.M., just prior to Ford's acceptance speech (McDougall 1977, 87).

After the convention, Bailey-Deardourff hired adman Malcolm MacDougall as creative director of advertising, and MacDougall asked Spiegel to put together another version of the convention film to show on election eve. The completed film replayed the general election spot advertisements that appeared in the convention film, along with footage from the Republican National Convention, followed by a "live," ten-minute Ford speech. It aired at 8:30 P.M. on ABC, 9:30 P.M. on CBS, and 10:30 P.M. on NBC, in each case following Carter's election-eve program.

The Ford film, a hallmark of the presidential campaign film's shift from the classical documentary to the hybrid documentary-advertisement, aims to create a positive feeling about America and Gerald Ford. While following the structural conventions of the biographical campaign documentary, the Ford film also incorporates the aesthetics of television advertising. A prototype of subsequent Republican campaign films, it combines upbeat music and narration, along with idyllic images of America and its people, intercut with "documentary" footage. For example, as the film opens, Ford accepts his party's nomination at the Republican National Convention (with "Hail to the Chief" playing in the background). Patriotic yet unrelated images of the Tall Ships at the Fourth of July celebration, and Ford ringing the bell on the deck of the USS *Forrestral*, follow this scene. These images of renewal have no referential context in the film, yet they help create positive images of Gerald Ford and the country he represents. The juxtaposition of images persuade people to "buy" idealized images of the candidate, country, and themselves.

The film, which consists of 16mm film and videotape, exploits the perceived immediacy of television. It admixes "live" appearances by Joe Garagiola and Gerald Ford, prerecorded interviews, news clips, fabricated images, archival footage, and still-photographs. It begins with an on-camera introduction by sports figure Joe Garagiola, seated inside *Air Force One*. But *Air Force One*, while a powerful symbol of the presidency, served as the setting out of necessity rather than design. As the election-eve film neared completion, the producers realized that a live appearance by Ford would bring the film up to the moment and give it a sense of urgency. But Ford's advance people were unable to schedule a time other than the Saturday before the election, as Ford and Garagiola, who was assisting the candidate by moderating a series of panel discussion programs, flew from Houston to New York. Thus, the sound of the plane's engine that accompanied Garagiola's introduction was not a fabrication; both Garagiola's introduction and Ford's final speech were shot in the air. The sounds of a plane in flight distract the viewer, as does the turbulence that rocked the plane as Ford spoke; at the same time, the plane in motion does convey a sense of Ford as a man of action. A slight continuity problem is also apparent to perceptive viewers. Jamieson notes that although these "live" portions were supposedly taking place on election eve, the shots of the plane that served as transitions throughout the film were obviously taken in broad daylight (1984, 373).

In terms of content, the film establishes Ford's leadership, competence, and accomplishments while humanizing him as an ordinary American. Whereas past Republican candidates more often stressed their leadership, this campaign tried to present Ford as simultaneously a leader and a man of the people. This shift coincided with the Republicans' appropriation of Democratic symbolism, but it was also a necessity in this election in order to combat Carter's populist appeal. Endorsements from "down-to-earth" celebrities such as Garagiola and Pearl Bailey help accomplish this task. Celebrities "above the people" stand up for Gerald Ford, but only those who are folksy representatives of the common person. Pearl Bailey, speaking extemporaneously from a television studio in a prerecorded segment, comments, "Oh, he's made some mistakes honey. You better believe he has." She may have intended to show the candidate as a flawed man in order to humanize him, but instead her remark serves as an implicit reminder of Ford's big mistake—his pardon of Nixon, a negative issue not addressed by the Ford campaign or the film. According to Deardourff, lingering public suspicion about Ford's motives for pardoning Nixon went against the campaign's effort to portray him as a man of integrity. Ford's political advisers opted not to bring it up during the campaign, but its omission amid Ms. Bailey's reminder, left a substantive hole in the film as well as the campaign.

In many ways the film obeyed classical presidential campaign film conventions. Like most presidential candidates, Ford was born into a loving family that taught him the obligation to serve his community, and he was dedicated to his wife and children. More screen time was devoted to family than in any previous campaign film, a harbinger of the family values theme that would dominate succeeding elections. Home movies, a breakfast sequence with the Ford family, and interviews with Ford and his children show his human dimension and traditional values. Along with home movies and still-photographs of the Ford family celebrating daughter Susan's birthday, the family interviews reinforce that he is a good father, and is loved and admired by his offspring. The narrator declares that Gerald and Betty "are a love story," and in a brash appeal to the emotions, the film replays clips from Gerald and Betty Ford's news conference regarding her mastectomy. This creates empathy and subtly reminds viewers of the Fords' ability to overcome crisis.

The film emphasizes Ford's leadership qualities by depicting socially notable achievements from youth to adult. The anonymous narrator cites Ford's personal accomplishments, from National Honor Society member to Eagle Scout to captain of the high school football team. As in classical campaign films, friends and colleagues provide verbal support for the candidate. Willis Ward, a black teammate from Ford's University of Michigan football team testifies to his forcefulness of character, claiming that Ford blocked a player from Georgia (an oblique reference to Carter) who had made a racist remark, causing the player to have to leave the game. The film moves on to Ford's career at Yale Law School. Class-mate William Scranton attests to Ford's hard work and discipline, and the narrator informs viewers that Ford finished in the top third of an extraordinarily high-achieving class.

Archival World War II footage of the navy carrier *Monterey* mythologizes Ford as a war hero. The image is complete with footage of uniformed soldiers engaged in battle and sounds of gunfire. Gunnery officer John Caldwalder, in color and located in the present, informs viewers about Lt. Ford's leadership and courage during battle. Still-photographs depict Ford's first election campaign for Congress, then a wedding photograph with Betty. As Betty remarks upon how hard Ford worked to win elections, their home movies show Ford the family man, frolicking with his young children in the back yard. Democratic Congresswoman Edith Green, in an attempt to imply nonpartisan support for Ford, testifies to Ford's competent leadership and decency of character; still-photographs of Ford in Congress accompany her words.

Great pains are taken to contrast Ford's egalitarian governing style with Nixon's imperialistic manner. Ford assures voters that he has a democratic governing style, while pictures show him listening to advisers. A photograph of Ford conferring with his cabinet was actually taken during the ill-fated *Mayaguez* incident, although the photograph's reference was not mentioned (Drew 1981, 401). Appointments Secretary Terry O'Donnell and Secretary of Transportation William Coleman appear on-camera to testify to Ford's openness and willingness to accept disagreement, while Chief of Staff Richard Cheney assures voters that, although Ford listens, he also knows when to make a decision. Throughout the film, testimonials come from Ford's cabinet members and colleagues rather than ordinary Americans.

Other film clips depict Ford as an active president at work. Still-photographs depict the loneliness of the office; in one photograph, he leans over a table with his back to the camera, an allusion to a famous, similar photograph of John Kennedy. The narrator also cites Ford's domestic accomplishments to induce belief in his credibility as a leader: reduced government spending, less inflation, more jobs. The narrator's assertion of positive economic changes brought about by Ford's leadership occurs against a backdrop of rousing music. Active verbs suggest that he alone controlled circumstances with firm, decisive action: "President Ford cut spending by over 9 billion dollars. He cut inflation in half. . . . Ford unshackled the private sector, providing an unparalleled 4 million new jobs in one and a half years." There is a break from the literal representation that has structured much of the rest of the film. Images of construction workers and farmers tilling soil, not anchored to time or place, accompany the narrator's words. These are the stereotypical Americans whom Gerald Ford represents.

The film also emphasizes Ford's stature as a world leader, and implicitly contrasts him with Carter, who had no foreign policy experience. He meets with Brezhnev and Chou En-lai; he negotiates a settlement to the Israeli-Egyptian conflict. Yet, he also represents America's military renewal. Again, the film rejects literal representation: images and sounds of missiles firing appear as Ford claims the need for a strong defense, and the scene ends with generic World War II battle footage. The narrator boasts that Ford has increased the military budget and reversed a ten-year downward trend. He implies that the public need not fear another Vietnam under Ford's stewardship.

Overall, the film attempts to present Ford as an integrated leader and a man of the people who presides over an America where crises have been resolved. For the Republicans, candidates embracing both opposing images coincides with an increasingly optimistic vision of America where the candidate can fit everyone's idealized image. In the tradition of Republican candidates before him, Ford evokes troubled times from the past in order to indicate their resolution in the present. Negative images predominate throughout Goldwater's *Choice*, they open Nixon's *Change Without Chaos*, and Ford's film tucks them into a brief sequence in the middle. A film montage depicts bombs exploding, the Ku Klux Klan, soldiers in Vietnam, students demonstrating and holding peace signs, and police marching to restore order. Both the 1972 Nixon and Ford films cut from images of discord to a shot of the White House, with the incumbent president seated securely within its confines. Ford's narrator asserts, "In these troubled times, a distressed nation was stirred by a new and candid voice." Gerald Ford, in a speech clip, assures the American people that the nightmare is over. The narrator blames liberal practices without mentioning them by name, as he goes on to criticize high government spending, taxes, inflation, and ever-increasing government programs of the past.

While Nixon's *Change Without Chaos* conveys the dynamic image of a president achieving change, the Ford film attempts to depict a renewed America. Beginning with Ford, the Republicans appropriate the positive vision of hope and market it, while the Democrats, bereft of symbols after the "failure" of the Great Society, increasingly lapse into the vision of despair. Ford announces in a clip from his acceptance speech, "Something wonderful happened to this country of ours the past two years. We all came to realize it on the Fourth of July. Together after our years of turmoil and tragedy, Americans recaptured the spirit of 1776."

Later, as the narrator recites a litany of Ford's accomplishments, symbols of abundance accompany his voice: shots of spewing wheat, fields being harvested, fruit being picked from a tree, and melons being harvested. A close-up depicts french fries being mass produced, followed by a shot of potatoes on a conveyor belt.

The Ford film both speaks to and creates images of the resurgent American people. It addresses the generalized middle classes, whom Ford acknowledges in another clip from his acceptance speech: "You are the people who pay the taxes and obey the law. You are the people who make our system work. You are the people who make America what it is." These are not the angry, rebellious Americans from the troubled past, but the virtuous citizens from the increasingly prosperous present. He reassures them that he has increased jobs, but it is more a statement about law and order than a promise of employment. The narrator asserts, "America started back to work with meaningful, proud jobs, not dependent on government handouts." The illustrative images show construction workers, implicitly equating blacks and welfare by including a black construction worker in a film where few other minorities appear.

Ford's vision of resurgence is visually reinforced as the film nears the end with a marching band and an upbeat, uplifting song, "I'm Feeling Good About America." The song, written by Bob Gardner, was initially used as a spot advertisement with different versions in different parts of the country. The inserted advertisement preceded Ford's "live" appearance in the film, while the song's final rendition at the film's conclusion was accompanied by images of America shot from a plane, including mountains, streams, farmland, the New York City skyline, and the Statue of Liberty. According to Deardourff, "It may still to this day be the best piece of presidential campaign music ever done. It captured exactly the feeling we wanted to convey. It allowed us to use a lot of visuals. . . . it was the only thing that even came close to capturing the sense that things were getting better and would continue to get better if Ford were reelected." The song's final line, "I'm feelin' good about me," is a harbinger of the eighties and the Reagan ideology.

While the film largely followed the expository documentary conventions of chronological ordering and illustrative proof, it also began to create an image of an upbeat, optimistic America that the candidate represented. Yet, it may have been too soon after Watergate and the turbulent 1960s for most Americans to accept its premise. Moreover, the filmmakers were not happy with the final product. MacDougall complained that it looked like, and was, "film-by-committee" (1977, 224). Different people shot most of the footage, Ed Spiegel was a filmmaker with little political expertise, and Bailey and Deardourff were too busy with the spot ads, panel discussion programs, and running other political campaigns to closely supervise production of the film. Spiegel preferred the aesthetics of film to tape, and the film was a mixture of both. It was difficult to make major editorial changes quickly on film, and thus by the end they were locked into an approach.

Deardourff stated, "As I look back, that film is a serious disappointment to me. We weren't able to pull it off from a production standpoint in the way I would have liked, but I think it had creative problems as well. There were conceptual problems that we didn't take as seriously as we should have." The film rehashed old material rather than made a final statement that punctuated the entire campaign. Ford failed to provide a vision during the campaign, and the filmmakers looked to him to do so in his final "live," ten-minute speech. But the candidate spoke only in generalities; he was hoarse, exhausted, and clearly uncomfortable speaking directly to camera. Ford, already regarded as a poor speaker, had no time to practice his speech, and turbulence rocked the plane as he spoke. Deardourff recalls that they pleaded with him to redo the speech, but he was too mentally and physically exhausted after the arduous campaign to do so.

## THE CARTER CAMPAIGN

While Ford's campaign continued the Republican tradition of hiring political professionals whose aims were to win above all else, Carter continued the Democratic trend to work with longtime friends and loyal supporters personally committed to the candidate. Carter's advisers, Hamilton Jordan and Jody Powell, with him from his governorship in Georgia, headed his primary and general election campaign team. In contrast to Bailey-Deardourff's strictly business relationship with their client, Carter's personal friend and adviser, Gerald Rafshoon, directed his media campaign during the primary and general election. Rafshoon, an Atlanta based consultant with an advertising background, had worked with Carter since the candidate's unsuccessful bid for governor of Georgia in 1966. Rafshoon ran Carter's winning campaign for governor in 1970 and served as his adviser ever since. Rafshoon had such authority within the campaign that he was able to produce and air commercials during the primaries before Carter ever saw them.

Pollster Pat Caddell, who worked for McGovern in 1972, was one of the few Democratic mainstays. Bob Squier, an ex-television producer who worked on Humphrey's 1968 campaign, was the only media consultant on the team with prior presidential campaign experience. Consequently, their efforts led Caddell to reflect, "The 1976 General Election was at best a mediocre effort. . . . We tried to run a national primary campaign, which was our experience. We did not run a conceptual strategic campaign, we did not try to lay out a conceptual framework of messages, issues, signals, or definitions. Rather than a conceptual strategy, we had a strategy of tactics" (Drew 1981, 407).

The Carter campaign tried to take advantage of post-Watergate sentiment. Caddell's polls found that integrity and competence, rather than issues, were most important to the electorate. These became Carter's campaign themes, bolstered by the message that he was an anti-Washington, antiestablishment candidate. Carter had positioned himself as a political outsider in his 1966 gubernatorial race in Georgia, and the time was right for him to use the same approach in his run for the presidency. His campaign headquarters were in Georgia, not in Washington. Rafshoon's media stressed his small town, rural image; he was a populist man of the people, and the peanut was used to symbolize his campaign because of its "humble" quality. As the general election campaign progressed, Rafshoon also attempted to portray Carter as presidential material by stressing his leadership abilities and foreign policy experience. The campaign produced one hybrid-documentary campaign film, *Jimmy Who?*

### Jimmy Who?

*Jimmy Who?* was a biographical campaign film, narrated by E. G. Marshall, that aired before Carter's acceptance speech at the Democratic National Convention and again during the general election campaign. Rafshoon shot much of the material over a three-year period before Carter's presidential run, and contracted the rest to Rod Goodwin, head of Magus Productions in Philadelphia. Rafshoon selected Goodwin for his ability to unobtrusively follow the candidate with a camera crew; thus, Rafshoon had in mind the cinema verité style characteristic of the classical films. Three camera crews shot footage during the convention; during the general election, an expanded half-hour version incorporated clips from Carter's acceptance speech and the convention itself. Parts of the film were also cut into spot commercials. But Carter opted for a "live," issue-oriented, telethon-type program on election eve, making one last attempt to combat charges that he was "fuzzy" on substantive issues.

Gerald Rafshoon, producer of *Jimmy Who?*, professed a preference for cinema verité, where nothing is staged or shot in a studio. He stated:

When we talk about the tenets of political advertising, we are of course referring to accurate representation. We are not talking about selling a candidate like a bar of soap. The implementation is quite different. It must be based around intimacy and simplicity. You have to validate on the air what you are doing on the street. In general, elaborate and expensive production techniques should be out of the question. In short, what you see is what you get (1976, 43).

Yet, *Jimmy Who?* radically departed from the conventional classical documentary form and exemplified the hybrid documentary-advertisement genre. It admixed documentary footage that recorded the progress of Carter's primary campaign with more innovative televisual techniques. Although Rafshoon paid lip service to cinema verité, the film was a hybrid that used flashy visual techniques to entrance viewers, while its representational images anchored it in "reality." Its slick form contrasted with the simplicity of its contents.

The postconvention film opens with documentary footage of Carter's acceptance speech at the Democratic National Convention. The film then cuts to an animated drawing of Jimmy Carter at the podium of the National Press Club, where he is introduced as "the next president of the United States." The graphic dissolves into a "live" image of Carter, who introduces himself by describing his academic background. Dissolve to the train depot in small-town Plains, Georgia, and then Jimmy Carter, in checkered shirt, walks through a wheat field as the narrator provides his biography. In another scene, Carter meets with Americans around the country while Dionne Warwick sings "What Do You Get When You Fall in Love?" Despite the attempt at cinema verité styling of the images here, at least one of these meetings is staged; close viewing reveals a woman waiting in a doorway who emerges just in time for Carter to "spontaneously" greet her.

At one point, the film severs all ties to representation. The narrator states, "The primaries came in rapid succession like firecrackers on the Fourth of July," and fireworks appear to shoot out of the lens of the camera and onto the television screen. The film reproduces animated pictures of Republican and Democratic symbols, other candidates, campaign paraphernalia, and then political cartoons about Jimmy Carter. Back to Plains and the candidate walking through corn fields, and then a scene where Carter recites from his acceptance speech, accompanied by a montage of American people superimposed against landscapes of different geographical locations that again shifts the film out of the realm of actuality. The film closes with the Carter campaign song, also the title of his print autobiography, "Why Not the Best" playing behind "realistic" images that illustrate the progress of the Democratic primary campaign. Video freeze frames, superimpositions, animation, graphics, songs, and other special effects distinguish *Jimmy Who?* from other campaign films.

The films also nods to television by including it as part of the film. After narrator E. G. Marshall announces Carter's primary victory, footage depicts Jimmy Carter getting the election results as he sits with Dan Rather in the anchor booth of the CBS news studio. *Jimmy Who?* incorporates television coverage of the campaign as part of its story; Jimmy Carter, like the rest of the American people, learns about reality by watching television.

Although the general election campaign made an attempt to portray Carter as a "presidential" leader, the film made little effort to do so. Both the pre- and postconvention versions of *Jimmy Who?* emphasize Carter's status as a political outsider, an unknown underdog whose candidacy is an American success story. As the film opens, Carter recalls the skepticism voiced by the *Atlanta Constitution*—his home state newspaper—about the announcement of his candidacy; there is a freeze frame, the title comes up, and the narrator reminds viewers that few people outside Georgia knew his name when he entered the race. The sequence is meant to illustrate Carter's rise from unknown contender to presidential candidate, but it can also be read as the self-deprecation typical of Democratic candidates.

Carter's qualifications and experience were secondary; most important, he was a humble, virtuous, plain-speaking man of the people with roots in the soil who, as wife Rosalynn avers on camera, "has never had any hint of scandal in his personal or public life." The film presents the millionaire businessman as a small-town peanut farmer who worked the family land. Carter wanders through fields of grain and vegetables, inspecting the produce, or scooping handfuls of peanuts as they are mass produced. He gets his hands dirty like any farmer. The narrator informs viewers that Carter left a promising navy career to return to the land and resume the work of his parents, and Carter declares on camera: "Nobody in my family before my generation ever had a chance to finish high school. We've always worked for a living. We know what it means to work."

The Carter campaign was aware that perceptions of the candidate's character, rather than specific issues, were central in this campaign. In an opening vignette, people on the street mostly comment upon Carter's personal characteristics rather than qualifications. These supporters also reiterate the major themes of the film. One woman says, "I think he's sexy," while another adds, "I think he has a nice smile." Several of those questioned don't know who he is; one man thinks he's a baseball player. They describe him as a peanut farmer rather than governor of Georgia, and one young woman is apologetic, "I don't think it makes any difference whether he's a peanut farmer or not. I mean, there's nothing wrong with peanuts as far as I'm concerned." Comments by these ordinary Americans also reinforce that Carter is a man of the people. One man says, "He's a people's man," while a woman with a working class accent surmises, "I picture him like one of us, one of the working people, one of the common people."

Carter campaigns by going directly to the people and introducing himself, in contrast to Nixon or the incumbent Ford who made little direct contact with voters. He is assisted by the Georgia "Peanut Brigade," made up of volunteers who travel to New Hampshire to canvass for the primary. At one point, Carter notes, "The ultimate political influence rests not with the power brokers, but with the people"; and he further aligns himself with ordinary Americans in a voice-over that says, "I see a president who is not isolated from our people, but who feels your pain and who shares your dreams." His America is one that is in pain rather than resurgent.

Carter's America merges rural and urban, North and South, into one community with a united citizenry. He alludes to past scandals and corruption, although the film is generally upbeat and forward-moving. Carter suggests that although the country is presently troubled, it can be healed through compassion. He speaks of government's need to reflect the competence, compassion, and simple decency of the people. In many ways, his image is the antithesis of Richard Nixon's and much of the film can be read as a refutation of Nixon—and all that he represented—rather than Gerald Ford.

While Ford's film represents few ordinary Americans on camera, Carter's film represents little else. Young, middle-aged, elderly, black, white, male, and female citizens, rarely identifiable by occupation or class, populate the screen. Although Carter is associated with rural land, people are interviewed in Central Park and Carter is shown campaigning mainly on city streets. In addition, the New Hampshire primary illustrates not only Carter's first significant victory, but a meeting point of North and South. There are the requisite construction workers and farmers in the film, and at one point Carter shakes hands outside an auto shop. The locations the narrator claims Carter visits are encompassing: towns, cities, meeting halls, factories, supermarkets, sidewalks; Carter states that he went to shopping centers, factory shift lines, colleges, beauty parlors and barber shops, farmer's markets, and union halls. But the greater preponderance of young people in this film than in other campaign films and the emphasis on popular music aligns Carter with youth, change, and vitality.

Carter narrowly beat Ford in the election, and no doubt the public's inability to forgive the Republicans for Watergate contributed to his victory. His first term in office, however, was beleaguered by domestic and international problems. By 1980 the public mood had shifted, and, once again, disgruntled voters were looking for change. Most importantly, they were susceptible to images of a resurgent America, a mythic land of hope and opportunity promised by the Republicans.

## THE 1980 ELECTION

Republican challenger Ronald Reagan and Independent John Anderson battled incumbent President Carter in 1980. The end of four years of the Carter presidency was marked by economic disarray at home. An energy crisis exacerbated the usual problems of inflation and high unemployment. Moreover, American impotence in the face of the OPEC nations' move to control the world oil supply, and then the seizure of American hostages in Iran, reinforced impressions of a power in decline. By the end of the 1980 primary campaign, Carter's pollster Pat Caddell's surveys found that despite rebuffing a nomination challenge from Ted Kennedy, Carter's popularity was at an all time low, and the majority of people did not want him as their president.

To a large extent, the 1980 campaign was an implicit debate between those who believed that the American Dream was still a possibility, and those who believed in the inevitability of privation and declining expectations (Burnham 1981, 107). Caddell, taking surveys throughout the Carter presidency, surmised that the nation was undergoing a moral and spiritual crisis; people were pessimistic, anxious, lacking confidence, and alienated from the political process (Perry 1984, 60–61). Reagan's pollster Richard Wirthlin came to similar conclusions. Throughout most of 1978 and 1979, Wirthlin's polling firm, Decision Making Information, conducted comprehensive studies of public attitudes. In a June memo, he wrote that the public had been "severely battered" by Vietnam, Watergate, assassinations, riots, black revolts, and the alienation of youth. The result was "the shattering of traditional confidence in America," where throughout the seventies, the majority felt that the country was on the wrong track. People believed that everything was moving too fast, there were no fast rules anymore, and the values of their parents no longer held (Goldman and Fuller 1984, 35). The general election campaign began with a nation in despair, lacking confidence in their president, their government, and themselves.

## THE REAGAN CAMPAIGN

Ronald Reagan, the Republican front-runner, had been preparing for the Republican nomination since his unsuccessful attempt to unseat Gerald Ford in 1976. His initial team of advisers consisted of campaign veterans with him since his election as governor of California: chief-of-staff Edwin Meese, consultant Michael Deaver, and pollster Richard Wirthlin. Campaign manager John Sears, a lawyer involved in Nixon's 1968 campaign, had already managed Reagan's attempt to wrest the nomination from Gerald Ford in 1976. The team was fraught with internal strife between the Californians and party insiders. Deaver "resigned" early on after a confrontation with Sears; Wirthlin battled with Sears over control of campaign strategy. Just before the primary, Reagan fired Sears along with two of his supporters. William Casey became campaign manager, Wirthlin was put in charge of strategy, and Deaver later returned to the campaign.

Sears hired Los Angeles adman Peter Dailey, who also headed Nixon's 1972 November Group and Ford's 1976 primary campaign, to produce media communications. As was typical with Republican campaigns, Dailey formed an ad hoc advertising agency, Campaign '80, by recruiting top talent from Madison Avenue. Bill Carruthers, a documentary filmmaker who worked on the Nixon and Ford campaigns, provided his expertise on longer films and videotapes. Shortly after Sears left, Richard O'Reilly replaced John Savage as the general manager of Campaign '80. Dailey remained, although Deaver and other campaign insiders criticized his advertisements and he was not rehired in 1984.

The Republicans aimed to expand their base to reach both undecided independents and disaffected Democrats. After Nixon's resignation in 1974, the Republican party invested in computers to raise funds and rebuild the party, and they used their investments in sophisticated ways. Pollster Richard Wirthlin had been developing a computerized campaign simulation model, Political Information System (PINS), since 1969. The model, first used by the military and political scientists to simulate war scenarios in the fifties, then adapted by marketing firms, aimed to predict the effect of particular strategy choices. PINS analyzed poll and census data, historical voting patterns, economic conditions, and political experts' assessments to continually track the progress of the campaign; its computerized simulation even predicted Reagan's victory. In contrast, the Carter campaign did almost no testing (Jamieson 1984, 397).

PINS was the most sophisticated technology used yet in a presidential campaign; throughout 1978 and 1979, Wirthlin conducted comprehensive, in-depth studies of public attitudes to secure a data base; throughout the campaign, daily tracking polls enabled them to make strategy adjustments. Most importantly, unlike less complex systems that could only measure voters' responses to candidates' positions on the issues, PINS could assess reactions to particular presentations of the candidate's character. Wirthlin found that leadership was the key issue for voters. His firm categorized every aspect of the electorate's ideal image of a leader so that Reagan could act out any features that didn't fit the ideal until they became perceived as "natural" (Perry 1984, 83).

PINS also revealed Reagan's negatives: many people perceived Reagan primarily as an actor rather than a competent leader, and they were concerned that he was too militant. In a confidential campaign memo written in June, Wirthlin wrote that the campaign needed to "reinforce the image strengths that embody the Presidential values a majority of Americans think are important. . . . At the same time, minimize the perception that he is dangerous and uncaring" (Blumenthal 1981, 43). The strategy was to overcome doubts about Reagan's leadership abilities, then turn the election into a referendum on Carter's leadership.

The campaign advertisements were thoroughly marketed and tested. The Reagan strategists ran focus groups on 800 to 1000 people in Los Angeles, Cleveland, Baltimore, Detroit and New York; they also pretested their advertisements on selected markets, and compared audience responses to their own and Carter's ads. In order to make Reagan known to voters and to establish him as a competent leader, the early advertisements were issue-oriented spots that stressed Reagan's record as governor; they also made extensive use of five-minute documentary-advertisements throughout the campaign. The ads were purposely low-key rather than slick and glossy. According to Dailey, they wanted to produce ads with an "amateurish" quality: "You do it with execution that wasn't so great—a little bit corny maybe or maybe the lighting isn't so good" (Devlin 1981, 5). These "unprofessional" ads dissociated the presidential candidate from the Hollywood actor.

## The Reagan Record

Dailey produced a short biographical documentary called *The Reagan Record* that embodied Wirthlin's strategy recommendations. The

8 1/2-minute film preceded Reagan's nomination acceptance address at the Republican National Convention, and then was recut into a five-minute spot aired repeatedly until the final weeks of the campaign. It also provided the basis for shorter commercials aired on television. The film later won praise within the industry by winning a Storck Award for noteworthy achievement in the political advertising arts.

*The Reagan Record*, the keystone of Reagan's campaign, depicted Reagan as both a hero who "saved" the state of California during his tenure as governor, and as a man of the people, a natural-born leader who emerged out of America's heartland. The film lauds Reagan's record as governor of California as vindication of his beliefs in a decentralized federal government, tax cuts, welfare reform, and a renewed faith in the American Dream. It shows him as a strong administrator of a state "five times the size of Georgia," in order to highlight his ability to govern a country and to dispel widespread perceptions that he was merely an actor. The film, pretested on undecided Democrats, presented Reagan as a benign leader, in contrast to the Carter campaign's depiction of him as a dangerous aggressor who posed a threat to world peace.

The film unfolds in the straightforward manner of the classical documentary, beginning with Reagan accepting the Republican nomination. The film then cuts to America's heartland, small-town Illinois. After it depicts his early years through a series of still-photographs, the film cuts to Hollywood, "where he appealed to audiences because he was so clearly one of them." His military service as an air force captain on a special air force film training unit is cited, after which he returns to Hollywood, dedicated to "improving the lot of every working man and woman." After he won the race for governor of California in 1966, the film claims that he resolved California's crisis and got the state "back on track."

On the surface, *The Reagan Record* obeys traditional documentary conventions, yet it subtly manipulates visual images to imply leadership. For instance, group photographs are doctored so that Reagan, shaded blue, stands out from the black-and-white crowd. It is also replete with factual inaccuracies or exaggerations of his record as governor. The narrator claims that California was on the brink of bankruptcy before Reagan worked his budgetary magic, and graphics on-screen quote a *San Francisco Examiner* editorial that says, "We exaggerate very little when we say Governor Reagan has saved the state from bankruptcy." More accurately, the state had a cash flow problem because there was no state income withholding tax, so they had to borrow from other state funds. There was no danger of bankruptcy, and only the editorial, which in the first version of the film was erroneously credited to the *San Francisco Chronicle*, made any such suggestion. In addition, the narrator states that Governor Reagan was the greatest tax reformer in California history, providing property tax relief of over $2 billion. But these tax reforms were the product of the largely Democratic legislature; Reagan's proposals were rejected. The narrator also asserts that by the time Reagan left office, the deficit had been turned into a surplus. But no mention was made that this accomplishment resulted from tax increases, which Reagan as presidential candidate ostensibly opposed. Reagan also claimed that his gubernatorial administration increased money for student loans, but the federal government, rather than the state, financed the loans. The film then proclaimed his environmental protection program as, "the nation's toughest." But Reagan opposed formation of the Redwoods National Park, expansion of state parks, and fired two members of the state Natural Resources Board for being too tough on industry. The film quotes the head of the California Federation of Labor, who commends Reagan's labor record. However, the labor leader, John Henning, protested that his remark was taken out of context and asked that the statement be removed from the ad (Turner 1980, B17).

In a final irony, according to the *New York Times* (29 September 1980, D13) a scene purportedly depicting Reagan signing a bill to cut taxes is actually showing him signing a bill to liberalize the right to abortion. He later renounced his position on abortion, claiming that he opposed abortion and was sorry he ever signed the bill.

Despite the film's emphasis upon exposition, it was too late to regress to the past. The Reagan campaign recognized the utility of emphasizing hope and affirmation rather than futility and despair; thus, *The Reagan Record* ends on an uplifting note that attempts to stir patriotic emotions. In a final image montage similar to the conclusion of the Ford film, the campaign theme song, "The Time Is Now" accompanies rhetorical depictions of America: rocky seacoasts, farmland, bunting-draped small towns, the Statue of Liberty, still-photographs of Reagan delivering campaign addresses. He initiates the theme of 1984: "Together . . . A New Beginning." These images were familiar, and thus reassuring, to the majority of Americans who yearned for a simpler past. Reagan offered the promise of a "return" to a new beginning. His promise was alluring to the throngs of downtrodden and disenchanted Americans.

### This Man, This Office

Carter's 1980 campaign employed virtually the same team of advisors and strategists that he had in 1976: Hamilton Jordan, pollster Pat Caddell, and media consultant Gerald Rafshoon. The campaign produced one documentary, *This Man, This Office*, made by consultant Bob Squier in October 1979 and shown on ABC in early January. During the primary, thirty- and sixty-second spots were cut from the film. Rafshoon later added footage from Carter's Camp David Accords between Israel and Egypt, and they used the film to introduce Carter before his nomination acceptance address. It was replayed yet again at 8:30 P.M. on election eve, though only in key states.

*This Man, This Office* demonstrates the way that images of a candidate may shift as they move from challenger to incumbent. Carter's *Jimmy Who?* portrayed him as a man of the people, but the latter film tries to present him as an experienced leader. The film wraps Carter in symbols of the presidency, such as the White House, Oval Office, and *Air Force One*. High profile Democrats endorse his presidency: Arizona Governor Bruce Babbitt, House Speaker Tip O'Neill, Hawaiian Senator Daniel Inouye, House Majority Leader Jim Wright, New York Governor Mario Cuomo, Arizona Representative Morris Udall, San Francisco Mayor Diane Feinstein, and even former Secretary of State Cyrus Vance (though he was forced to resign from office before the film was made). These eminent public figures lend Carter their credibility through their association with him. They either cite his accomplishments or remind people that an unpopular president is not necessarily a bad one. Mario Cuomo, for example, offers Carter a double-edged compliment, "When he got low in the polls, that to me was his badge of honor. Because I knew that he was low in the polls meant that he was willing to do the right thing, even if it wasn't, for the moment, the popular thing."

Along with the attempt to present Carter as an authoritative figure supported by his colleagues, there are some positive images that attempt to associate him with the American people: a factory worker, a welder, children, a farmer pitching hay, construction workers, houses being built, a tractor moving through a field. These images appear briefly, and do not contribute to the overall tone of the film. Four years later, the Republicans appropriated these mythic images of traditional America as the Democrats relinquished them.

*This Man, This Office* depicts Carter as a leader, but largely at the expense of his image as a man of the people. In another sequence, ordinary Americans appear on-screen to voice the qualities they'd like a president to have. In a sequence of person-on-the-street interviews they cite Carteresque attributes such as morality, loyalty, consistency, God-fearingness, patience, sincerity, credibility, concern, and caring. Significantly, none mention Carter by name.

The film attempts to defend Carter's unpopularity and perceptions of his unorthodox style of governing primarily by relating him to past presidential leaders and stressing the burdens of the office. The film opens with a camera panning around icons such as the Lincoln Memorial and Washington Monument. The narrator reports the hardships of being president, stating "there's no end to the chains that bind him," a comment that sets the film's implied theme of Carter as Christ-like martyr. The scene cuts to outside the White House, then to Carter as he enters the Oval Office. He sits at his desk, pressing his fist to his forehead and writing furiously. In reality, he rarely used the room (Drew 1981, 258). The image is one of despondency, befitting the dominant tone of the entire film.

The film associates Carter to, mostly dead, Democratic and Republican presidents through statues, film footage, and portraits. Footage of previous presidents depicts them stating unpopular positions, and portraits of nineteenth century presidents appear as the narrator recites unfavorable comments directed against them. He offers an almost apologetic explanation of the Carter presidency, "No president has been entirely beloved in his own time." The emphasis upon past history and visual images of cultural artifacts appear defensive, almost an acknowledgement of defeat before the campaign had even begun. The film fails to create the impression of a dynamic forward-moving campaign.

The film tries to associate Carter with the glory of America's past rather than its present. But the film conveys a vision of malaise almost despite itself. As in other modern films, images and symbols representative of mythic America attempt to create a positive aura that surrounds the candidate. As the film opens, the "Battle Hymn of the Republic" plays as the narrator recounts the settlement of the New World. Shots of the ocean, seagrass rippling in the breeze, a sunset, mountains in clouds, Niagara Falls, and the desert with a silhouette of a man on horseback appear on screen. Dissolve to a shot of the Constitution, then a fast-paced montage of shots of neons, marquees, taxis, kiosks, and skyscrapers in Times Square as the narrator lauds the Constitution for allowing "people to transfer real power without killing each other." A clip of Mayor Koch appears in which he says, "This city can survive anything." New York City serves as a metaphor for modern America, yet it is hardly a celebratory image, especially as the city had recently almost gone bankrupt.

*This Man, This Office* addresses America and implies all is not well: a black woman stands in a disgruntled crowd and complains to reporters, "There's no hope for the black people." As guitar and drums play, men march with picket signs, people throw frisbees in the confines of Central Park, people run en masse in the New York Marathon, and police with guns occupy a building.

The film appears to admit defeat. Even Carter, attending a black church service in Cleveland, says in an understatement, "I don't claim that we've yet reached the Promised Land." The music that concludes the film is a dirge. Tones of lamentation accompany a shot of a lone, overworked president ensconced in paperwork, while a cacophony of voices culled from the film bombard him with "He doesn't always do what's popular," or "He's not a conventional president." The message, like the candidate, failed to inspire enthusiasm.

## SUMMARY

Television's centrality as source of campaign information, the media consultants' commercial marketing orientation, a conception of the voter as viewer/consumer, and the political state of affairs contributed to a new emphasis upon image in the modern films. Montague Kern noted that 1976 marked the "triumph" of the thirty-second spot in both commercial and political advertising, and cited research that indicated a decline in messages designed primarily to inform voters about candidate positions. Appeals that aimed to entertain viewers superseded those that served to inform voters, and even when issues were mentioned, they primarily functioned to build a favorable candidate image (1989, 48–49).

Images of the country reflected candidates' images in the modern presidential campaign films. After the Watergate debacle, and in the midst of an economic recession, both the Ford and Carter films envisioned not crisis but movement toward resolution in 1976. Both films broke away from the conventions of classical campaign films, and used modern televisual techniques to capture viewers' attention. Neither were substantive. *Jimmy Who?* lightheartedly ignored social and economic problems as it celebrated Jimmy Carter, while the Ford film continued Nixon's message by assuring Americans that social discord was past. It symbolized a reborn America while it emphasized the candidate's honest family values and accomplishments in office.

Although Carter succeeded in getting elected president, the Ford film was a more successful campaign film. The Carter film may have been too incoherent a potpourri of visual techniques; even Carter's 1980 reelection campaign film, again produced by Gerald Rafshoon, did not emulate its techniques. While later Republican campaign films have built on the Ford effort, Democratic films after1976 reverted to the tone and technique of the classical campaign films characteristic of the military model. The result created an irony: while the Democrats, out of office, promoted themselves as the party of change, their film techniques reverted to the out-of-date expository more appropriate for a military style campaign. The Republicans, on the other hand, perfected their craft.

In 1980, a more somber tone prevailed and both Reagan's and Carter's film reverted to more traditional styles. Jimmy Carter stopped smiling and Ronald Reagan's "new beginning" began in earnest. Carter's *This Man, This Office* returned to the themes of incompetency and fallibility characteristic of Humphrey's and McGovern's films. The film acknowledged Carter's unpopularity and served as an apology for the first four years of his presidency. It provided little to vote *for*. Even the Carter campaign did not seem convinced by the candidate. The Reagan biography, however, drew from Ford's 1976 depiction of resurgence. The Reagan campaign recognized the utility of emphasizing hope and affirmation rather than despondency and despair. It celebrated American renewal in the outlines of a picture that took full shape in 1984. As the presidential campaign films attempted to resonate with the mood of the electorate, as discerned by polls, they became increasingly representative of a world where reality was mass produced; in effect, the resulting clusters of images, giving public expression to otherwise inchoate hopes and fears, created the reality that they ostensibly represented.

# Chapter 6

# The Generic Hybrid Ascends, 1984–1988

Ronald Reagan ran for reelection in 1984 as an unopposed incumbent with a successful first term in office. The country was at peace and relatively prosperous—despite a recession that clouded the early days of the Reagan administration, the economy was on the rebound, bolstered largely by borrowed capital and increases in defense spending that strengthened the country militarily. Inflation and unemployment were decreasing, and the Republicans widely proclaimed that Ronald Reagan's economic reforms had induced a recovery. The public mood was hopeful, confident and optimistic; whereas a 1980 Gallup poll found that only 12% of those surveyed were satisfied with the direction in which the country was headed, by 1984, 50% responded in the affirmative.

In contrast to a unified Republican party, Democratic nominee Walter Mondale headed a party in disarray. Much of its traditional blue-collar base had gravitated to the Republican party in 1980, and the Democratic message of New Deal liberalism held little suasory power with the new generation of voters accustomed to scarce resources and wary of big government. While Democratic election reforms enabled political outsiders to secure the nominations in 1972 and 1976, Mondale was a party insider who secured the nomination the old-fashioned way: by having a well-planned organization that began its work long before the election. Even so, he received strong primary challenges from Gary Hart and Jesse Jackson that derailed his campaign. It never recovered.

The 1984 presidential election campaign continued the battle between the old- and new-style politics, the military and the merchandising models of campaigns. Walter Mondale, the party Democrat who had worked his way up through its ranks, attempted to marshall the troops; Ronald Reagan, a movie star and television narrator propelled into politics, offered himself as a commodity to a nation of consumers. Mondale underemphasized television, while the entire Reagan campaign was a made-for-television production.

## THE REAGAN CAMPAIGN

Reagan's reelection team had ample time to plan and organize his campaign. Chief of staff James Baker and adviser Michael Deaver oversaw strategy, assisted by a team of Republican advisers seasoned from previous campaigns: senior director Ed Rollins, deputy director Lee Atwater, director of polling and planning Richard Wirthlin, senior consultant and marketing director Robert Teeter, and outside consultant Stuart Spencer. The campaign took full advantage of marketing techniques to test, analyze, and target their advertising. Wirthlin developed a technique, Values in Strategic Assessment, that measured voter behavior and response to the Reagan media campaign. In June, they began telephone surveys that tracked viewers' moods; these continued nightly throughout the election. The results of these conversations, along with in-depth focus group interviews, allowed them to develop campaign themes, which they then pretested on target groups and modified accordingly. Wirthlin used survey data as input into simulation models and perceptual mapping schemas in a manner more sophisticated than in 1980. Computers combined Nielson or Arbitron ratings with census data, zip codes, previous voting preferences, and lifestyle profiles to determine what programs potential voters were likely to watch, so that advertisements could be placed with maximum benefit.

The Republicans aimed to reach the same groups that voted for Ronald Reagan in 1980: the traditionally Democratic, working people who were losing faith in the American Dream. Many of these disgruntled Americans formed the religious New Right, located primarily in the South and Midwest. Richard Nixon began to harness this "Silent Majority" in 1968; by 1980, newly politicized and energized around a variety of socially conservative causes, they supported Ronald Reagan, and the 1984 campaign sought to convince them of the veracity of their decision. The campaign stressed Reagan's leadership and accomplishments in office, while espousing broad, traditional American values and linking Reagan to symbols that defined and inspired the majority of American voters. His campaign was largely a positive celebration of traditional America. According to Reagan's assistant Richard Darman:

What we were doing with symbols—which admittedly can be called trite—was in effect saying this election is about America's concept of itself. In the 1960s and 1970s, for a whole host of reasons touched upon, we lost confidence in ourselves. We think it's a central part of America's defining characteristic, that it is a confident nation, confident now, confident about its future. I'm going beyond just the faith, family, work dimension that we have talked about and that are long-standing. In emphasizing America's symbols in the way that we did, we tried to underline that America has a special mission. We should be proud of that again. We are in some special sense a land of opportunity. We are in some special sense a protector of freedom. We are in some special sense a pioneer of new frontiers. And it's important that we feel that way about ourselves (Moore 1986, 248).

To achieve their aims through paid media, the Reagan campaign carried on the Republican tradition, started with Richard Nixon's 1968 November Group, of using an ad hoc team of creative advertising experts. In this case they chose forty of the most talented Madison Avenue figures. The Tuesday Team, as they became known, was headed by advertising executive Jim Travis, with Sig Rogich and Walter Carey the major officers. Rogich, a close friend of Reagan supporter Paul Laxalt, was an ex-advertising man who went on to become instrumental in George Bush's 1988 presidential effort. Roger Ailes, a Republican adviser since 1968, served as consultant. Vice-president of BBD&O Phil Dusenberry, who was on the advisory committee, eventually produced the campaign film. Tom Messner, who later wrote and filmed much of George Bush's 1988 campaign film, was also a member of the Tuesday Team who contributed extensively to the 1984 Reagan film.

Both Michael Deaver and Nancy Reagan were disappointed with the 1980 commercials, and wanted high-quality, high-production value advertisements befitting a president. Deaver, widely reported as obsessed with stagecraft, wanted advertisements with high-production values whose visuals meshed with words. He stated, "We absolutely thought of ourselves when we got into the national campaign as producers. We tried to create the most interesting, visually attractive scene to fill that box, so that the cameras from the networks would have to use it. . . . We became Hollywood producers" (Moyers 1989). They set out to create innovative advertisements that would break through political apathy. This was particularly important because Reagan had a significant lead over Mondale in the polls, and the Republicans did not want to lose the election because of voter complacency. In an environment where the economy was sound and the nation was at peace, the Republicans wanted to keep Americans feeling good about themselves, their country, and their president.

### A New Beginning

During the primaries, the Tuesday Team produced patriotic, reassuring, and optimistic ads that evoked traditional America. Later, some of these images were cut into an eighteen-minute "documentary" film, *A New Beginning*. This film proved a landmark in presidential filmmaking that seamlessly intermeshed documentary and advertising forms (Morreale 1991). Michael Deaver initiated this film, along with another about Nancy Reagan. Produced by Phil Dusenberry, a creative advertising expert from BBD&O with no previous presidential campaign experience, *A New Beginning* became the cornerstone of the campaign. It had higher production values and a greater aesthetic sensibility than any previous campaign film. It was shot on 35 mm film rather than videotape, lighting and camera techniques received meticulous attention, they used sophisticated editing and dubbing techniques, the film incorporated a best-selling country music video, and Dusenberry hired an orchestra to play the originally composed film score. Referred to as a "docudramatic salute," it cost about $1 million to produce when factors such as the film crews' overseas travel (conducted before the reelection campaign officially began) were considered (Diamond 1984, 58). Eighty hours of film were edited down to eighteen minutes for the convention film, which the Republicans planned to air immediately before Reagan's nomination acceptance address.

*A New Beginning*, while retaining documentary codes and conventions, reproduced commercial advertising images whose positive associations were familiar to viewers. Luntz (1988, 207) quotes Nicholas Lemann: "The makers of the [Reagan] ads quite openly modeled them on successful campaigns for companies such as Pepsi Cola and McDonald's, because commercial testing methods indicated that voters would respond best to this style of advertising." The Republicans intermeshed the fantasy of advertising with the perceived reality of documentary, both synthesized in the figure of Ronald Reagan. The following analysis of the film illustrates this technique (see Morreale 1991). Footage from Reagan's 1980 inauguration appears. Images and sounds of traditional America are crosscut within this replay of an actual event. A plow furrows the rich soil, implying fertility and productivity. The image dissolves to a pristine white farmhouse; the sun rises, a rooster crows, flowers bloom, and there is work to do, as indicated by a truck with an empty bed moving out of frame. These images evoke a pure, agrarian America; its connotations resonate with the literal image of Ronald Reagan that surrounds them. A cowboy and his horse dissolve into an image of a city laborer, unifying country and city in the world of work. The laborer gestures upward as he directs a crane; his movement, mimicked by similar gestures and camera movements throughout the film, suggests optimism. A traffic policeman guides a group of workers as they cross the street, while the chief justice's off-camera voice says the word "defend" as part of the oath of office. The picture and narration invite associations with law and order, protection and defense. Reagan's voice promises to "preserve and protect," while children gaze upward at a flag being hoisted in a wooded camp. Thus, the scene could imply that Reagan preserves and protects the environment, although he makes no such claim. Then Reagan repeats the word "defend," and there is a cut to a close-up of a child's face. Again, the association is with defending children. By juxtaposing the "documentary" image of the Reagan inauguration with these "fictional" images, Ronald Reagan shares their connotations, the positive qualities of traditional America: fecundity, beauty, and hope, while also reminding Americans of the need for a strong defense. The scene ends with a shot of the White House, the unifying center of political authority that links the preceding images with Ronald Reagan's presidency. The White House dissolves into an image of Ronald Reagan positioned securely within its confines, seated at his desk in the Oval Office.

Virtually all of the film's scenes make implicative points. The next scene depicts Reagan at work; he mentions the "image" of the loneliness of the job, and there is a long shot of Reagan alone at his desk. He then reminds Americans that he seeks opinions of his advisers and opponents—negating any suggestions of an imperial presidency. George Bush appears on camera to express his support for Reagan and his feeling about "a new beginning"; then the first set of interviews with "ordinary" Americans follows. These are the members of Reagan's America: traditionally Democratic black and ethnic construction workers, a young ethnic woman, and a middle-American man. All express gratitude to Reagan for restoring pride, patriotism, and jobs. The final interviewee introduces the campaign song, Lee Greenwood's "God Bless the U.S.A." The incorporation of this popular song, which was nominated for Best Country Grammy in 1984, further dissolved the thin boundaries that differentiated politics and entertainment.

The image montage that accompanies "Proud to Be an American," is pure spectacle, with little direct relation to Ronald Reagan. While throughout the film, camera movements pan upward, their direction is even more pronounced here. As Greenwood sings, images of traditional America representative of its values appear: a cityscape, yacht, child hugging her father, traditional wedding, house under construction, family moving out of their house, welder at work, plow furrowing earth, flag, child saluting flag, Statue of Liberty (under repair), cowboys conversing, a picnic, Reagan attending a military funeral, policeman hoisting flag, woman hugging soldier, a still-photograph of Americans waving flags, and finally, Reagan surrounded by the flag.

Reagan then lauds the new patriotism in America, matched by footage of his trip to the Korean Demilitarized Zone. This also functions to support his military build-up to protect "freedom." Afterwards, middle-American men and women appear on-camera to proclaim their support for his strong defense policies and the economic recovery. Throughout the film, a heavy reliance on female interviewees attempted to redress a perceived gender gap, for many women voters were believed to prefer Mondale. In the half hour version, scenes from a short documentary about Nancy Reagan are included. They end as Ronald Reagan muses, "I can't imagine life without her," and violins play in the background. The value of a close-knit family plays a part in most campaign films, and Reagan, campaigning as the champion of family values, was no exception. Although Reagan could not realistically play up the tight bonds of his own estranged family, the campaign could, and did, emphasize his close relationship with his wife.

The film does include some substantive claims and addresses some issues with regard to the economy: Reagan appears on camera and takes credit for reduced inflation, interest rates, and unemployment during his administration. He neglects to mention the burgeoning federal deficit. Newspaper headlines from the early eighties substantiate his optimistic words, as do "fictional" images of houses under construction, a waitress taking an order at a diner, two men weighing fish, workers giving thumbs-up signs, and the same family that appeared earlier during Greenwood's song moving into a larger house and buying a new truck.

While most campaign films depict military heroism to illustrate the candidate's leadership and qualifications for office, *A New Beginning* uses the assassination attempt on Reagan's life instead. News footage taken at the time appears in lieu of the archival battle footage of past films. Typically, a grateful soldier comments on the candidate's bravery. Here, Reagan himself faces the camera and recollects the incident. Reagan recalls his meeting with the recently deceased Cardinal Cooke while he was recuperating after the incident. He stares into the camera and announces his realization that his remaining time now belongs to . . . Someone Else.

The film briefly depicts Reagan's visit to his ancestral home in Ireland, his precampaign trips to Japan, Korea, and China, then his emotional Normandy speech delivered to D day veterans at the commemoration ceremony. Whereas classical campaign films simply show footage of the candidate's oratory, the Normandy speech is a dramatic event that was planned with the television cameras in mind. Reagan reads from a letter sent to him by a young woman whose father, a veteran, recently died of cancer. The camera captures her sobs, cutting from her back to Reagan, who speaks from the podium, surrounded by a set design of colorful flowers. Symphonic music provides the final emotional touch.

The film ends with a scene of the Reagans relaxing on their Santa Barbara ranch, where they ride horses and gambol in the yard. Then President Reagan, at his second home in the White House, takes viewers on a tour and explains his reasons for running for a second term. "God Bless the U.S.A." provides a final summary of the symbolic, if clichéd, images that appeared throughout the film (with some new images): a river gushing in the mountains, a cityscape, a policeman hoisting the flag, the space shuttle lifting off, veterans saluting at Normandy, flags and crosses at the military cemetery in Normandy, Reagan in a still-photograph with the 1984 U.S. Olympic team, the Statue of Liberty under repair, and Ronald Reagan and George Bush walking outside the White House with their backs to the camera. The montage then closes with a still-photograph of Ronald Reagan with his hands clasped over his head in a victory sign. The half-hour version then cuts to Reagan's acceptance address and Ray Charles singing at the Republican National Convention, intercut with filmed images of "America the Beautiful."

Through a combination of visual and verbal codes, *A New Beginning* constructed a unified American community of adherents to mythic Main Street America and the positive values of hope and optimism—all in the context of a strong defense. Ronald Reagan provided a screen that reflected desirable images of America and Americans; as many observers have noted, he mirrored America's idealized image of itself. *A New Beginning*'s carefully produced images reproduced clichéd, and thus comforting, television images of America rather than representing extra-televisual reality. Like all rhetorical depictions, viewers need not analyze or interpret these images; their meaning was already imprinted on the minds of most Americans.

The resultant film's hybrid nature did not escape the notice of the networks, which had already announced that they would only broadcast "newsworthy" events. Although the Republicans exerted pressure on them to air the film—Ronald Reagan reportedly made personal phone calls to ask that the networks show the film, and the Republicans dimmed the lights on the convention hall floor so that reporters couldn't conduct interviews while the film was running—the networks largely condemned the film as a commercial rather than a news event, a decision reinforced by letters of complaint from prominent Democrats. The Republicans claimed that the film was, in effect, their introductory speech for the candidate, and since the networks had aired Senator Kennedy's introductory speech for Walter Mondale, their introduction should be aired in the interests of fairness. In the end, only NBC, CNN, and C-Span broadcast the film in its entirety.

Many television viewers did see the film, however, in whole or part. Scenes from *A New Beginning* were first aired as commercials during the primary campaign, and other scenes were cut into commercials that aired during the fall. The film was also shown as a prelude to Reagan's live appearances throughout the general election campaign, and in one instance, the Democrats complained because KPAZ-TV, a religious broadcasting station in Phoenix, showed the film over and over again. In a more subtle case, Greenwood produced a music video to accompany his song that used virtually the same images that appeared in the Reagan film, without any explicit reference to Reagan or the presidential campaign.

The extended version of *A New Beginning* was broadcast as a paid political program that kicked off the general election advertising campaign on September 11. The Republicans roadblocked all three major news networks as well as ESPN, CBN, and WTBS by airing the film on all stations at 8:00 P.M. They tried to buy time on CNN, MTV, USA, the Nashville Network, and Metromedia stations, but couldn't because of their scheduling policies. As a result, they received an extraordinary 25.6 rating and a 46 market share on the three major networks alone, while its duration and documentary form led many viewers to believe that it was media news coverage of the campaign rather than paid media. Reagan's campaign team did not underestimate the film's significance. According to Jim Travis, kicking off the campaign with the film was a key strategic move that influenced the entire campaign (O'Connor 1984, 111).

## THE MONDALE CAMPAIGN

The Mondale campaign remained ensconced in the military model. Rather than focusing on media, Mondale hoped to win the nomination and then election by dint of superior organization. In a significant move, the pro-Mondale Hunt Commission challenged Democratic party reforms initiated by McGovern and Carter, so that it became more difficult for party outsiders to win the nomination. Primaries occurred early across the United States, so that the candidate with the most money and name recognition was likely to win.

Yet, after winning the battle for the Democratic nomination, old-school Democrat Walter Mondale could not compete with the Reagan campaign's highly orchestrated and technologically sophisticated media campaign. While Reagan employed a total of 300 paid professionals, Mondale had only 150. His campaign organization had few television-savvy holdovers from earlier Democratic efforts. His inner circle of advisers consisted of old-line Democrats: James Johnson, his campaign chairman, controlled the operation, while manager Robert Beckel handled the practical, day-to-day matters. Two Washington lawyers, Richard Moe and John Reilly, served as advisers, as did Democrat party leader Robert Strauss. Peter Hart was pollster, although Pat Caddell came on board later to assist the faltering campaign.

Consultant Roy Spence conducted Mondale's primary and general election media effort, called Campaign '84, while Richard Leone, a former state treasurer of New Jersey who once ran unsuccessfully for the Senate, served as media strategist. Spence wanted to present Mondale as a man of strength and principle. In a strategy memo, he stated: "The national image of Walter Mondale is [that he is] 'a nice guy, a typical old-fashioned politician, a politician whose heart is in the right place, but has no real *depth*, no real inner strength, no real backbone—a politician who is so tied up on old answers he is not up to the job of leading a *New America*'" (Goldman 1984, 41). However, Spence could not convince the political advisers to work on changing the candidate's image. They clung to the misguided belief that superior campaign organization, rather than an altered perception of Mondale's character, could win the campaign.

It took Mondale a full two months after the convention to put together a media team, which eventually consisted of a group of agencies: Spence, David Sawyer Associates, Frank Greer Associates, and McCaffrey and McCall. There was little time to plan an advertising strategy; moreover, Mondale wanted a "collegial" approach to campaign media, where his team made decisions collectively. As a result, consultant David Garth, who was asked but refused to join the campaign, referred to Mondale advertisements as inconsistent and lacking continuity and a core. The Republicans later criticized the campaign as themeless and visionless, without even a slogan to define Mondale's message. Mondale only produced twenty different spot commercials, half as many as Reagan, and he spent less than the Republicans did on television ($20 to $25 million), despite the fact that the Republicans, with the advantage of incumbency, had more free media exposure.

Hart's early polls found that many people liked Reagan, but they took Mondale's side on the big issues, such as the deficit, arms race, and environment. Although this data could also have been interpreted to mean that people wanted a leader regardless of position on the issues, they decided to run an issue-based campaign that shook people out of their complacency. They decided that Reagan was vulnerable on two issues: the deficit and war. Yet, the commercials produced during the first half of the campaign tried to explain the deficit, an issue too complicated, dry, and cerebral for television. While the Mondale campaign defended their advertisements as gritty, realistic, and issue-oriented, they were often criticized as primitive. They were shot on 16 mm film, and were poorly lit. Campaign '84 seemed to have little understanding of visual images. The images appeared as mere filler for the more important words.

## The (Untitled) Mondale Film

Mondale's campaign film conveyed his inability to use television to present himself effectively. It had more in common with the classical campaign films tied to a military model of campaigns than with modern merchandising campaigns. The eleven-minute biographical convention film was not strategically placed within the Democratic convention, and the Democrats were not able to convince the networks to show the film. It followed rather than preceded the candidate's acceptance address; therefore, the networks did not feel compelled to show it as part of their news coverage. Moreover, the Democrats did not air it again in its entirety during the general election campaign, despite the fact that one of Pat Caddell's strategy memos, written by Labor Day, suggested that one of Mondale's major problems was that people didn't *know* him (Goldman and Fuller 1984, 101). They cut the film into sixty-second and five-minute spots, but did not deem it worthwhile to show the original or a reedited version on national television. Mondale's director of media operations, Judy Press Brenner, when asked if the campaign would follow the Republicans' example and roadblock the networks with a half-hour presentation, replied, "I don't consider it a useful media vehicle. It really just makes the troops feel good. Generally, the only people who watch it are those already on your side" (Saltzman 10 September 1984, 6) Ultimately, the Democrats did roadblock the networks with a five-minute spot on 28 October at 10:55 P.M.

The film was representative of the candidate's lack of positive vision, coherent message, and attention to visual images. Just as the candidate was a throwback to an earlier era, the film was an expository narrative that appeared amateurish in comparison to the Reagan effort. It combined biography and statements of Mondale's positions with some image montages. The film opens with a scene where children say what they want to be when they grow up, interspersed with Mondale walking through the woods as he provides an account of his early years to an invisible cameraperson. He wears a checkered woodsman's shirt, typical attire for "off-duty" presidential candidates. An example of his unwillingness to craft an image for the electorate came as he discussed his high school football career. He begins by informing viewers that he was captain his senior year. Then he adds, "We had a (pause) *fair* record." "What was your nickname in high school?" the narrator asks. "Crazy Legs," Mondale responds, with a self-deprecating laugh. Although the moniker does refer to a well-known football player, the symbolic message he conveys about his leadership skills is far from reassuring.

An image montage covers the primary campaign; both the film style—fast, with tilted camera, the use of graphics to indicate the different states in which he won victories, magazine covers and headlines to indicate the progress of the primary campaign, and the insertion of political cartoons—were reminiscent of some of the techniques used in *Jimmy Who?* The film depicts him as a family man in a scene where he fries fish and picnics with his wife and children. As if to pound the point home, he states, "The campaign really taught us the importance of family." There is the requisite black-and-white documentary footage of his early career as a young senator. A commendation by anthropologist Margaret Mead is cited, although she was probably not a figure well-known to the majority of Americans. The narrator cites a litany of the candidate's accomplishments as "the Children's Senator," among them a nutrition program, support of Headstart, and introduction of the Elementary and Secondary Education Act. These were not particularly popular achievements or important issues for the majority of voters in 1984, who associated them with the excessive government spending and the failed Great Society projects of liberalism.

Ostensibly back in the present, Mondale sits with a group of young children while his voice-over, probably a speech excerpt, repeats his commitment to education. In a scene entirely lacking in visual appeal, Mondale rides in a car with a woman who represents the "ordinary American." He hardly appears on-screen; the shot depicts her at the steering wheel, driving and talking simultaneously. She complains about the high incidence of chemical contamination in her neighborhood, and notes that two children died from leukemia last year. Dead babies are not typical topics in campaign films. She provides testimony for Mondale, commending him for his fight to clean up toxic waste. The camera cuts to polluted waters, a trash-strewn dump site, and a fence with a sign reading "Danger." In a film where viewers could be inspired by Walter Mondale, instead they are treated to pictures of garbage. This is not to belittle the importance of these matters, it is just that such images contributed to perceptions of Walter Mondale as the "doom and gloom" candidate whose vision of malaise offered nothing positive.

Finally, Mondale meets with his campaign staff in a staged scene, and there are brief shots of the candidate meeting with foreign leaders. He attends a human rights meeting in Vienna with representatives of the South African government, speaks for democracy in Manila, and visits Egypt just before the historic Camp David Accord. The narrator asserts that Mondale "has made a difference," as an army man, senator, and second in line as commander-in-chief. The film does not stress that he was Jimmy Carter's vice-president, wisely dissociating him from one of the most unpopular presidents in American history. The film concludes with another shot of Mondale walking in the woods. He gives his version of the American Dream: "We have a duty to make America better. That's what America's all about—to give every child a chance to fulfill his or her dreams." That may be what Mondale thinks America is all about, but that is not the image of America conveyed by the film. While Reagan's America is sun-filled and pristine clean, Mondale's America is polluted and trash-laden. Toxic waste dumps and children with leukemia are dominant images, rather than children attaining their hopes and dreams.

There is a final image montage of America, by 1984 a presidential campaign film convention that was one of the Mondale campaign's few concessions to the visual, symbolic language of television. The Mondale film was not deemed successful, even by his own campaign. One member of Frank Greer and Associates, the consulting firm that made Mondale's film, stated, "We just groaned when that thing played on television."

After the election, Mondale acknowledged his shortcomings as a television candidate in a candid "Meet the Press" interview:

I do not think I communicated effectively, that in fact that's what the 1984 campaign was all about. This is partly how you shape the case, but it's also how you communicate. I do not think that I matched Reagan's genius at television, his genius at communicating the symbolism of the presidency, and we must find a candidate who, in addition to being right on these issues and stating them correctly, can master this modern challenge of communications in this huge country of ours (Sunday, 7 April 1985).

Mondale's realistic appraisal of his own campaign was also a succinct statement of the problems faced by the next Democratic presidential candidates. Michael Dukakis, the Democratic candidate in 1988, failed to learn Mondale's lesson. George Bush, on the other hand, demonstrated that his years as apprentice to the master were not wasted.

## THE 1988 CAMPAIGN

Despite Reagan's successful eight years in office, and a climate of peace and perceptions of prosperity, cracks in the facade were beginning to show as the 1988 election neared. Polls suggested a strain of anxiety beneath proclamations of contentment; the Wall Street Panic of November 1987 suggested that the economy had peaked and crashed; the federal deficit had escalated to $2.4 trillion; and the Iran-Contra scandal had once again raised public suspicions about government corruption.

## THE BUSH CAMPAIGN

George Bush, as the incumbent vice-president, was by no means assured of a November victory. As the general election campaign began, George Bush faced several disadvantages. The last two-term vice-president to win election was Martin Van Buren in 1836; moreover, many voters did not believe that Bush, in Reagan's shadow for the past eight years, was strong, tough, or assertive enough for the presidency. Gallup polls taken in the spring showed that for every person who liked Bush, another one didn't. But for every five people who said they liked Dukakis, only one didn't. By Memorial Day, Bush trailed Dukakis by fifteen points in the polls (Schieffer and Gates 1989, 359).

Bush's ensuing presidential campaign underscored the way that artful use of television could shape impressions. George Bush repeated the Reagan formula. His close circle of advisers, Jim Baker, Lee Atwater, pollster Robert Teeter, and communications director Roger Ailes, all worked on the Reagan 1984 campaign. Even his media team consisted of holdovers from the Tuesday Team: creative director Jim Weller, publicity director Sig Rogich, and producers Tom Messner and Barry Vetere. The media campaign was well financed, experienced, and highly organized. While many presidential campaigns (including Dukakis's) were poorly organized and fractured by internal dissent between political advisers and consultants, Bush's circle of advisors made decisions by consensual agreement.

Bush's staff knew their candidate was all but certain to win the Republican nomination. This confidence allowed them time to carefully develop their media strategy. The Bush convention film indicates that the vice-president's campaign strategy was determined before the general election campaign had even begun. At a staff meeting on Memorial Day, his advisers decided to define him as strong and tough—through images, and by attacking Dukakis early and hard. At the same time, they would reassure voters, especially women, by advocating a kinder, gentler nation and presenting Bush as a genial, trustworthy family man. These conflicting themes posed no problem for television viewers by now accustomed to fragmented meanings from one image to the next.

### The (Untitled) Bush Film

Bush's highly produced seven-minute convention film was a collaborative effort. Roger Ailes and Sig Rogich filmed interviews with the Bush family months before the campaign began. Tom Messner and Barry Vetere, heads of a Madison Avenue advertising firm, shot other footage and wrote the script. Clay Rossen, Ailes's assistant, oversaw production to assure a coherent portrait. The convention film took only three weeks to put together, and an expanded version, televised on election eve, was completed in four weeks. Bush's film introduced his themes at the convention, replayed them as advertisements during the campaign, and then reprised the campaign with a twenty-minute version of the film on election eve, followed by a brief address to the nation. Like its predecessor, *A New Beginning*, it was shot on 35 mm film rather than videotape to give it a lush, rich, professional quality, and the original music was meticulously arranged. The film was essentially an advertisement in documentary form. According to Rossen, they designed the last sixty seconds as a perfect commercial that could be lifted intact. The commercial, called *Family/Children*, opened the general election campaign and media director Janet Mullins claimed that it was the most effective advertisement of the campaign (Devlin 1989, 393).

The Bush film's opening scene illustrates that the film was a hybrid documentary-advertisement whereby verbal and visual communication supported each other and created the image of "George Bush" planned by his strategists. It begins with the title, "August 1988," on a blank screen, ostensibly locating the viewer in present time. As the title fades, a blond toddler runs through brilliant green grass in slow motion. The child is in soft focus, and sentimental music accompanies the image.

Quickly, this gentle Madison Avenue image of childhood dissolves to white and is replaced by another headline that locates the viewer in the distant past, December 1941. The film consists almost entirely of dissolves to white rather than cuts between images. Dissolves bring a soft, nostalgic feel to the film, and dissolves to white rather than black help to unify otherwise disparate images. Here, harsh, pounding music accompanies stark black-and-white newsreel footage. As this shot too dissolves to white, the anonymous narrator announces that America has faced many challenges throughout the twentieth century, and has found many people to meet those challenges. The implication, of course, is that George Bush is one of those people. The narrator's voice accompanies archival footage of soldiers kissing their loved ones goodbye as they leave for war (at one point, the camera slowly pans up the back of a woman's leg, obliquely echoing the presentation of women in Hollywood fiction films). Rather than addressing current challenges, such as the still unresolved federal deficit, the film returns viewers to the nostalgic site of a former, successfully met challenge.

Newsreel footage and still-photographs in lieu of moving images signal authenticity. Bush takes over the film's narration—subtly indicating that he is in control—and he explains that he joined the army at the young age of eighteen because he wanted to be a pilot. Two still-photographs corroborate his words: the young civilian poses with his wife Barbara, then he appears in a pilot's cap and air force uniform. Bush maintains his modesty and does not mention that he became a war hero; instead, the off-screen narrator's voice returns to recount that Bush earned the Distinguished Flying Cross on a bombing run. Grainy, black-and-white archival images of aerial combat illustrate the narrator's words. Although this generic battle footage gives no indication of Bush's squadron, it implicitly makes a claim for the authenticity of his war experience. The war footage is dramatic and exciting; it evokes patriotic sentiments that viewers associate with the candidate—and these become all the more powerful given Bush's charge that Dukakis was unpatriotic.

Then, a disjunctive cut occurs in the film and Bush's voice and image are united in one shot. Color indicates a shift to the present, as Bush, seated comfortably in the Oval Office of the White House (where he is "at home"), relates in detail his adventure as a war hero. Scratched and faded black-and-white images labeled "Government File Footage" verify his words, followed by a shot of the young George Bush as he is rescued after his crash landing in the Pacific Ocean. This same footage was used in an advertisement during Bush's unsuccessful bid for the presidential nomination in 1980. Authenticity is doubly signalled here, both by the nature of the footage and the printed graphic. Bush's image symbolizes strength—in this case, a real life exploit demonstrates the candidate's qualifications as a courageous leader.

The film's form and images implicitly set up George Bush's two-pronged campaign strategy, where he is a candidate who is "kind and gentle," yet strong and prepared to represent the American people—he is both an empathic man of the people and a leader. Both the child who opens the film and the dissolves that link shots imply softness and delicacy, while the footage of Bush's World War II mission is a metaphorical as well as literal exposition of his strength of character. After more images showing victory celebrations that marked the end of World War II, the film again returns to the present. Bush speaks on-camera from the White House and articulates his desire to unify all Americans, to make all a part of the same team effort that resulted in victory in World War II. Barbara Bush briefly takes over the narration to give the film a "woman's touch" and assure viewers that her husband is indeed a caring man.

Ronald Reagan appears on-camera to voice his support for the candidate, and the film replays footage from Reagan's own 1984 campaign film. Images culled from the Reagan film emphasize the continuity between the two men; both the convention film and the expanded version repeat the same images of prosperity and resurgence that appeared in 1984. Bush maintained his connection with the still popular Reagan while defining himself apart from the president.

Bush's convention film closes with the small child who opened the film finally reaching her destination as George Bush scoops her off the ground. It becomes apparent that she is his grandchild as they both join his extended family gathered for an outdoor picnic. George Bush, ordinary American, steams corn in the kitchen and barbecues in the backyard. Dressed casually, he sits in the midst of abundance, chomping on a hamburger while his adoring grandchildren gather round his feet. The Bush campaign was well aware of the power of family to define their candidate as a nice guy who could identify with the common experiences of the American people. The viewer becomes a member of his clan, privy to knowledge of the "real" George Bush relaxing at home. This final sixty seconds of the film became the successful *Family/Children* spot advertisement.

The expanded version of the film shown on election eve includes footage of Bush's acceptance address where he cites the accomplishments of the last eight years, intercut with interviews with the Bush family and images of America and Americans. Although Bush stresses his continuity with Reagan, he does not maintain Reagan's focus on the present, or the unadulterated optimism of the "new beginning." The extended version brings viewers back to images of America's troubled past, with images of Vietnam and people demonstrating for civil rights. The narrator claims that George Bush always stood for civil rights, although the Vietnam War is not mentioned.

There is a chronological account of the campaign, introduced with titles that indicate its stages: the primary, general campaign, and election eve, bringing the viewer up to the present. For the first time since Barry Goldwater's *Choice*, Bush injects negative campaigning into the "documentary" film. He impugns Dukakis' patriotism in a scene where schoolchildren salute the flag. His voice-over narration asks the question, "Should public school teachers be required to lead our children in the pledge of allegiance?" Without explicating, he recites, "My opponent says no, I say yes." Throughout the campaign, Bush made an issue out of Dukakis's refusal to make the pledge of allegiance mandatory in Massachusetts public schools. Although Dukakis's stand was based on legal grounds, the Republicans used the largely symbolic issue to criticize the candidate. After a similar attack on Dukakis for refusing to endorse prayer or a "moment of silence" in schools, Bush implies that Dukakis is soft on crime while drawing on racist sentiments. First, he presents footage where the Springfield, Massachusetts, police officers and Boston Patrolman's Association Union, among others, endorse George Bush. Despite the fact that this conservative group traditionally supports the Republican presidential candidate, the scene implies that Dukakis, soft on crime, lacks the support of the law enforcement agencies in his own state. Then without mentioning Willie Horton, the subject of one of Bush's most controversial ads during the campaign, Bush makes his point. The image portrays Bush shaking hands with police officers while he claims, "I'm the one who believes that it is a scandal to give a weekend furlough to a hardened first degree killer who hasn't even served enough time to be eligible for a parole." Early on in the campaign, focus groups reacted strongly when they were told that convicted murderer Willie Horton had committed a brutal rape and murder when on a weekend furlough condoned by Dukakis. This, too, became a symbolic issue that haunted Dukakis throughout the campaign, even though many other states had similar programs.

When the campaign arrives at election eve, Bush gives a "live" speech, in the tradition of Richard Nixon and Gerald Ford. The Bush film, more so than any other campaign film, served as a representative anecdote for the campaign. George Bush defeated Michael Dukakis by running a campaign largely on symbolic issues, all of which were reiterated in this film. Even the issue of family values, described in a clip from the debates between the two candidates, appeared again in the film. Not only was Bush surrounded by his grandchildren, but his wife and children appeared on camera to describe what a warm and caring family man "Grampy" was. "This campaign has brought us closer together as a family," Dorothy Bush states earnestly. "He can be very nice and friendly but in a competitive setting no one is going to outhustle or outwork him," says son Jeb, reemphasizing the kind and gentle, yet strong and prepared theme. Overall, the Bush film, in both form and content, reinforced the unity and sophistication of the campaign.

## THE DUKAKIS CAMPAIGN

John Sasso, Dukakis's campaign manager during Boston's gubernatorial elections in 1982 and 1986, convinced the governor of Massachusetts to run for president in 1988. Pollster Tubby Harrison determined that people wanted competence and leadership, a solid person they could trust. Sasso determined that Dukakis could run on the "issues" of character and competence, combined with a highly organized campaign and enough funds to buy the nomination. Dukakis was relatively unknown to voters, but benefited from a primary race where several candidates self-destructed.

The Dukakis campaign also came close to self-immolation. In an incident that may have ultimately doomed the Dukakis campaign, Sasso was made to resign. Sasso admitted leaking news to the press about rival candidate Joe Biden plagiarizing parts of a campaign speech, and Dukakis was forced to punish the indiscretion after publicly insisting that his campaign had nothing to do with the leak. Yet Sasso was the only person Dukakis trusted to run his campaign. His aides talked him into hiring Susan Estrich, a Harvard law professor, as campaign manager, although she had never run a national campaign. The result was a campaign in disarray after Sasso's departure. It lacked a tightly structured chain of command, and for the most part, the staff was composed of "very bright Bostonians with very little experience in national politics" (Hershey 1989, 87). Dukakis never had confidence in Estrich, he stipulated that no one advertising person was in charge, and his staff could make no decisions without his approval. As a result, although the campaign produced many ads, they had no thematic unity and no one could decide which to air.

Thus, unlike his opponent, Michael Dukakis did not have the benefit of an experienced team of political experts whose operations for the general election were in place during the primaries. Moreover, neither Dukakis nor his staff took the advice of seasoned Democratic political advisers. They did not seek the advice of losing campaigns, and thus they tended to repeat the same mistakes.

During the primaries, Dukakis worked with local Boston consultants, but decided to follow the Republican model and hire an ad hoc group of Madison Avenue advertisers during the general election. The Future Group consisted of well-known advertising professionals such as Scott Miller, Ed McCabe, and Gary Susnjara. Dukakis was the first Democratic party candidate to attempt to go to Madison Avenue since Hubert Humphrey used Doyle, Dane and Bernbach (DDB) in 1968. Humphrey fired the Madison Avenue agency midway through the campaign at political consultant Joe Napolitan's request; similarly, when Dukakis rehired John Sasso in the fall to get his campaign back on track, Sasso hired advertising director David D'Alessandro from Baltimore as advertising director, and most of the Madison Avenue personnel quit.

Dukakis also lacked the visual advantages of incumbency, which provided the Bush campaign with free footage of the candidate at work in the White House or interacting comfortably with world leaders such as Mikhail Gorbachev or Margaret Thatcher. The Dukakis campaign spent more than the Bush campaign on production of television materials— roughly $6.5 million to $3.5 million, no doubt because they had less footage to begin with (Devlin 1989, 391).

## Snowblower

Boston consultant Dan Payne produced the seven-minute Dukakis convention film, *Snowblower*, just before Dukakis's ill-fated switch to Madison Avenue. The film, a low-key effort shot in one day, lacked the production values of the Bush film. It cost only $20,000—a low figure compared, for example, to the Reagan 1984 film, which cost an estimated $500,000. *Snowblower* aired at the Democratic convention as a prelude to Dukakis's acceptance speech and was never used again. No other campaign film was produced.

One function of a campaign film shown during the convention is to familiarize voters with a candidate. Dukakis was not well known to the majority of the American people and needed campaign materials that told voters who he was and what he stood for. Polls taken during the primaries showed that even people in favor of Dukakis were unclear about his record or proposals. Joe Napolitan, a Democratic political consultant who worked on the Kennedy and Humphrey presidential campaigns, recalled that he wrote to the candidate about the necessity and importance of a lengthy biographical film to introduce him to voters, but his advice was not heeded. The campaign's inability to clarify who the candidate was and what he represented left him vulnerable to the Republicans' distortions of his identity and positions in the ensuing campaign. In a postelection interview, Roger Ailes commented, "Every single thing I did from debates to rhetoric to speeches to media was designed to define the two candidates and push them further apart" (Devlin 1989, 392).

The Bush film illustrated the campaign's well-planned strategy, but no strategy at all could be discerned from *Snowblower*. It barely accorded with the conventions of the political campaign film. There were the requisite still-photographs of the candidate as a youth, in a picture with his father, as a high school athlete, and as a soldier in army uniform. However, while most films—and not just the Bush film— include an anecdote that illustrates the candidate's patriotism by recounting one of his heroic exploits while in the service, with stock World War II battle footage cut in, this film merely mentions that Dukakis was in the army.

No live footage of Dukakis or his immediate family appears anywhere. The candidate's cousin, the actress Olympia Dukakis, serves as on-camera narrator who reminisces about the candidate from a personal, anecdotal point of view. Wearing khaki pants and a plain blouse— the kind of casual clothes that "ordinary folk" wear, she describes her personal remembrances of Dukakis's life in the chatty, down-to-earth manner of a big sister. Her folksy style and dialogue attempt to present Dukakis as a man of the people. According to Payne, she had input into the dialogue and improvised her comments at some points. It would have been unthinkable for an actress with no political experience to have such clout in the carefully controlled Republican production.

Olympia appears in virtually every shot of the film. Although presidential candidates traditionally use familiar celebrity voices to narrate campaign films, these stars rarely, if ever, appear on-camera as they do so. Moreover, Olympia was not a star of major stature who could lure her admirers to the Dukakis camp. Her performance in *Moonstruck* was nominated for an Oscar that year, but this was her first major film role.

The personable, down-to-earth relative of the candidate does not convey the authority of the omniscient narrator, nor is she well versed in the film narrator's functions. The traditional narrator creates the illusion of unity through linguistic binding terms such as "we," "let's," and "us" that refer to all viewers. Olympia Dukakis, however, states early on, "*We Greeks* are good at marathons." (According to Payne, this was an improvised bit.) Her words divide rather than unify; she emphasizes Dukakis's Greek rather than American heritage and differentiates one ethnic group from the majority of Americans.

*Snowblower*'s overall style is more linear than visual. As Olympia narrates, she literally and metaphorically "walks" viewers through the film as she takes them on a tour of Dukakis's hometown in Brookline, Massachusetts. The word *pedestrian* describes the narrator, the film, and by association, the candidate. Ironically, in the original script for Reagan's 1984 campaign film, Charlton Heston appeared on camera and took viewers on a tour of the White House. Phil Dusenberry, who produced the film that was eventually made, fired the scriptwriter who came up with such a "horrendous" idea. In another scene that seemed to quote from Walter Mondale's 1984 convention film, Olympia narrates from behind the wheel of a car, talking as she drives through Brookline, then on to Brookline High School, and then to her cousin's house. In the Mondale film, a woman drives past toxic waste dumps and laments the state of the union. Neither shot showed any degree of visual sophistication.

Dukakis's film evidences even less sense of the symbolic nature of the presidential election campaign than the Mondale film. The film emphasizes Dukakis's suburban roots as a native of Brookline, Massachusetts, in an attempt to contrast him with Bush, a native of no one state in particular. However, in a national campaign, the candidate needs to be associated with a place that resonates with the public in a dramatic fashion. The Brookline High School gymnasium, or the hospital where the candidate's father worked, are hardly such loaded symbols. Moreover, Olympia spends almost as much time discussing her memories of the candidate's father as she does the candidate himself. While the Bush campaign clearly understood the power of family, there are no pictures, let alone film footage, of Dukakis's wife or children. Most importantly, viewers get a brief glimpse of his tree-shrouded home, but they are not invited inside. They only see it from a distance—the camera position is inside the car driven by Olympia, who pulls up alongside the curb outside. Then she walks through the backyard and into the garage—not traditional loci of domestic intimacy. Viewers are not welcome in his home.

Dukakis ran on the theme of competence. Yet, the visual form and content of the campaign film contradict the verbal claims. The film provides little sense of his competence as a candidate for president. Airing the film as a prelude to the acceptance speech provided Dukakis with perhaps the largest nonpartisan audience of the entire campaign, yet neither he nor his campaign staff were able to exploit the situation. The film does nothing to alter perceptions that he was a cold, distant techno-crat, removed from the people. The one visual symbol that represents Dukakis's character is a rusted snowblower that Olympia claims is twenty-five years old. "He gives a new meaning to the word frugal," she says. Presumably the image and her comment were intended to highlight his managerial skills: he was good at saving money, a boon considering the huge federal deficit the next president would face. But of all the symbols to parade out of Dukakis's home, the snowblower suggests that frugality is his most impressive personality trait, and frugality is not a quality that wins elections. George Bush is caring, daring, a man with a mission. Michael Dukakis is thrifty.

Dukakis avers that he is a man of the people, yet he is not fluent in their language. He is oblivious to the shaping and unifying power of televisual communication. As succinctly stated by one Bush adviser, "An election campaign is in part a national tribal ritual, a rite of renewal, and if you don't respond in a way that says you know it, you send a subliminal message that you are really outside of the mainstream culture" (Hershey 1989, 86).

## SUMMARY

Although the Bush campaign received well-deserved criticism for its negative, even deceptive attacks on Dukakis as the campaign progressed, the failures of the Dukakis campaign held lessons for the 1992 candidates. Given that television is here to stay, it is essential to be conversant with its grammar and syntax. Astute politicians use the medium according to its strengths and capabilities. Television is dramatic, visceral, and impressionistic. The juxtaposition and association of words, sounds, and images make implicative claims that cannot be held to traditional criteria of evidence and proof (see Morreale 1991; Jamieson 1988). Television can communicate the myths and values that define and unify members of a community, but it is less suited to conveying the complexities of deliberative argument or to elucidating the intricacies of pressing issues that may divide the candidates. By 1992, Democratic candidate Bill Clinton became the first Democratic candidate since John Kennedy to use the medium of television to his advantage, while the floundering incumbent George Bush attempted to follow suit.

# Chapter 7

# Generic Transformation, 1992

By 1992, the gossamer filaments of the Reagan administration's "new beginning" were becoming apparent. The prosperity of the 1980s had come to an abrupt end, the economy was in a state of torpor, and it was painfully apparent that the Reagan Revolution, supported by George Bush, was a failure. Although the Bush administration could point to successes in the realm of foreign policy—most notably, its invasion of Iraq and the end of the Cold War signaled by the dissolution of the Soviet Union—domestic issues dominated the national agenda. As the election approached, traditional Democratic issues, such as health care and education, were frequently cited concerns. The first four years of the Bush administration had not yielded significant improvements in these areas. Unemployment was soaring and Bush's popularity was at an all time low. Whereas in 1988 only five in ten Americans believed the country was on the wrong track, by 1992 nearly eight in ten Americans believed that this was the case (*New York Times*, 26 July 1992, 22).

In the context of a floundering Bush presidency, Democratic challenger Bill Clinton became his party's nominee. During the primaries, both candidates were threatened when Ross Perot, a billionaire businessman, secured a large following of disgruntled Americans by promising to dispense with "business as usual" in American politics. The relatively unknown Perot's enthusiastic reception made it apparent that the national mood was anti-status quo. Both Bush and Clinton took their cues and claimed that they were candidates who represented change. When the theme of change became untenable for an incumbent candidate, Bush shifted to trust and leadership. Clinton presented himself as a moderate who would hopefully win back the Democrats who had turned to Ronald Reagan in 1980, while Bush tried to paint him as a "high-taxing, big-spending liberal who could not be trusted with the nation's security" (Rosenthal 1992, 1).

The 1992 presidential campaign was unconventional by many standards. Although Perot dropped out of the race on the final day of the Democratic National Convention, declaring that a revitalized Democratic party made it unnecessary for him to run, he later reentered the race in October, making 1992 the first three-candidate race since 1980. In addition, polls revealed that the majority of voters were disenchanted with the highly produced, emotion-based appeals that characterized the past two Republican elections. In fact, "Willie Horton" became a code word for describing the untoward tactics the Republicans used in 1988. Thus, as in the aftermath of Watergate in 1976, "authenticity," albeit contrived, dominated both campaigns. More so than ever before, the candidates exploited popular culture forums, such as talk shows, where they could appear to voters as "themselves" and circumvent the scrutiny of the news media. To avoid charges of overt manipulation, they disdained the use of flashy, soft-sell advertising techniques. The atmosphere affected both political advertising and campaign films. As in the past, Clinton and then Bush had short convention films that presented their candidacies to the American people. The Clinton film attempted to define the candidate's character by presenting and updating myths of the presidential candidate, while an extended election-eve version added material that stressed the campaign themes and vision. The Bush convention film, captive to rhetorical exigencies of the campaign, shifted the campaign film away from personal biography or resumé to a new category that combined elements of both. In an uncharacteristic move for a Republican candidate, a scrambling Bush campaign cancelled plans for an election-eve presentation, opting instead to spend the money on local advertising. Although Ross Perot aired a series of half-hour *infomercials*, a term developed to account for advertisements that borrow stylistically from news programs, he did not air a campaign film. His campaign strategist, Hamilton Jordan, hired a Dallas filmmaker to make a Perot biographical film, but upon seeing the five-minute rough cut, an ill-tempered Perot declared, "This is crap," and the project was scrapped (Goldman and Mathews November/December 1992, 75). Jordan resigned from the campaign the next day.

Both the Clinton and Bush films broke from the conventions of past campaign films, which was appropriate in an unconventional election year. The Clinton and Bush films were very different in terms of style and strategy, yet both demonstrated an understanding of televisual communication and exploited the capacities of the medium. The modern presidential campaign film reached maturity in 1992.

## THE CLINTON CAMPAIGN

Bill Clinton won the Democratic primary after a long and bloody struggle in which many pundits prematurely counted him out of the race. The primary campaign demonstrated once and for all that candidates' characters, rather than issues, had come to dominate presidential politics. Clinton was dubbed "Slick Willie," a man who would say anything to get elected, and he was dogged with accusations of draft-dodging, philandering, and marijuana smoking. Yet, the candidate persevered, and his nomination at the Democratic National Convention made 1992 the first presidential election with a baby boomer candidate shaped by the Vietnam War rather than World War II.

Clinton had a well-organized staff made up of young political operatives, seasoned Democratic consultants, and Madison Avenue advertisers. His communications director, George Stephanopoulos, and campaign manager, David Wilhelm, were both under thirty-five, although Stephanopoulos had worked on Dukakis's 1988 presidential campaign. Wilhelm coordinated political strategy, Stephanopoulos oversaw advertising and public relations issues, and consultant James Carville emerged as chief strategist. Frank Greer, who had also worked for Walter Mondale in 1984, headed the advertising team, although his associate, Mandy Grunwald, became chief advertising strategist. Roy Spence, also on Mondale's team, came out of retirement from politics to serve as creative advertising adviser. In addition, Squier, Eskew, Knapp, and Ochs, the top Pennsylvania Avenue Democratic consulting firm, came on board. Bob Squier was a veteran of past presidential campaigns, first working as television producer for Hubert Humphrey in 1968. Squier also produced Jimmy Carter's *This Man, This Office* in 1980. The campaign hired one Madison Avenue advertising agency, Deutsch, Inc., known for producing controversial, cutting-edge advertisements. Clinton's longtime friends, television producers Harry Thomason and Linda Bloodworth-Thomason (creators of the television series "Designing Women") were responsible for producing televisual campaign materials, in particular the biographical campaign film *The Man From Hope*.

*The Man From Hope* articulated the campaign objectives outlined in a strategy memo written by Carville, Greer, and pollster Stan Greenberg in late April. Their focus group research revealed that Clinton's major problem was that people didn't know or trust him. In an election year dominated by a public mood of pessimism and cynicism, voters perceived him as a typical politician who "wouldn't look you straight in the eye" (Kelly, 14 November 1992, 9). The campaign memo set out a strategy to change public perceptions of Clinton by "repositioning" him as a warm, honest, plain-folks idealist; this would be accomplished simply by using elements of his life story. Their "image modification plan" provided the basis for the campaign film and the entire fall campaign. There were two basic tenets: the candidate needed to communicate in a way that sounded less political, and they needed to convey an image of Clinton as an aggressive, middle-class agent of change who was ready to stand up to special interest groups (Kelly, 14 November 1992, 9). The convention film, *The Man From Hope*, was one of the most coherent manifestations of the attempt to repackage Clinton to make him more palatable to voters. It was broadcast prior to Clinton's acceptance speech, sent to supporters to show their friends, and then recast as part of a thirty-minute, election-eve special.

### The Man From Hope

The Thomasons produced the fourteen-minute version of *The Man From Hope* from ten hours of film and 1000 pages of written text. Although the Thomasons had no experience in national politics, they were seasoned television producers who understood the requirements of emotional televisual communication that could inscribe the candidate within American mythology. They used the film to create an image of Bill Clinton as "a man with a modest, small town background, no stranger to adversity, who matured into a man who believes deeply in family and country" (Grimes 1992, A11). The personal, unslick, documentary-style production provided Clinton's life story in a low-key, interview setting. Structured as a series of seemingly casual on-camera interviews with Clinton and his family, every scene and conversation sought to dispel the negative impressions of Bill Clinton that were formed during the primary campaign by establishing him as a man of character and principle.

The film affirmed itself as a hybrid documentary-advertisement by taking the form of a documentary while retaining the purpose of an advertisement. It corresponded with what Steve Dworin, president of Deutsch Inc., declared as the aim of the image advertisements—to depict Clinton as "a man with a great deal of conviction who really cares about people" (Elliot 1992, 7). In a campaign which sought to dispel charges of slickness, any Madison Avenue-type associations were avoided. The film's structure was similar to *Richard Nixon: A Self-Portrait,* a film developed with similar goals in mind for Richard Nixon in 1968. Whereas the Nixon film consisted of a single interview with the candidate in different locations, intercut with illustrative still-photographs, the Clinton film consisted of a series of interviews with the candidate and his mother, wife, mother-in-law, daughter, and brother. Film footage as well as still-photographs demonstrated the points individual family members were making, and the film had high production values. Clinton was framed in soft, low-key lighting, increasing the impression of earnestness and sincerity. Dissolves linked many of the shots, giving the film a soft, unified feel. Clinton was often shot in close-up, or the camera would tighten in as he spoke, allowing viewers full access to his facial features and expressions. The music was slow and sentimental, helping to guide viewers' emotions and feelings of identification with the candidate. It was a more polished media production than previous Democratic candidates' films.

The film presented a carefully choreographed image of the candidate. Its style was democratic—no single point of view dominated, even that of the candidate. There was no omniscient narrator, only the characters who relayed their versions of experiences. In some cases, Clinton would begin relating a story, and the camera would cut to another character who would finish the story. As with most Democratic candidates' films, Clinton was a man of the people, defined by those around him rather than an authoritative leader who defined himself.

Former Reagan speechwriter Peggy Noonan (1992, 32) criticized the Democrats as a party obsessed with death and dead heroes of the past, and the Clinton film was no exception to this tradition. In order to imply leadership, Clinton was associated with martyred Democratic heroes of the sixties who formed his political philosophy. In archival footage that was clearly a coup for the Clinton campaign, the young Bill Clinton, visiting Washington as a representative of Boy's Nation, shakes hands with then President Kennedy. The impressive footage symbolically presents the revered Democratic leader annointing the candidate, while simultaneously affirming the part of the American Dream where anyone can be president. In a scene cleverly inserted to bring back the ideals of the 1960s, Clinton's brother recalls that Bill idolized Martin Luther King, and memorized every word of his "I Have a Dream" speech. Footage of King giving his famous speech accompanies his words. There are shots of Robert Kennedy, during which Clinton recalls the impact these deaths had on his generation. Shots such as these simulate reality; they make the case for Clinton's leadership by linking him to these figures with whom he had only a tenuous real-life connection.

As with many presidential candidates, Clinton came from a humble background in a small town. In fact, one of the film's purposes was to dispel the misconception that Clinton, a Yale Law School graduate, had been born wealthy. Wife Hillary accomplishes this task in one of her filmed sequences. She declares, "Some people think that Bill must have been born wealthy, that he had all of the privileges that you could ever imagine. Well, instead of being born with a silver spoon in his mouth, he was really born into a house with an outhouse in the backyard." Hillary's mention of a silver spoon is a reference to George Bush, who was castigated at the 1984 Democratic convention for having been born with a "silver foot" in his mouth. Her remark also places her husband within the rags-to-riches corpus of American mythology. Clinton's mother also describes him as a precocious youth who learned to read at a young age and professed interest in serving others. She recalls an anecdote where the seven-year-old Bill stated his determination to improve Arkansas' national standing in education, "if they'll only let me." At the same time, the film was careful to dispel notions that the candidate was overly ambitious. In a scene where Clinton remembers his first meeting with Hillary, he mentions that he had no desire to serve on the *Yale Law Journal*. When pressed by his classmates, he responded by saying, "I'm not going to get a big Wall Street job. I'm not going to go work on the Supreme Court. I'm going home to be a country lawyer."

While in many ways conforming to the conventions of the classical campaign film, new twists on its content suggested further evolution of the genre. While Clinton's grandparents and mother were presented as self-sacrificing and dedicated to the young child's welfare, and Bill Clinton was a loving husband and committed father, the film departed from the whitewashed images of happy families that typically characterize presidential campaign films. The film read almost like a confessional "I'm dysfunctional, you're dysfunctional" paean to contemporary mores. Instead of the idyllic family, Clinton acknowledged that he came from a single parent family. His widowed mother had to leave him with his grandparents while she went back to nursing school, and one of his most poignant childhood memories was of his mother falling to her knees and sobbing as he was leaving after a visit. His mother eventually remarried, but his stepfather was an abusive alcoholic who become violent with his mother (only once, Clinton and his mother claim in the film). The result led to another critical comment by Peggy Noonan, "Why do modern Democrats have to declare to each other that they have suffered, that they are victims? In group therapy this is known as saying hello, but—this is government. The real pain in a person's life is interior; the anguish unveiled in these speeches seems a surrogate for genuine pain, and the device seems not revelatory but deceptive" (1992, 32). Yet, Clinton maintains that he always felt love and compassion for his stepfather, and his mother asserts that his stepfather felt deep love for Bill. The film dents the myth of the happy loving family, but does not desiccate it entirely.

As in all campaign films, the candidate and his wife are presented as a happily married couple. However, Bill and Hillary Clinton acknowledge that their marriage has had problems and they refer to their interview on national television where they discussed the issue in the presence of their daughter Chelsea. "It was pretty painful," Clinton reports. But the experience turned out to be cathartic. "What do you think?" he asked when it was over. "I think I'm glad you're my parents," came the reply. The film may intimate that Clinton is a flawed husband, but the imperfections do not extend to his relationship with his daughter. He describes her birth as one of the most moving experiences of his life, Hillary conveys an anecdote about the young, naive father believing that his infant daughter understood gravity, and Chelsea describes his overinvolvement at her softball games. Film footage depicts them practicing softball in the backyard, playing by a lakeside, and dancing. Chelsea declares on camera, "What I would like America to know about my mother and father is that they're great people and great parents." As she speaks, the entire family relaxes in a hammock, arms clasped around one another. Despite occasional lapses, the Clintons are an intact unit. They represent the modern family.

By focusing solely on Clinton the man, issues, qualifications, and the candidate's vision of America are not explicitly addressed. The convention film intentionally emphasizes character rather than issues. Yet, it is also an adventurous film that uses Bill Clinton's relationship to his family as a metaphor for his relationship to his country. Two telling anecdotes illustrate this point. First, he is presented as the big brother who took care of his younger brother Roger. Several still-photographs depict him with his arm protectively around Roger, who comments, "You know I have to smile when I hear my brother say in the campaign that we have to be one country, because that's the way he always felt about our family." Throughout the film, Clinton is the anchor that grounds his less-than-perfect family. He is a leader within the context of the family, whether his own or the American nation. In another instance, he stands up to his alcoholic stepfather who is about to hit his mother, and his stepfather backs down. Later in the film, he uses hitting as a metaphor both to explain his own fate (getting "beat up" by the press) and that of the

American people (taking "hits" from the Republican administration), which becomes, by implication, the abusive dysfunctional stepfather. He says, "What I want you to know is that the hits I took during this election are nothing compared to the hits that the people in this state and this country are taking every day of their lives under this administration. We no longer should have a country where I worry about me and you worry about you and they worry about them. . . . We've got to be one country again, going up or down together again." Later, Clinton makes the connection again, "I hope that every day from this day forward we could be a nation coming together instead of coming apart." Clinton's yearning for a unified country where no one gets hit or stands divided represents his desire for a unified family without abuse and fractiousness.

Clinton's longing for the ideal family, expressed by his references to the real father he never knew, corresponds to his longing for an ideal America of the past. Clinton's America is represented by his recollections of growing up in Hope, Arkansas, where everyone was happy, safe, and secure. He describes it as "a place and a time where nobody ever locked their doors at night, everybody showed up for the parade on Main Street, and kids like me could dream of being part of something bigger than themselves." In this way, his nostalgic vision of America is not unlike Ronald Reagan's urge for a return to a "traditional" America that existed in a purer, more innocent time. Clinton reappropriates former Republican terms such as hope and optimism—fortuitiously assisted by his birthplace, which allowed him to conclude the film with the comment, "I still believe in a place called Hope." Whereas Republican candidates associate malaise with the liberal Democratic policies of the sixties, Clinton associates malaise with the deaths of his heroes—John Kennedy, Robert Kennedy, and Martin Luther King. After a scene describing the personal impact of King's death on him, Clinton states, "It was a terrible time and it just broke my heart and the spirits of millions of people. It was only two months later when Robert Kennedy was killed. Those were two deaths that changed a lot of things for my generation, for this country. And if both those men had lived, I think the last twenty years would've been a lot different for America, and much better." Clinton gives a Democratic cast to the myth of Paradise Lost.

As evidenced by *The Man From Hope*, the Clinton campaign learned from the failures and successes of past candidacies, both Democratic and Republican. Clinton reappropriated territory and symbols that had been the province of Republicans since 1980. The candidate stressed hope and optimism in a better future, while he characterized the status quo in terms of malaise. The Clinton campaign reclaimed the ambiguous "family values," recognizing that this largely symbolic issue struck a chord with the majority of Americans. Clinton's film both reaffirmed and challenged the traditional myth of the president and provided a modern version of the candidate and the family values that he represented. The election-eve version of the film replayed the Clinton biography, but added more substantive material to convince Americans that Clinton had a vision and a plan. Whereas Dukakis had taken the time after the convention to rest and relax, Clinton and his vice-presidential candidate, Al Gore, went on a cross-country bus tour that was organized to convey a melange of hitherto Republican images: people waving flags, happy families gathered by the roadside, idyllic farms along the way. These images were reminiscent of those that characterized Ronald Reagan's 1984 campaign. Farmers, construction workers, children, Americans of all stripes and colors greet the candidates as they cross through small towns and farmlands. Unlike Reagan, however, Clinton is shown grasping the hands of the throngs who gather to greet him. He is a man in touch with the people (in contrast, too, to George Bush, who was criticized throughout the campaign as "out of touch").

Clinton's commitment to education, job creation, welfare reform, and health care are some of the issues mentioned, while the words "change," "trust," and "plan" are uttered by the candidate himself, his running mate, Al Gore, and the people who endorse his candidacy. Traditional Republicans, such as Admiral William Crowe and several CEOs of major corporations, state their support for Clinton, implicitly dispelling conceptions that Democrats lack the support of the military and business. As in many campaign films, people in the street—men, women, young, old, black, white, southern, northern, self-proclaimed working class, and those in business suits, all assert their support for candidate Clinton. The camera does not hide the fact that these people are attending a Democratic rally, perhaps to contrast the Clinton campaign's "honesty" with the Bush campaign's deceptive tactics. During the campaign, the Bush operation was charged with using friends and relatives of campaign workers as supposedly neutral people on the street who endorsed the candidate. In traditional fashion, the film closed with Clinton making a "live" speech to voters, followed by a montage of images that recapped the film.

## THE BUSH CAMPAIGN

George Bush followed the pattern of Republican candidates before him, although his campaign lacked the tight organization and cohesion of those in the past. Bush's problems resulted from his own reluctance to campaign, his failure to take Clinton seriously until it was too late, his inability to gauge the country's mood, and from the misguided belief that he could defeat Clinton by running a negative campaign based on "family values," much as he had done in 1988. Bush also suffered from the loss of the key political operatives who had masterminded his 1988 campaign. Bush had no one like Reagan's Michael Deaver to orchestrate his campaign. His former campaign manager, James Baker, was serving as secretary of state and had no desire to rejoin a political campaign. Media consultant Roger Ailes declined to formally participate although he served as informal adviser, and master strategist Lee Atwater died the year before from a brain tumor. Moreover, many veterans of the Reagan and Bush campaigns served in new and unfamiliar capacities in the Bush 1992 campaign. The campaign was composed of many operatives in their positions for the first time. Pollster Robert Teeter, active in Republican presidential politics since Richard Nixon's 1972 campaign, became campaign chairman for the first time, while Fred Steeper took over as pollster. Up until the Republican convention in August, Teeter shared control of the campaign with Chief of Staff Sam Skinner, but the resulting dual structure meant that no one figure was in charge. Until James Baker's reluctant return as campaign chief of staff in August, the campaign lacked leadership. The campaign followed the previous Republican models and recruited a team of creative advertising experts from Madison Avenue called the November Company. The November Company was headed by Martin Puris, who had no previous experience producing political advertisements, while only two creative members of the November Company had worked on political campaigns before. The November Company's advertisements were not deemed successful. Unlike the past three Republican presidential elections, strategy was not coordinated from the top and the inexperienced media team received little direction.

The flawed advertising was only part of a campaign that lacked overall integration and a unified positive message. Republican political consultant and presidential campaign veteran Ed Rollins referred to the 1992 Bush effort as "the worst campaign ever seen" (Dowd, 5 November 1992, 1). The Bush campaign film, aired only at the convention, reflected the lack of cohesion and control in the upper echelons of the campaign.

### The (Untitled) Bush Film

Bush's convention campaign film was made before Baker's return to manage the campaign. As with most convention films, the film introduced Bush's nomination acceptance speech, but it was broadcast only on CNN, C-SPAN, and PBS. The film was something of a departure from the traditional subgeneric presidential campaign film categories of biographical, resumé, and visionary films. Incumbents rarely use biographical films the second time they run for office, unless their campaigns are specifically attempting to redefine the candidate's persona. The Nixon campaign used *Richard Nixon: Portrait of a President* and, to a lesser extent, *The Nixon Years: Change Without Chaos* to present him to voters as a personally warm, humane, and compassionate man. But Bush's problems went deeper than voters' perceptions of his personality defects. Under usual circumstances he would have a resumé film that highlighted his accomplishments in office. But the end of his first term produced an economy in shambles, a disgruntled electorate, and widespread perceptions that he was a foreign affairs president who had neglected the domestic arena. The president who promised, "Read my lips—no new taxes" in 1988, had signed one of the largest tax increases in history into effect, the "education" president had passed no legislation to reform the schools, and unemployment was steadily rising. Even Bush's foreign policy successes were tenuous. Though his popularity rating was extraordinarily high during the United States' invasion of Iraq, since then public enthusiasm had waned, especially as Saddam Hussein remained in power in Iraq. Only the break-up of the Soviet Union and the fall of the Berlin Wall, events that merely occurred on Bush's watch, could be touted as evidence of his success. Thus, a resumé film would only reinforce voters' perceptions of Bush's failings, and a visionary film seemed impossible for a president whom critics contended had no agenda and offered no compelling reason why he should be president. Both Democrats and fellow Republicans criticized him for failing to redefine himself to the public. Clinton campaign pollster Stan Greenberg observed, "He made the fatal error of not reintroducing himself to the American people. . . . He didn't give people positive reasons to see him as a domestic leader" (Fineman 1992, 9). Bush administration official William J. Bennett admonished, "The first thing is to decide who you are, and they never did that. It's hard to communicate if you've got nothing to communicate" (Bedard 1992, 36).

The resulting film was not quite biography, not quite resumé, and not visionary at all. It intentionally departed from the soft-focus sentimentality of Bush's 1988 film and even Reagan's 1984 campaign film, as well as from the Clinton film that ran at the 1992 Democratic convention. In an election year where people claimed that they were turned off by slick and manipulative campaign tactics, the Bush campaign disassociated itself from the "Madison Avenue" styling, characteristic of their earlier efforts. The film was a bipartisan biography of great American presidents whose qualities embodied the ambiguous "American spirit." Its style borrowed from new trends in television documentary filmmaking that began with Ken Burns' extremely successful *Civil War* series. As in the *Civil War* series, the Bush film consisted entirely of still-photographs, lithographs, paintings, and archival film footage. Illustrative images appeared on screen as different voices animated significant quotations from former great presidents, such as George Washington, Abraham Lincoln, Theodore Roosevelt, Franklin Delano Roosevelt, and John Kennedy. Only the once-maligned Richard Nixon, resuscitated in the film and heralded for his determination, and Ronald Reagan, hailed for his leadership, spoke for themselves. Actor Robert Mitchum's voice provided narration that linked the various sequences.

Despite the use of documentary rather than slick advertising techniques, the film was not a throwback to earlier modes of presidential campaign communication. It was made for a video generation inured to a visual bombardment. The music was almost a character in this film. Harsh, edgy, and forceful, it was uncharacteristic of the soft music that usually appears in campaign films. There were no cuts—all of the shots in the entire film were linked by dissolves. Images overwhelmed the minimal narration and appeared on screen at record-breaking speed, so much so that it was impossible to assimilate them all in one viewing. In contrast to the classical films where the narration explicated the flow of images, the visuals that appeared here received no explication. The use of dissolves and fast cuts masked the fact that the pictures' connection to the narration was at times tenuous and often obscure. The film left a great deal of space for interpretation. In one instance, the narrator states, "America needs a president who tackles challenges head-on." The language implies a vigorous leader, while the images depict a school bus climbing up a hill towards the camera, then a dissolve to a small group of black children with one writing in the foreground. The pictures could bring any number of references to mind—the school busing controversy of the seventies or the problems of educating minorities. School busing was not an issue explicitly linked to George Bush, nor had he earned plaudits for his advancements in education. At worst, the scene has racist overtones; one implication is that only blacks in America provide challenges or need improved education. In either case, the images have no readily apparent reference, yet they do not seem overtly incongruous in the context of a film where images constantly flash on and off screen within seconds.

Despite the Bush film's innovative style, the film reflected the flailing campaign's weaknesses. The concentration upon the past only emphasized that Bush had no forward moving vision. While the Clinton film was almost entirely "live," this film was made up of dead images and icons—most reminiscent of Carter's *This Man, This Office* in 1980. A section on 1960s history even inexplicably included a sequence of images of Elvis Presley, James Dean, Fidel Castro, and Martin Luther King.

The film failed to highlight George Bush the candidate. Unlike most campaign films, it did not mythologize him as a leader, man of the people, or both. Instead, he was presented as a *keeper* of the flame, a maintenance man rather than inspired leader or Cincinnatus called from the plow. The narration described the qualities of all of the great presidents: fairness, courage, grit, resolve, wisdom, imagination, determination, and leadership, and suggested that George Bush possessed these qualities that embody the American spirit. But George Bush was hardly mentioned until the film's conclusion, when the narrator merely asserted that he had these qualities. No evidence, pictorial or otherwise, supported this unconvincing claim.

In a scene where Bush could have claimed success due to the fall of the Berlin Wall, the credit seems to go more to Ronald Reagan. Reagan's voice says, "Mr. Gorbachev, tear down that wall," accompanied by images of Germans avidly destroying the great barrier. The narrator reports, "Today the wall is down. The Cold War is over. And because of America's leadership, more of the world enjoys the sweet taste of freedom than ever before." America, not George Bush, is lauded for its leadership, and the text even implies that Ronald Reagan, rather than George Bush, was responsible for the fall of the Berlin Wall. The film offered no good argument for reelecting the candidate, other than continuity with a tradition.

Even the quotations culled from the various great presidents speak primarily to the theme of continuity. According to Theodore Roosevelt, "It's not the critic who counts. Not the man who points out how the strong man stumbles or where the deed could have been done better. The credit belongs to the man who is actually in the arena, whose face is marred by doubt and sweat and blood, who strives, who spends himself in a worthy cause."

The film obliquely admits that all is not well, and for the first time in years, a Republican candidate speaks to malaise. "Through our best times and our worst the keepers of the flame have been our presidents," the film begins. As is conventional in campaign films, images of the worst times harken back to the depression rather than the present, and these images are balanced by dynamic shots of the Statue of Liberty with fireworks exploding behind her. Yet, the film goes on to refer to Reagan's "new beginning" as something less than the fulfillment of America's promise. The narrator states, "Today as a new dawn breaks over America, we face tough challenges and unprecedented opportunities." As he speaks, an eagle soars over treetops, followed by images reminiscent of the previous Reagan and Bush films—a construction worker, now in silhouette, bangs a nail into a house, and a cowboy rounds a steer on the range. Other than the repetition of the flag and Statue of Liberty, there are no other symbols that recall the hope and optimism of the past twelve years. The suggestion of tough times is more predominant. In Dwight D. Eisenhower's words used to illustrate wisdom: "No easy problems have ever come to the president of the United States. If they are easy to solve, someone else has already solved them."

Bush's campaign film demonstrates the lack of direction and authority that characterized the 1992 campaign. The film, while technologically sophisticated and artistically made, failed to display the organizational and strategic strengths that had catapulted him to the presidency in 1988. It did not address Americans' concerns or give them any new information about George Bush. It may have impressed them with its wizardry, but it did not provide a positive, commanding image of the president.

## SUMMARY

The 1992 presidential campaign films made it apparent that genres are dynamic as well as static. Both the content and form of the presidential campaign transformed to accord with political exigencies and the cultural milieu. The Clinton and Bush films broke away from past conventions. Clinton's campaign film redefined images of ideal candidates and their backgrounds. The Bush film provided little information about the candidate's personal biography, accomplishments in office, or future vision. Instead, it provided a panorama of American history and tradition, with the candidate tacked on at the very end.

Both films remained hybrid documentary-advertisements, although they responded to the political climate by downplaying advertising codes and embracing those characteristic of the modern television documentary. The shift in emphasis from documentary to advertisement paralleled another shift. Clinton learned from his predecessors and adopted the Republicans' tactics, while the Republicans lost the narrative thread that had carried past elections. It seemed that their story had nowhere to go, while Clinton began one of his own. Bill Clinton's story came to life with the campaign film, which defined him as an imperfect, if sincere man, symbolically born in Hope, Arkansas. Bush's story, which presented him as the last of a long line of ex-presidents, appeared to end.

# Chapter 8

# Afterword: The Presidential Campaign Film as Cultural Artifact

This historical survey of the presidential campaign film provides a rich vein of material for analyzing the interrelation of contemporary American culture and politics. Campaign films have become integral to the campaign ritual, certainly aired before the candidate's acceptance speech, and typically rebroadcast in some form during the general election campaign. The films often serve as representative anecdotes that reflect campaign strategy, exemplifying both its strengths and weakness. Although they cannot predict winners and losers, they lay bare the ways that presidential images are constructed, and the extent to which images are essential to American politics.

The films shift from the classical expository documentary form, characteristic of military-style campaigns, to the hybrid documentary-advertisement, characteristic of merchandising campaigns. Through the years, they become more technologically sophisticated and geared to the demands of an audience reared on television. The films develop to take the changing nature of their audiences into account, from partisan gatherings of supporters to impartial mass television audiences with potentially short attention spans. As the films become more audience-centered, they employ the familiar codes of television programs made to entertain audiences rather than to inform voters, whether they culminate in the highly personal form favored by Bill Clinton or the impersonal version employed by George Bush.

This analysis of presidential campaign films indicated the Democrats' and Republicans' divergent approaches to presidential image making. The films generally fell into two production categories that coincided with the candidates' mythic visions: high-technology production techniques, characteristic of the hybrid documentary-advertisement, typically affirmed a regressive, idealized vision of "traditional" America, while conventional, less highly produced films were apt to envision malaise, crisis, and the need for change. The former, most evident in the films produced for Republican candidates, reflected an audience-centered approach to political communication that relied upon marketing principles and sophisticated televisual communication to construct political images. The latter, most characteristic of Democratic candidates' films up until 1992, remained candidate-centered; they did not fully exploit marketing techniques or take advantage of television's communicative strengths and capabilities. As a result, the Republicans more readily adapted their films to a culture dominated by television, while the Democrats typically remained impervious to the requirements of a televisual, consumption-based culture.

Republican candidates in the age of television have reaped the organizational and financial benefits of incumbency more often than Democrats. Since at least 1968, the Republicans have benefited from a steady pool of political consultants and Madison Avenue advertisers. They have been able to refine and develop their marketing techniques, as demonstrated by their thematic consistency through the years and by the evolving form and functions of their campaign films. While both Democrats and Republicans draw from the corpus of American mythology, the Democrats' marketing and televisual communication techniques lag behind the Republicans. Historically, the Republicans draw on previous campaigns' research to project images and evoke myths that address deep-seated yearnings, while the more candidate-centered Democrats produce images of the candidate that are less dependent upon the hopes and desires that fuel the American psyche. This analysis of campaign films suggests that the Republicans are far more fluent in the language of television; their visual and verbal messages support one another and provide the glue to bind their constituencies, while the Democrats more often undercut visual messages with incongruent visual forms and images. The party of progress most often sells its candidate with regressive communication strategies, while the party of tradition markets its vision with advanced technological tools. The Democrats began to reverse this trend in 1992, but it remains to be seen whether this election marked a turning point or an anomaly.

Despite the historic formal differences in the films produced for Democratic and Republican candidates, this study makes apparent how mythic images and values are promoted within a culture under the guise of "history," and how little myths concerning the president and country have changed. Presidential candidates' self-images remain relatively constant as versions of American myth, with the candidate presented as a leader, man of the people, or both simultaneously. For the Republicans, candidates embracing both opposing images coincided with an increasingly optimistic vision of an America where crises have been resolved, and the candidates represent all things to all people. But the Republican vision faded in 1992, a victim of circumstance and the incumbent's inability to inspire confidence in its veracity. The Democrats co-opted hope and optimism, and represented their candidate as both leader and man of the people. In so doing, they also managed to redefine the ideal American as one that emerges from a less than perfect family, and who may himself fall prey to weaknesses, but who emerges stronger for it.

Ever since the publication of Andrew Jackson's biography for the 1828 campaign, presidential candidates have played upon the Jackson narrative, based upon a belief in America's ability to fulfill its promise of liberty, justice, and equality, as well as a pessimistic fear that corruption, decay, and loss of moral virtue threaten the American Dream. Candidates either promise salvation or warn of impending doom. In the 1960s, a period of significant cultural transformation, the Republicans appropriated the positive side of the American Dream and sold it to the American people. The films produced for Republican candidates developed a coherent set of themes and images as they addressed an imaginary audience of unified Americans. The Republican vision moved from apocalypse to redemption as it provided Americans with the figures of hope and reassurance they craved, defined against the background of the other—black, urban, poor, liberal, progressive Americans. The American Dream was taken for granted in Eisenhower's *Report to Ike*; after turbulent social changes, it fell under siege in Barry Goldwater's *Choice*. Nixon and Ford suggested that they were in the process of overcoming the threat and were working toward achievement of the dream, Ronald Reagan articulated its fulfillment and synthesized opposing myths of the president, and George Bush perpetuated the Reagan vision in 1988, though he peppered it with negative reminders of the America represented by liberal democracy. In 1992, however, Bush surrendered hope and optimism to the Democrats. The Republican narrative played itself out.

Until recently, the Democrats, a coalition party that until 1992 seemed to be losing its coalitions, seemed unable to construct a positive vision of what they represented. Increasingly bereft of symbols after the "failure" of the Great Society, they lapsed into a vision of despair. Democratic candidates from 1968 to 1988 reflected the pessimistic side of the

American Dream; they presented themselves as flawed representatives of a country in crisis. They were frequently defined by what they stood against. The Democratic vision of malaise reflected a party in disarray. Salvation came in 1992 with the construction and marketing of a positive, if ambiguous, vision of forward-moving change represented by the youthful Clinton and his runnning mate, Al Gore.

Despite presidential campaign films' usefulness for examining American politics and culture, they pose ethical problems that need to be addressed. The films exemplify changes from a print to a video culture, one dominated by consumerism and the desire to "buy" the best image. Although campaigns have always used images and entertainment, there is no longer any ground to distinguish image from reality. The image conveyed on television *is* the campaign. Politics and entertainment have imploded in the age of the image. Instead of substantive political discourse that enlightens and edifies, the politics of image entices and cajoles. Critical questions are not raised; as the presidential campaign films so aptly illustrate, only familiar, easily codified aspects of a candidate's life and record are highlighted, and vacuous symbols such as freedom, patriotism, and the flag define candidates. It is easy to fabricate a truth with pictures, or at least to only tell part of the story. The use and abuse of the "arational" television medium in a political culture that calls for "rational" judgment is a long-term problem. Television and democratic self-government are ill-matched partners. However, in the short term it becomes all the more necessary to use images and symbols to counter images and symbols; to demonstrate leadership and competency by making use of all of the tools at one's disposal. The Democrats learned this lesson in 1992, just as the public and news media became more wary of manipulative campaign tactics. We can only be sure that the battle will wage on in 1996, and we can only hope that an increasingly televisually literate electorate will learn to look beyond the seduction of images.

# Filmography

Ailes, R. (Executive Producer). 1988. *Bush Campaign Film*. [Film on videotape]. Available from Political Commercial Archives, University of Oklahoma, Norman, OK.

Brown Brothers. (Producers). 1928. *Master of Emergencies*. [Film]. Available from Herbert Hoover Presidential Library, West Branch, IA.

Dailey, P. (Producer). 1980. *The Reagan Record*. [Film]. Available from Republican National Committee, Washington, D.C.

DeNove, J. (Producer). 1960. *The New Frontier*. [Film on videotape]. Available from Kennedy Presidential Library, Boston, MA.

deRochemont, L. (Producer). 1948. *The Dewey Story* . [Film on videotape]. Available for viewing at Schuck Collection, Kennedy Presidential Library, Boston, MA.

Dusenberry, P. (Producer). 1984. *A New Beginning*. [Film on videotape]. Available from Republican National Committee, Washington, D.C.

Fox, W. (Producer). 1923. *The Life of Calvin Coolidge*. [Film]. Available from National Archives, Washington, D.C.

Greer, F., and associates. (Producers). 1984. *Mondale Convention Film*. [Videotape]. Available from Cable News Network Tape Library, Atlanta, GA.

Guggenheim, C. (Producer). 1972. *The McGovern Story*. [Film on videotape]. Available from Nixon Presidential Materials, div. of National Archives, Alexandria, VA.

Hearst-Metronome News. (Producer). 1940. *The Presidential Campaign of Wendell Wilkie*. [Film]. Available from National Archives, Washington, D.C.

Hubschman, A. (Producer). 1936. *Roosevelt Campaign Film*. [Film]. Available from Franklin Delano Roosevelt Presidential Library, Hyde Park, NY.

Kimberly, H. S. (Producer). 1928. *Upbuilding with Prosperity*. [Film]. Available from Herbert Hoover Presidential Library, West Branch, IA.

Macdougall, M. (Producer). 1976 *Ford Election-eve Campaign Film*. [Videotape]. Available from Gerald Ford Presidential Library, Ann Arbor, MI.

Napolitan, J. (Executive Producer). 1968. *What Manner of Man*. [Film on videotape]. Available from Minnesota Historical Society, St. Paul, MN.

Payne, D. (Producer). 1988. *Dukakis Convention Film*. [Film on videotape]. Available from Public Affairs Video Archives, Purdue University, West Lafayette, IN.

Pryor, A. (Producer). 1956. *Election-eve Report to Ike*. [Videotape]. Available from Dwight D. Eisenhower Presidential Library, Abilene, KS.

Puris, M. (Executive Producer). 1992. *Bush Convention Film*. [Film on videotape]. Available from Public Affairs Video Archives, Purdue University, West Lafayette, IN.

Rafshoon, G. (Producer). 1976. *Jimmy Who?* [Videotape]. Available from Consolidated Productions, Washington, D.C.

____. 1980. *This Man, This Office*. [Videotape]. Available from Consolidated Productions, Washington, D.C.

Shakespeare, F. (Executive Producer). 1968. *Richard Nixon: A Self-Portrait*. [Film on videotape]. Available from Nixon Presidential Materials, div. of National Archives, Alexandria, VA.

Thomason, H., and L. Bloodworth-Thomason. 1992. *The Man from Hope*. [Videotape]. (Available from Public Affairs Video Archives, Purdue University, West Lafayette, IN.

Universal Pictures and International News. (Producers). 1948. *The Truman Story*. [Film]. Available from National Archives, Washington, D.C.

Walton, R. (Producer). 1964. *Choice*. [Film on videotape]. Available from Public Affairs Video Archives, University of Oklahoma, Norman, OK.

Wolper, D. (Producer). 1972. *The Nixon Years: Change Without Chaos*. [Film on videotape]. Available from Nixon Presidential Materials, div. of National Archives, Alexandria, VA.

____. 1972. *Richard Nixon: Portrait of a President*. [Film on videotape]. Available from Nixon Presidential Materials, div. of National Archives, Alexandria, VA.

Wyckoff, G., and Filmac (Paramount) Productions. (Producers). 1960. *Ambassador of Friendship*. Available from Kennedy Presidential Library, Boston, MA.

# Bibliography

Agranoff, R. 1972. *The new style in election campaigns.* Boston: Holbrook Press.

Apple, R. W. 1972. O'Brien reproves lax effort. *New York Times*, 1 September, 1, 6.

Barnouw, E. 1979. *Documentary: A history of the non-fiction film.* New York: Oxford University Press.

Bedard, P. 1992. They'd rather be hunting: Campaign wizard James Baker turned out to be his chief's never-present help in time of trouble. *National Review*, 30 November, 34–37.

Bell, B. T. 1972. Nov. 7: It's a clear choice all right, but what's the real difference. *Contemporary Review*, 15 October, 177–83.

Bernays, E. 1952. *Public relations.* Norman, OK: University of Oklahoma Press.

Berry, J. P. 1987. *JFK and the media: The first television president.* Lanham, MD: University of America Press.

Biocca, F., ed. 1991. *Television and political advertising.* Vols. I & II. Hillsdale, NJ: Lawrence Erlbaum.

Bloom, M. 1973. *Public relations and presidential campaigns: A crisis in democracy.* New York: Thomas Y. Crowell Co.

Blumenthal, S. 1981. Marketing the president. *New York Times Magazine*, 13 September, 43ff.

Boorstin, D. 1961. *The image: A guide to pseudo-events in America.* New York: Harper and Row.

Brown, W. B. 1960. *The people's choice: The presidential image in the campaign biography.* Baton Rouge, LA: Louisiana State University Press.

Burke, K. 1955. *A grammar of motives.* New York: George Braziller.

Burnham, W. D. 1981. The 1980 earthquake: realignment, reaction, or what? In *The hidden election: politics and economics in the 1980 presidential campaign.* Ed. T. Ferguson and J. Rogers. New York: Pantheon Books.

Bush, G. 1991. *Lord of attention: Gerald Stanley Lee and the crowd metaphor in industrializing America.* Amherst: University of Massachusetts Press.

Campaign '72: Continuing dispute over broadcasts. 1972. *Congressional Quarterly*, 29 January, 204–8.

Campbell, Joseph. 1988. *The Power of Myth* with Bill Moyers. New York: Doubleday.

Casey, R. D. 1937. Republican propaganda in the 1936 campaign. *Public Opinion Quarterly*, Vol. I (2), April, 27–34.

Chester, E. W. 1969. *Radio, television, and American politics*. New York: Sheed and Ward.

Chester, L., G. Hodgson, and B. Page. 1969. *An American melodrama: The presidential campaign of 1968*. New York: Viking Press.

Cockburn, A., and J. Ridgeway. 1981. The world of appearance: The public campaign. In *The hidden election: politics and economics in the 1980 presidential campaign*, 65–97. Ed. T. Ferguson and J. Rogers. New York: Pantheon Books.

Cotler, G. 1952. That plague of spots on Madison Ave. *Reporter*, November, 7–8.

Craig, R. 1954. "Distinctive features of radio-television in the 1952 presidential election." Master's thesis, University of Iowa.

Denton, R. E., Jr. 1982. *The symbolic dimensions of the presidency: Description and analysis*. Prospect Heights, IL: Waveland Press.

Devlin, L. Patrick. 1981. Reagan's and Carter's ad men review the 1980 television campaigns. *Communication Quarterly*, Vol. 30, No. 1, Winter, 3–12.

_____. 1989. Contrasts in presidential campaign commercials of 1988. *American Behavioral Scientist*, March/April.

Diamond, E. 1984. Amid 11 clashing creative egos, Tuesday Team's strategy unfolds. *Adweek*, 27 August, 1, 58.

Diamond, E., and Bates, S. 1984. *The spot: The rise of political advertising on television*. Cambridge, MA: MIT Press.

Donath, B. 1976. The adman behind Jimmy Carter: A decade of dedication paying off. *Advertising Age*, 12 July, 113–15.

_____. 1976. Ford's adman plans election turnaround strategy. *Advertising Age*, 23 August, 1, 182.

Dowd, M. 1992. Sifting strategies: What went wrong, and right. *New York Times*, 5 November, 1, B5.

Drew, E. 1976. *American journal: The events of 1976*. New York: Random House.

_____. 1981. *Portrait of an election: The 1980 presidential campaign*. New York: Simon and Schuster.

Edelman, M. 1988. *Constructing the political spectacle*. Chicago: University of Chicago Press.

Elliot, S. 1992. Bold ad firm is chosen to build Clinton's image. *New York Times*, 4 July, 7.

Ellis, J. 1989. *The documentary idea: A critical history of English-language documentary film and video*. Englewood Cliffs, NJ: Prentice Hall.

Ellul, J. 1973. *Propaganda: The formation of men's attitudes*. New York: Vintage Books.

Elson, R. T. 1971. DeRochemont's The March of Time. In *The documentary tradition: From Nanook to Woodstock*, 104–11. Ed. L. Jacobs. New York: Hopkinson and Blake.

Evans, R., and R. Novak. 1964. High Command Split: Goldwater's advisers were divided on whether to show TV movie. *Los Angeles Times*, 8 November, E7.

Fielding, R. 1972. *The American newsreel: 1911–67*. Norman, OK: University of Oklahoma Press.

Fineman, H. 1992. The Torch Passes. *Newsweek Election Extra*, November/December, 4–10.

Fischer, R. A. 1988. *Tippecanoe and trinkets too: The material culture of American presidential campaigns, 1828–1924*. Chicago: University of Chicago Press.

Fisher, W. 1973. Reaffirmation and subversion of the American dream. *Quarterly Journal of Speech* 59, 160–67.

____. 1980. Rhetorical fiction and the presidency. *Quarterly Journal of Speech* 66, 119–26.

Foltz, K. 1992. Bringing Madison Avenue polish to Bush's campaign ads. *New York Times*, 19 June, D5.

Ford to take high road on campaign advertising. 1976. *Broadcasting*, 6 September, 27–30.

Fox, S. 1985. *The mirror makers: A history of American advertising and its creators*. New York: Vintage Books.

Frankel, M. 1972. It's a clear choice all right, but what's the real difference? *New York Times Magazine*, Section VI, 15 October, 34ff.

Gilbert, R. 1972. *Television and presidential politics*. North Quincy, MA: Christopher Publishing House.

Golden, D. 1992. The president's point man. *New York Times Magazine*, 19 April, 14ff.

Goldman, P., T. Fuller and the Newsweek Special Election Team. 1984. Avalanche: The Reagan mandate and how he will use it. *Newsweek Election Extra*, November/December, 1–112

Goldman, P., and T. Mathews. 1992. 'Manhattan Project,' 1992. *Newsweek Election Extra*, November/December, 40–56.

____. 1992. Superhero. *Newsweek Election Extra*, November/December, 70–77.

Goldman, P., T. Mathews, and the Newsweek Special Election Team. 1989. *The quest for the presidency: The 1988 campaign*. New York: Simon and Schuster.

Grimes, W. 1992. Film tribute to Clinton focuses on simple values. *New York Times*, 17 July, A11.

Gronbeck, B. 1989. Mythic portraiture in the 1988 Iowa caucus bio-ads. *American Behavioral Scientist* 32, March/April, 351–64.

Gronbeck, B., and A. Miller. 1993. *American self-images and the presidential campaign*. Boulder, CO: Westview Press.

Heale, M. J. 1982. *The presidential quest: Candidates and images in American political culture: 1787–1852*. New York: Longman.

Hershey, M. R. 1989. The Campaign and the Media. In *The Election of 1988: Reports and Interpretations*. Chatham, NJ: Chatham House Publishers.

Irwin, D. 1964. Morality film by Barry: Revision of movie planned. *Los Angeles Times*, 22 October, 1, 25.

Jacobs, L. 1971. Precursors and prototypes (1894-1922). In *The documentary tradition: From Nanook to Woodstock*, 2–9. Ed. L. Jacobs. New York: Hopkinson and Blake.

Jamieson, K. H. 1984. *Packaging the presidency: A history and criticism of presidential campaign advertising*. New York: Oxford University Press.

____. 1988. *Eloquence in an Electronic Age: The Transformation of Political Speechmaking*. New York: Oxford University Press.

Kelley, S., Jr. 1956. *Professional public relations and political power*. Baltimore: Johns Hopkins University Press.

Kelly, M. 1992. The making of a first family: A blueprint. *New York Times*, 14 November, 1, 9.

Kern, M. 1989. *Political advertising in the eighties*. New York: Praeger.

Kintner, R. E. 1965. Television and the world of politics. *Harper's Magazine*, May, 121–32.

Kurtz, H. 1992. GOP ad veterans cut from Bush team. *Washington Post*, 9 February, A16.

Lee, R. 1993. Images of civic virtue in the new political rhetoric. In *Presidential campaigning and American self-images*. Ed. B. Gronbeck and A. Miller. Boulder, CO: Westview Press.

Luntz, F. 1988. *Candidates, consultants, and campaigns*. New York: Basil Blackwell.

MacDougall, M. 1977. *We almost made it*. New York: Crown Publishers.

Martineau, P. 1957. *Motivation in advertising: Motives that make people buy*. New York: McGraw Hill.

May, E., and J. Fraser, ed. 1973. *Campaign '72: The managers speak*. Cambridge, MA: Harvard University Press.

McGee, M. 1975. In search of "the people:" A rhetorical alternative. *Quarterly Journal of Speech* 61 (4), 235–49.

McGinnis, J., ed. 1970. *The selling of the president, 1968*. New York: Pocket Books.

McNeil, R. 1968. *The people machine*. New York: Harper and Row.

Merelman, Richard. 1976. The dramaturgy of politics. In *Drama in life: The uses of communication in society*, 285–301. Ed. J. E. Combs and M. W. Mansfield. New York: Hastings House.

Mickelson, S. 1989. *From whistlestop to sound bite: Four decades of politics and television*. New York: Praeger.

Mondale, W. 1985. Interview on "Meet the press," 7 April, Washington, DC: Kelly Press.

Moore, J. 1986. *Campaign for president: The managers look at '84*. Dover, MA: Auburn House.

Moore, J., and J. Fraser. 1977. *Campaign for president: The managers look at '76*. Cambridge, MA: Ballinger Publishing Co.

Morreale, J. 1991. *A new beginning: A textual frame analysis of the political campaign film*. New York: SUNY Press.

Mortenson, C. 1967. *Comparative Analysis of Political Persuasion on 4 Telecast Program Formats in the 1960 and 1964 Campaigns*. Doctoral dissertation, University of Minnesota.

Moyers, B. 1989. The illusion of news. *The public mind*. PBS Television.

Murray-Brown, J. 1991. Video ergo sum. In *Video icons and values*. Ed. A. Olson, C. Parr, and D. Parr. New York: SUNY Press.

Napolitan, J. 1972. *The election game and how to win it*. Garden City, NY: Doubleday.

Navasky, V. S. 1972. The making of the candidate. *New York Times Magazine*, 7 May, 27ff.

Nichols, B. 1981. *Ideology and the image*. Bloomington: University of Indiana Press.

_____. 1991. *Representing reality: Issues and concepts in documentary.* Bloomington: University of Indiana Press.

Nimmo, D., and J. E. Combs. 1983. *Mediated political realities.* New York: Longman.

Nimmo, D., and K. Sanders. 1981. *Handbook of Political Communication.* Beverly Hills: Sage Publications.

Noonan, P. 1992. Behind enemy lines. *Newsweek,* 27 July, 32–33.

Nuccio, S. 1964. Advertising: Post-mortem on GOP drive. *New York Times,* 5 November, 64.

O'Connor, J. J. 1984. Tuesday's winners. *Advertising Age,* 12 November, 1, 111.

Osborn, M. 1986. Rhetorical depiction. In *Form, genre and the study of political discourse,* 79–100. Ed. H. W. Simons and A. Aghazarian. Columbia: University of South Carolina Press.

O'Shaughnessy, N. 1990. *The phenomenon of political marketing.* New York: St. Martin's Press.

Patterson, T. E., and R. E. McClure. 1976. *The unseeing eye.* New York: Putnams.

Perry, R. 1984. *Hidden power: The programming of the president.* New York: Beaufort Books.

Rafshoon, G. 1976. Agencies: Don't shun political candidates. *Advertising Age,* 16 August, 43–44.

Redding, J. 1958. *Inside the democratic party.* New York: Bobbs-Merrill.

Republicans: Well organized, well financed in 1972. 1972. *Congressional Quarterly,* 12 August, 1984–1987.

Ritter, K. W. 1980. American political rhetoric and the American jeremiad tradition. *Central States Speech Journal* 31, 153–71.

Robertson, N. 1964. GOP film depicts moral decay. *New York Times,* 21 October, 35.

Rosenthal, A. 1992. GOP plotting 2-edged effort to bolster Bush. *New York Times,* 19 July, 1.

Runkel, D. R., ed. 1989. *Campaign for president: The managers look at '88.* Dover, MA: Auburn House.

Sabato, L. 1981. *The Rise of Political Consultants.* New York: Basic Books.

Saltzman, A. 1984. Tuesday Team's debut: $1 million half-hour on Tuesday night. *Adweek,* 10 September, 1, 6.

Schieffer, B., and G. P. Gates. 1989. *The acting president: Ronald Reagan and the supporting players who helped him create the illusion that held America spellbound.* New York: Dutton.

Schram, M. 1987. *The great American video game: Presidential politics in the television age.* New York: William Morrow.

Schwartz, T. 1974. *The responsive chord.* New York: Anchor Books.

Seldes, G. 1952. Television and the Voter. *Saturday Review,* 6 December, 17ff.

Selling the president '72. 1972. *Newsweek,* 31 July, 55B.

Thomson, C. A. 1966. Mass media performance. In *The national election of 1964,* 111–57. Ed. M. C. Cummings, Jr. Washington, DC: Brookings Institute.

Thum, G., and M. Thum. 1972. *The Persuaders: Propaganda in war and peace.* New York: Atheneum.

Toner, R. 1992. At dawn of new politics, challenges for both parties. *New York Times,* 5 November, B1.

Trent, J. S., and R. V. Friedenberg. 1983. *Political campaign communication: Principles and practices.* New York: Praeger.

Turner, W. 1980. Exaggerations found in comparing Reagan ad with his record as governor. *New York Times,* 30 October, B17.

Tyler, P. 1971. Documentary technique in film fiction. In *The documentary tradition: From Nanook to Woodstock,* 251–71. Ed. L. Jacobs. New York: Hopkinson and Blake.

Weisbord, M. 1964. *Campaigning for president: A new look at the road to the White House.* Washington, DC: Public Affairs Press.

Westbrook, R. 1983. Politics as consumption. In *The Culture of consumption: Critical essays in American history 1880–1980,* 143–73. Ed. R. Wightman Fox and T. J. Lears. New York: Pantheon.

*We the people: The American people and their government.* 1975. Washington, DC: Smithsonian Institute Press.

White, T. 1961. *The making of the president, 1960.* New York: Atheneum.

_____. 1965. *The making of the president, 1964.* New York: Atheneum.

_____. 1969. *The making of the president, 1968.* New York: Atheneum.

_____. 1973. *The making of the president, 1972.* New York: Atheneum.

Witcover, J. 1977. *Marathon: The pursuit of the presidency, 1972–1976.* New York: Viking Press.

Wyckoff, G. 1968. *The image candidates: American politics in the age of television.* New York: McMillan Co.

# Index

ABC television: and campaign film broadcast, 116, 132; and convention coverage, 77–78

Academy Award, 79

Actors, in campaign films, 36, 47, 52, 156. *See also* Reenactment strategies

Actuality film, 3, 32, 82, 123–124

Adams, John Quincy, 26, 27, 28

Advertisements, product, 3, 6, 31, 47–48, 130; behavioral psychology and, 39–40; celebrity endorsements and, 39–40, 51; The Daisy commercial, 76; and documentary format, 15, 17–18, 25, 38–43, 57, 85, 117, 121–122, 124, 140–144, 164–169, 170–174, 177–180; during Great Depression, 39–40; informercials and, 162; and mankind's redemption, 39; negative, 56; old-style campaigns and, 27–32; and television, 46–48, 56, 91–92, 100, 113–116, 143–144, 162, 163–164, 165, 170, 171–172. *See also* Image-making, presidential; Spot advertisement, presidential

*Advertising Age*, 40

Advertising agencies, 39–40, 46, 48, 58, 63, 70, 71, 75, 80, 85, 99, 114, 122–123, 128, 139, 145, 149, 155, 162, 163–164, 165, 170, 171–172. *See also names of individual agencies*

Advocacy propaganda, 28–32; and surrogate speakers, 30. *See also* Persuasion; Propaganda

AFL-CIO, 93

Agitative propaganda, 25–26. *See also* Persuasion; Propaganda

Agrarian myth, use of, 10

Ailes, Roger, 85, 139, 156, 170

Air Force One, 132

Allied Expeditionary Force (AEF), 36

*Ambassador of Friendship* (film), 12, 17, 37, 63–66. *See also* Nixon, Richard

American Association of Political Consultants, 3. *See also* Political consulting

American Dream, 8, 13; Clinton and, 165; family and, 9–10; Kennedy and, 63, 165; Mondale and, 148; mythic motifs, 13–14, 60, 83, 87, 96, 99, 120–121, 158–159, 164–169, 172, 179; nostalgia and, 10–11; Reagan and, 127–129, 130, 138, 143. *See also* Image-making, presidential; Myth, American; Symbolism

Anderson, John, 127

Anderson, Morgan, DeSantis and Ball agency, 71

*A New Beginning* (film), 15, 140–144, 150. *See also* Reagan, Ronald

Antebellum period, 6

Anti-Biography, old-style campaign, 28. *See also* Propaganda

Arbitron ratings, 138. *See also* Polls, opinion

Archetypal imagery, 6–13

Aronson, Sidney, 80

Aspirations, 6

Athleticism, of presidential candidate, 7, 8, 118–119

*A Thousand Days* (film), 75

*Atlanta Constitution*, 125

Atwater, Lee, 138, 170

Audience manipulation: documentary format and, 11, 15, 16, 33–43, 47, 95–96; entertainment and, 42–43, 177; and motion picture industry, 36–37; old-style campaigns and, 27–32; political marketing and, 42–43, 46–48, 57, 95–96, 138–139, 143–144, 155–156, 163–165, 170–175; rhetoric and, 4, 17–18, 131; television and, 46–48, 50–52, 56–57, 112, 177; testimonials and, 17, 102–103

Authority, 5; depiction of, 47; lack of, 16

Babbitt, Bruce, 132

Baez, Joan, 79

Bailey, John M., 72

Bailey, Pearl, 118

Bailey-Deardourff agency, 114–115, 116, 122

Baker, James, 114, 138, 170

Baker, Robert G., 73

Balabar, Barney, 64

Ball, George, 47

Barker, Alton, 41

Basehart, Richard, 16, 103

Batten, Barton, Durstine and Osborne agency (BBD&O), 40, 48, 50, 55, 63, 114, 139

"Battle Hymn of the Republic," 133. *See also* Music, and campaign films

Baxter, Leona, 41–42

*Because It's Right* (film), 80, 81. *See*

*also* Humphrey, Hubert

Beckel, Robert, 145

Beliefs, 6

Bennett, William J., 171

Berlin Wall, fall of, 171, 173

Bernays, Edward, 41

Biden, Joe, 154

Biographical film genre, 3, 4–5, 35, 58–63, 82, 94–99, 123–127, 146–149, 162, 164–169, 171; American Dream motif in, 8, 9–11, 87–88, 96, 99, 120, 138, 140–141, 142–144, 151, 164, 165, 179; and candidate's upbringing, 7–8, 11, 35, 60, 87–88, 95, 103, 118, 125, 156, 166; and documentary footage, 12–13, 58–63, 66, 82, 91–94, 119–120, 123, 140–144, 164–169, 170–174; and family values, 7–10, 87–88, 142, 156–157, 164; heroism and, 10, 11, 59–60, 97, 119, 120, 130, 142, 151, 156, 172; historical impetus for, 27; nostalgia in, 10–11, 83. *See also* Documentary format; Propaganda; Rhetorical genre

Biography, old-style campaign, 28, 29–30. *See also* Propaganda

Bloodworth-Thomason, Linda, 163, 164

Boston Patrolman's Association Union, 153

Boy's Nation, 165

Brenner, Judy Press, 146

Brezhnev, Leonid, 120

Brookline, Massachusetts, 10

Brown brothers, 34

Bryan, William Jennings, 30, 31

Buchanan, James, 30

Budgets, of campaign films. *See* Films, presidential

Burch, Dean, 71, 72

Burns, Ken, 172

Bush, Barbara, 16, 151; and campaign film narration, 152

Bush, George, 8, 11, 12, 139, 149–150, 161, 166, 169–170, 179; campaign film techniques, 16, 20, 150–154, 159, 170–174; and incumbency, 149, 161–162, 169–170; and Vice

Presidency, 141, 149; and vision of resurgence, 14, 174
Bush, Jeb, 154

Caddell, Pat, 122–123, 127, 132, 145
Caldwalder, John, 119
Calhoun, John C., 27
California Federation of Labor, 131
Campaign Associates, 41–42
Campaign films, presidential: and advertising techniques, 15, 17–18, 25, 38–43, 46–48, 85, 100–106, 117, 140–146, 149–154, 164–169, 170–174; and American mythic imagery, 6–14, 96, 120, 138, 140–141, 142–144, 151, 179; classical film techniques and, 4, 15, 19–20, 94–99, 106, 123–124, 166; computer technology and, 40, 91–92, 128–129, 138; as cultural artifact, 177–180; and entertainment industry, 35–37, 139, 156–157, 164–169, 177; and foreign leaders, 12–13, 36, 50, 120, 132, 155; generalized mythic motifs in, 13–14, 18–19, 40, 154, 179; hybrid expository/documentary advertisement, 6, 15–21, 25, 32–38, 39–43, 49, 57, 108, 111–114, 123–127, 137–144, 164–169, 170–175; incumbents and, 5, 12, 14, 17, 19, 76–78, 91–92, 101–106, 140–144, 171; makers of, 3–4, 20, 31–38, 39–43, 48, 57, 58, 64–65, 71, 75, 79, 80, 94, 99, 100, 107, 116, 121–122, 123–124, 128–129, 138–140, 144–146, 149–150, 155, 162, 163–164, 165, 170, 171–172; and marketing principles, 4, 15–21, 32–38, 39–43, 49–53, 67, 85, 100–106, 117, 124, 138–146, 163–165, 170–175, 179; nostalgia and, 10–11; overview, 1–6; populist, 13, 123–127, 132; propaganda and, 25–26, 32–38, 40–43, 65–66, 95, 102; reenactments and, 36, 37; religious inferences in, 62, 71; as rhetorical genre, 4–6, 17–18, 131; structure and components of, 14–21, 32, 34–35, 50–52, 53–57, 58–62, 63–66, 71–75, 82–84, 85–89, 94–99, 100–106, 116–122, 123–127, 129–134, 140–144, 146–149, 150–154, 155–158, 164–169, 170–174; television and, 1–2, 37–38, 46–48, 49, 50–52, 65, 81, 85, 112–116, 125–127, 143–144, 149, 164–169, 170–175, 178; types of, 4–6, 15, 66, 92–93; use of family imagery in, 7–10, 35; and videotape technology, 19–20, 113, 144; war footage and, 11, 19, 33, 35, 36, 51, 61, 95, 97, 119, 120, 149, 151. See also Propaganda
Campaigning with Stevenson (film), 53–55, 66
Campaigns, presidential: and computer technology, 40, 42, 128–129, 138; and contrived pseudo-events, 29–32, 33, 38–43, 77, 143–144; as entertainment, 32, 42–43, 177; first national, 30; funds and allocations, 31, 35, 36, 42, 50, 53, 70, 71, 81, 92, 96, 112, 116, 140, 146, 155; military model of, 31, 38, 43, 45, 47, 58, 82, 106, 135, 137, 144, 146; old-style, 1, 4, 26–32, 137; party volunteerism and, 4, 28–29, 38, 126; themes and slogans, 42–43, 46, 52, 60, 61–62, 64, 72–73, 102–106, 131, 133, 138, 140–144, 145–146, 150–154, 155, 158, 161–163, 170–171. See also names of individual candidates
Camp David, 116; Accords, 132
Candidates, presidential: abortion rights and, 131; American myth and, 6–14, 17–18, 59–60, 74, 83–84, 87, 96, 120, 125, 127–129, 138, 140–144, 151, 164, 165; biographical films of, 3, 4, 5, 7–14, 19–20, 35–38, 58–63, 94–99, 102–103, 123–127, 146–149, 156–157, 162, 164–169; character construction of, 2, 5, 7, 8–14, 19–20, 27, 38–42, 45, 47, 49, 59–60, 83, 86–88, 92–94, 102, 119–121, 123, 125, 129, 132, 140–144, 162, 164–169, 170–174; children of, 9, 59, 102, 147, 152, 157, 165, 167;

commercialization of, 4, 15–21, 25, 32–38, 38–43, 46–48, 77, 85, 92, 100–106, 140, 143–144, 149–154, 164–169, 170–174; and common man, 10, 13, 17, 29–30, 50, 51, 75, 83, 95–96, 103, 106, 117, 124, 125, 140–141, 152, 156, 165, 166, 167–169; and cultural artifacts, 177–180; documentary format and, 3, 11, 15, 17–18, 19–20, 32–38, 39–43, 50–52, 58–63, 66, 91–94, 119–120, 123, 140–144, 164–169, 170–174; and entertainment industry, 35–37, 51, 66, 117, 139, 156–157, 163, 164–169, 177; environmental issues and, 131, 147–148; and expert image-makers, 31–43, 47, 48, 58, 63, 70, 71, 75, 85, 92, 94, 99–100, 114, 123–124, 128–129, 132, 137–139, 143–146, 149–150, 153, 154–155, 162, 163–164, 165, 170, 171–172; and foreign leaders, 12–13, 36, 50, 120, 132, 155; incumbent, 5–6, 12, 14, 17, 19, 28, 29, 57–58, 60, 76–78, 91–92, 101–106, 132, 140–144, 149, 161–162, 171; parents and upbringing, 7–8, 11, 35, 60, 87, 95, 103, 118, 125, 156, 166; propaganda and, 25–26, 28–31, 32–38, 39–43, 46–48, 92, 95, 153; resumé film and, 4–5, 12, 162; speechmaking and, 1, 19, 29, 30–32, 35, 46, 51–52, 58, 59, 60, 63, 121, 124, 130, 143, 153, 155, 169, 171; television and, 1, 3, 13, 37, 46–48, 50–66, 57–58, 63, 77, 81, 85, 91–92, 95–96, 112–116, 125–127, 137–139, 143–146, 149–150, 164–169, 170–174, 178; visionary film and, 4–5, 71; wartime heroism and, 11, 19, 33, 35, 36, 59, 97, 120, 151; wives of, 8–9, 34, 49, 50, 56, 59, 96, 118, 125, 142, 147, 151, 152, 157, 165, 166, 167. *See also* Image-making, presidential; *names of individual candidates*; Pseudo-events
Carey, Walter, 139
Carruthers, Bill, 128
Carson, Saul, 53

Carter, Jimmy, 8, 10, 12, 108, 111, 114, 116, 118, 120, 122–123, 145, 163; campaign film technique, 15, 16, 20, 123–127, 132–134, 173
Carter, Rosalynn, 8, 125
Carville, James, 163
Casey, William, 128
Castro, Fidel, 173
CBN television, 144
CBS television: and campaign film broadcasts, 70; and convention coverage, 56; election coverage and, 125; executives, 85
Character construction, presidential, 2, 5, 19, 83, 94, 140–144, 164–169; computer technology and, 129; family values and, 8–10, 125, 142, 151, 152, 154, 165, 166–167, 168; historical impetus for, 27; myth and, 7, 8, 59–60, 86–88, 103, 120, 151, 164–169; old-style campaigns and, 27–32; party orientation and, 13, 86, 123; perception and, 45, 49, 102, 149–150, 163–164; versus substantive issues, 26, 123, 151, 162, 164–169. *See also* Campaign film, presidential; Image-making, presidential
Chenoweth, Leonard, 96
*Choice* (film), 14, 37, 71–75, 120, 153, 179; narration of, 16. *See also* Goldwater, Barry
Christian principles, 7, 96
Churchill, Winston, 50
Cinématographe, 32
Cincinnatus image, 10, 28, 173. *See also* Image-making, presidential
Citizens for Eisenhower Committee, 50
Citizens for Goldwater-Miller Committee, 70, 71
Civil rights, 69, 77, 153; Hubert Humphrey and, 19, 84; and Martin Luther King, 76
*Civil War* (film series), 172
Clay, Henry, 27
Cleveland, Grover, 32, 41
Clinton, Bill, 163–164, 180; biographical depictions of, 7, 9, 10–11;

campaign film techniques, 16–17, 20, 159, 164–169, 175; Hillary Clinton and, 166, 167; and John Kennedy, 12, 165; and vision of malaise, 14, 168

Clinton, Chelsea, 9, 167

Clinton, Hillary, 7, 166, 167

Clinton, Roger, 167

CNN television, and campaign film broadcasts, 144, 171

Cold War, end of, 161, 173

*Colombian Observer*, 27

Colson, Charles, 99

Commercialization, campaign, 4, 25, 39–43, 47–48; as cultural artifact, 177–180; and infomercials, 162; political strategy in, 77, 82, 100–106, 128–130, 134, 137–139, 140, 143–144, 162, 164–169, 170–174; spot ads and, 46–48, 130. *See also* Marketing principles

Committee to Re-elect the President, 99, 103. *See also* Nixon, Richard

Communication, political: propaganda and, 25–26; televisual strategy and, 3–4, 148–149, 158, 162–163, 164, 177

Communism, 51; Kennedy and, 62; McGovern and, 93; Nixon and, 88, 104

Computer technology: and presidential market research, 40, 42, 128–129, 138; and television, 91–92. *See also* Polls, opinion

Conservative United Republicans of California, 73

Consultants, political. *See* Political consulting

Consumerism, 40, 74, 180; Kennedy on, 61

Contributions, campaign. *See* Campaigns, presidential

Conventions, political party: Bill Clinton and, 162; Democratic, 54, 56, 77, 79, 93, 94, 123, 155, 162; George Bush film and, 12, 162; Lyndon Johnson and, 75–76; Republican, 12, 77, 101, 115, 116, 117, 130; Richard Nixon and, 5, 101; Ronald Reagan film and,

140. *See also* Democratic party; Party, political; Republican party; Whig party

Cooke, Cardinal, 142

Coolidge, Calvin, 39, 41

Costs, of campaign films. *See* Films, presidential

Credibility, 5; by association, 12, 132; television and, 91. *See also* Kennedy, John F.; Testimonials, campaign film

Creel Commission on Public Information, 41

Critics, campaign film, 35, 52–53, 78, 85, 92, 144, 145, 158, 165, 166–167

"Cross of Gold speech," 30. *See also* Bryan, William Jennings

Crowe, Admiral William, 169

C-Span television, and campaign film, broadcasts, 144, 171

Cuomo, Mario, 132

Dailey, Peter, 99, 103, 114, 128

D'Alessandro, David, 155

Darman, Richard, 138–139

David Sawyer Associates agency, 145

Dean, James, 173

Deardourff, 115, 121, 122. *See also* Bailey-Deardourff agency

Deaver, Michael, 128, 138, 170

Decision Making Information, 127. *See also* Polls, opinion

Delegates: and film screening, 79; old-style campaigns and, 31; selection of, 112

Democracy: New Deal, 62, 137; and political campaigns, 91–92

Democratic Party: advertising/media experts and, 39, 40, 75, 122–123, 132, 149, 163–164, 165; American Dream and, 8, 13; campaign/political film technique and, 20, 36, 40, 53–55, 56–57, 72, 75, 79, 124–125, 132, 146–149, 155–158, 159, 162, 179–180; family values and, 9–10, 125, 147, 156–157, 165; McGovern and, 92–94; old-style campaign and, 29,

30, 146–149; populist imagery and, 13, 117–118, 123–127, 168–169; and publicity bureau, 41; Republican portrayal of, 51, 153; television and, 46, 47, 53, 56–57, 125, 144, 148–149, 178. *See also* Conventions, political party; Party, political; Republican party

Demographics: computer technology and, 91–92, 128–129, 138; voter identification and, 105–106

DeNove, Jack, 58

deRochemont, Louis, 36, 37

Deutsch, Inc. agency, 163, 164

Dewey, Thomas, 3, 46; and campaign film techniques, 35, 36, 37

Direct mail appeals, 42

Dissent, political, 93; images of, 102. *See also* Critics, campaign film; Protests

Distinguished Flying Cross, 151

Documentary format, 15, 32, 33, 91–94, 123, 147; cinematic, 16, 32–33, 106; and foreign leaders, 12–13, 120; fraud and, 33–38, 52–53, 65; as hybrid expository advertisement, 3, 15–16, 25, 38–43, 48, 49, 57, 111–114, 129–134, 140–144, 164–169, 170–175; and narrative techniques, 15–21, 54, 82; newsreels and, 33–37, 151; Oscar/Academy awards and, 19, 79; poetic, 38; and propaganda, 32–38, 39–43, 64, 65, 95; purpose of, 2–3; and spot ads, 3, 46–48, 50, 56–57, 100; television and, 16, 46–48, 49, 54, 58, 66, 92, 95, 143–144, 162, 163–164, 165, 170, 171–172. *See also* Expository advertisement film format

Dolan, South Dakota, 10

Douglas, Stephen, 30

Doyle, Dane and Bernbach agency, 75, 80, 155

Dramatizations, in campaign films, 37. *See also* Reenactment strategies

Duffy, Ben, 48

Dukakis, Michael, 8, 10, 149, 153, 154–155, 163, 169; and Bush campaign strategy, 153; campaign film techniques, 16, 155–158

Dukakis, Olympia, 10, 16, 156–157

Durante, Jimmy, 82

Dusenberry, Phil, 11, 139, 157

Dworin, Steve, 164

Eagleton, Thomas, 93

Eaton, John C., 3

Eaton, John H., 27

Economic conditions: and campaign style, 32, 62, 111, 137–138, 142, 149, 161–163; and image-making, 8, 10, 34, 39–40, 106, 108, 119, 127–129, 140–144, 149–150, 161, 171; and party patronage, 45

Education reform issue, 161, 171, 172. *See also* Issues, campaign

Eisenhower, Dwight D., 9, 11, 48, 50, 174; and campaign film techniques, 17, 35, 46, 48–53, 56, 66, 179

Eisenhower, Mamie, 49, 50, 56

*Eisenhower Answers America* (film series), 47

Elections: anti-war movement and, 93; documentary advertisement and, 3; image-building broadcasts and, 5, 116, 132, 152; old-style campaigns and, 4, 27, 29, 30, 31–32; reform, 31–32, 111–112, 137; ritual and, 14, 158, 177; and television influence, 1, 91–92, 177; two-term, 149

Elementary and Secondary Education Act, 147

Emotions, and commercialization, 39–43, 57

Entertainment industry: campaign as, 32, 42–43, 177; celebrity endorsements and, 39–40, 51, 66, 117, 156–157; and presidential campaign films, 35–36, 64, 118, 139, 157, 163, 164–169

Environmental issues, 131, 147–148. *See also* Issues, campaign

Equality, 13

Erlichman, John, 99, 102

Erwin, Wasey, Ruthrauff and Ryan agency, 70, 71

ESPN television, 144

Estrich, Susan, 154
Ethnicity, in campaign films, 105, 121,
    126, 134, 141, 157, 169, 172. *See*
    *also* Racism, in campaign films
Expository advertisement film format,
    15, 32–38, 58–63, 82–84; and
    advertisement, 15–16, 25, 117, 140–
    144, 152, 162, 163–164, 165, 170,
    171–172; as cultural artifact, 177–180;
    modern hybrid formulations of, 111–
    114, 123–127, 129–134, 140–144,
    146–149, 150–154, 155–158, 162–
    163, 164–169, 174–175; music in,
    20, 35, 37, 79, 114, 117, 121, 124,
    131, 133, 134, 140, 141, 144, 165,
    172; narration of, 16–17, 37, 50, 54,
    55, 74, 82–84, 97, 114, 120, 124,
    147, 151, 156–157, 165, 172, 173;
    original footage and, 19–20, 35, 58,
    59, 64–65, 167; reenactments and, 36,
    37, 49, 52; and rhetorical depictions,
    17–18, 131, 162; and special effects,
    20–21, 37, 74, 113, 114, 124–125,
    151, 172; stock footage and, 18–19,
    35, 36, 37, 50, 51, 59, 64–65, 103,
    165; structure and components, 14–16,
    32, 34–35, 50–52, 53–57, 58–62, 63–
    66, 82–84, 85–89, 94–99, 100–106,
    116–122, 123–127, 129–134, 140–
    144, 146–149, 150–154, 155–158,
    164–169, 170–174; testimonials in,
    17, 39–40, 49, 51, 52, 102–103, 117,
    132, 147, 156–157. *See also*
    Documentary format

*Family/Children* (film), 150, 152. *See*
    *also* Bush, George
Family values, depictions of, 8–10, 142,
    147, 151, 152, 154, 156–157, 165,
    166–167, 168, 170
Federal Communications Commission
    (FCC), 47; and candidate coverage, 57
Federal Election Campaign Act, 91–92,
    112
Feinstein, Diane, 132
Filmmakers, campaign. *See* Advertising
    agencies; Campaign films,
    presidential; Media specialists

Films, presidential: and advertising
    technique, 15, 17–18, 25, 38–43, 46–
    48, 85, 117, 140–144, 164–169, 170–
    174; biographical, 3, 4, 5, 7–14, 35,
    58–63, 82, 87–88, 94–99, 123–127,
    146–149, 162, 164–169, 171;
    classical film techniques and, 3–4, 6,
    15, 19–20, 94–99, 106, 134, 166;
    costs, funds and allocations, 31, 35,
    36, 42, 50, 53–54, 70, 71, 81, 92,
    140, 146, 155; as cultural artifact,
    177–180; documentary format and, 2–
    3, 15, 18–19, 32–38, 40, 49, 57, 66,
    94–99, 100–106, 123, 140–144, 147,
    172; and entertainment industry, 35–
    37, 64, 139, 156–157, 164–169, 177;
    and foreign leaders, 12–13, 36, 50,
    120, 132, 155; historical advent of, 2–
    4, 32–38, 39–43, 46–48; hybrid
    expository advertisement formats, 6,
    15–21, 25, 32–38, 39–43, 49, 57,
    108, 111–114, 123–127, 137–144,
    164–169, 170–175; incumbents and,
    5–6, 12, 14, 17, 19, 91–92, 101–106,
    132, 140–144, 149; and marketing
    principles, 4, 15–21, 32–38, 39–43,
    46–48, 67, 85, 91–92, 100–106, 113–
    116, 117, 124, 138–144, 163–165,
    170, 175; mythic imagery and, 6–14,
    18–19, 40, 59–60, 83–84, 96–97,
    120, 132, 138, 140–144, 179;
    nostalgia and, 10–11, 83; propaganda
    and, 25–26, 32–38, 40–43, 65, 95,
    102; reenactments and, 36, 37;
    religious inference and, 62, 71, 133,
    142; as rhetorical genre, 4–6, 17–18,
    131; structure and components, 14–21,
    32, 34–35, 50–52, 53–57, 58–62, 63–
    66, 71–75, 82–84, 85–89, 94–99,
    100–106, 116–122, 123–127, 129–
    134, 140–144, 146–149, 150–154,
    155–158, 164–169, 170–174;
    television and, 1–2, 16, 37–38, 46–
    48, 50–53, 65, 81, 85, 112–116, 125–
    127, 143–144, 149, 178; types of, 4–
    6, 15, 40; use of family imagery in,
    7–10, 35, 147, 151, 152; war footage
    and, 11, 19, 33, 36, 51, 61, 95, 97,

119, 120, 151. *See also* Campaign films, presidential; Candidates, presidential; Documentary format; Newsreels; Propaganda
"Films of merit," 35
Finch, Robert H., 99, 102
Flag, American, 17, 31, 174
Fletcher School of Government, 115
Ford, Betty, 8, 118
Ford, Gerald, 7, 8, 10, 11, 108, 111, 114–116, 126, 128; campaign film technique, 15, 16, 116–122, 134; and Nixon pardon, 118
*For You and Your Family* (film), 63. *See also* Nixon, Richard
Fox, William, 34
Frank Greer Associates agency, 145, 148, 163
Franklevey, Barbara, 106
Fraud, in campaign films, 37, 52–53, 65. *See also* Documentary format
Front porch campaigns, 31. *See also* Campaigns, presidential
Fuller, Smith and Ross agency, 85
Future Group agency, 155

Gallup, George, 47. *See also* Polls, opinion
Gambarelli, Maria, 51
Garagiola, Joe, 16, 117, 118
Gardner, Al, 78
Gardner, Bob, 121
Garfield, James A., 31
Garment, Leonard, 85, 102
Garth, David, 145
*Geisha Boy* (feature film), outtake shots from, 65
Genre, campaign film, 4–6; components of, 14–21. *See also* Rhetorical genre
Gimmicks, calculated use of, 42–43, 113; avoidance of, 86
"God Bless the U.S.A.," 20, 141, 143
Goldwater, Barry, 8, 12, 14, 69, 108, 120; campaign film techniques, 16, 36, 37, 70–75, 153, 179
Goldwater, Peggy, 8
Good will, publicity and, 41

Goodwin, Rod, 123
Gorbachev, Mikhail, 12, 155, 173
Gore, Al, 169, 180
Grasshoff, Alex, 101
Grassroots campaign, 92–93, 96
Great Debates, 57
Great Depression imagery, 8, 10, 83, 95; and media manipulation, 34, 39–40; and stock footage, 19, 35. *See also* Economic conditions
Green, Edith, 119
Greenberg, Stan, 163, 171. *See also* Polls, opinion
Greenwood, Lee, 20, 144
Grunwald, Mandy, 163
Guggenheim, Charles, 35, 57, 79, 80, 93–94, 100, 107
Guild, Buscom and Bonfigli agency, 58
Guylay, L. Richard, 55, 70

Haldeman, H. R., 85, 99
Hanna, Mark, 31. *See also* Media specialists
Harding, Warren G., 39
Harris, Louis, 61
Harrison, Benjamin, 31
Harrison, Tubby, 154. *See also* Polls, opinion
Harrison, William Henry, 29, 30. *See also* Whig party
Hart, Gary, 137
Hart, Robert, 145, 146. *See also* Polls, opinion
Headstart, 147
Health care issue, 161
Hearst-Metrotone News, 35
Henning, John, 131
Heroism, images of, 11, 28, 59–60, 130, 156; assassination attempt and, 142; calculated association with, 12, 28, 30, 33, 119, 172; stock footage and, 19, 97, 120, 151
Heston, Charlton, 157
Hiss, Alger, 51
Hitler, Adolf, 81
Hoffa, Jimmy, 60
Hoover, Herbert, and campaign film techniques, 34

Hope, Arkansas, 10, 168
Horton, Willie, 153, 162
Hubschman, Albert, 35
Hughes, Charles E., 39
Humphrey, Hubert, 10, 12, 14, 19, 76, 89, 156, 163; and campaign film techniques, 19, 78, 80–84, 122, 135, 155
Humphreys, Robert, 48–49
Hunt Commission, 144–145
Hussein, Saddam, 171
Hybrid documentary advertisement format. *See* Campaign films, presidential; Expository advertisement film format

Ideals, 6; American Dream and, 13, 14, 62–63, 99, 117, 165; of American male, 7, 8, 11; and common man, 10, 13, 29–30, 86, 168–169, 174; computer technology and, 129; construction of, 164–169; and ritual, 14, 158; of success, 8
Identity, American, 8–10; absence of, 64, 155–156, 171; and campaign film technique, 17, 163–164, 165; rhetorical depiction of, 17–18, 131, 165, 166, 167–169
Ideology, 6; American Dream and, 13, 88–89, 99, 121, 138–139; rhetorical depiction of, 18, 88, 131. *See also* Myth, American
*Ideology and the Image* (Nichols), 14
Image-making, presidential: biographical films and, 5, 7–14, 53–57, 58–62, 63–66, 83, 94–99, 146–149, 164–169, 170–175; campaign theme and, 47, 51, 92–94, 123, 133, 140–144, 146–149, 150–154, 164–169, 171; and cultural artifact, 177–180; Eisenhower and, 46–53; experts, 46, 48, 58, 63, 67, 70, 71, 75, 77, 80, 85, 99–100, 114, 122–123, 128–129, 132, 138–139, 143–146, 149–150, 154–155, 162, 163–164, 165, 170, 171–172; hybrid expository/advertisement and, 15–21, 25, 39–43, 49, 57, 116–122, 128–

131, 140–144, 150–154, 164–169, 170–175; old-style campaigns and, 26–27, 28–32, 144–146; overview, 1–6; patriotism and, 31, 60, 120, 131, 140–144, 141–142; propaganda and, 25–26, 28–31, 32–38, 40–43, 46, 102–103, 130–131, 164–169, 170–175; television and, 45, 46–48, 57–58, 60, 81, 91–92, 95–96, 112–116, 123–124, 143–144, 149–154, 158, 164–169, 180. *See also* Propaganda; Public relations, presidential; Spot advertisements, presidential
Images, presidential: alteration of, 5, 158–159, 161–162, 164, 170–171; archetypal, 6–13; and country/people, 13–14, 61, 95–96, 103, 117, 120–121, 133–134, 140–144, 150–154, 165, 166, 167–169; defined, 2; and documentary advertisement, 3, 140, 172; personal and party, 13, 59, 92–94, 100, 102–103, 132–134, 140–146, 147, 150–154, 156–157, 163, 165, 166, 167–169. *See also* Campaign films, presidential; Expository advertisement film format; Symbolism
"I'm Feeling Good About America," 121. *See also* Music, and campaign films
Immigrants, and party politics, 45
Incumbents: and campaign film techniques, 5–6, 12, 17, 76–78, 101–106, 140–144, 171; challengers and, 14, 28, 60, 111, 132, 140, 161–162; old-style campaign, 28, 29; and television, 91–92, 143–144, 149
Infomercials, 162. *See also* Perot, Ross
Information sources: advertising experts and, 38–43, 99–100; fraud and, 33–38; infomercials, 162; old-style campaigns and, 27, 28–32; statistics, 1, 46, 69, 77, 91; talk shows, 161; television as, 37–38, 77, 91–92, 125, 134. *See also* Newspapers; Newsreels; Radio
Inouye, Daniel, 132
Integrative propaganda, 25–26. *See also* Persuasion; Propaganda
Iran-Contra scandal, 149
Iraq, invasion of, 161, 171

Israel, 101, 120, 132

Issues, campaign: campaign themes and, 51–52, 61–62, 76, 84, 92–99, 123, 146, 151, 154–155, 161, 171, 180; candidate image as, 115, 123, 129, 151, 171; Democratic party and, 56–57, 123, 133–134, 146, 154–155; distillation of, 42–43; old-style speech-making and, 30; and public relations, 42, 146, 171; rhetorical depiction of, 18, 42, 46, 51, 60, 61–62, 64, 72–73, 76, 131. *See also* Candidates, presidential

Jackson, Andrew, 3, 13, 27, 179; Cincinnatus image of, 10, 28
Jackson, Jesse, 137
Jacobs, Lewis, 38
Jamieson, Kathleen, 81
Jefferson, Thomas, 12, 26
*Jimmy Who?* (film), 16, 20, 114, 147. *See also* Carter, Jimmy
Johnson, James, 145
Johnson, Lyndon B., 69, 74, 84; film tribute to, 100; political film techniques, 36, 40, 75–76
Jones, Eugene, 86
Jordan, Hamilton, 122, 132, 162
Jordan, Jim, 114
J. Walter Thompson agency, 39, 85

Kendall, Amos, 28. *See also* Media specialists
Kennedy, Jacqueline, 9
Kennedy, John F., 11, 59–60, 81, 156; assassination of, 69, 168; calculated association with, 12, 71, 79, 84, 97, 119, 165, 172; campaign film techniques, 36, 37, 58–63; as film narrator, 56; film tribute to, 19, 75, 100; and Great Debates, 57–58
Kennedy, Robert, 60, 76, 95
Kern, Montague, 134
Khrushchev, Nikita, 12, 65
*Khrushchev As I Know Him* (film), 63. *See also* Nixon, Richard
Kimberly, H. S., 34

King, Martin Luther, 76, 165, 173; assassination of, 168
Kintner, Robert, 70
Kissinger, Henry, 102
Kitchel, Denison, 71
Koch, Mayor, 133
Korean War, images of, 51, 142
KPAZ-TV (Phoenix), 144
Kudner Agency, 48
Ku Klux Klan, 120

Landon, Alf, 35
Lasker, Albert, 39
Laxalt, Paul, 139
Leadership, depiction of, 47, 142, 173. *See also* Heroism, images of
Lee, Ivy, 41
Lemann, Nicholas, 140
Lennon and Newell agency, 80
Leone, Richard, 145
Liberty, 13
Lincoln, Abraham, 12, 30, 61, 172
Literacy, 1
Long, Senator Huey, 51
Lorenz, Pare, 35
Luce, Clare Boothe, 49
Luce, Henry, 37
Ludwin, Henry, 71
Lumière brothers, 3, 32, 33

McCabe, Ed, 155
McCaffrey and McCall agency, 145
McCarthy, Eugene, 81
McDonald's advertising, 140
McEvoy, Bill, 97
McGinnis, Joe, 81, 85, 92
McGovern, Eleanor, 96
McGovern, George, 7, 10, 11, 12, 81, 91–92, 145; campaign film techniques and, 18, 35, 94–99, 135; substantive issues and, 92–94
MacGregor, Clark, 99
McKinley, William, 3, 31, 32
Magazine media, propagandistic, 39
Magus Productions, 123
Male, American, 7, 8
*Manahatta* (film), 38

Marketing principles, 4, 38–43, 91–92, 100–106, 143–144; advent of campaign films and, 32–38, 39–43, 46–48, 67; and modern campaign films, 113–116, 117, 124, 127–129, 138–142, 143–144, 163–165, 168–169, 170–175, 178; old-style campaigns and, 27–32; poetic documentary and, 38–43

Market research, 2, 78, 163–164; and computer technology, 40, 42, 113, 128–129, 138; consumer motivation and, 40; November Group and, 103; prosperity and, 47; and speech content, 46; telephone surveys and, 138

Marshall, E. G., 16, 123, 124

Massey, Raymond, 16, 74

*Master of Emergencies* (film), 34

*Mayaguez* incident, 119

MBS Radio, 53

Mead, Margaret, 147

Meaney, George, 93

Media coverage: calculated manipulation of, 34, 56, 77, 91–92, 100, 143–144, 162; fraud and, 33; free, 146, 155, 162; tapping, 5–6, 77, 162

Media specialists: advent of campaign films and, 33–38, 46–48, 94; advertising/image experts and, 38–43, 46–48, 67, 85, 99, 113–116, 122–123, 128–129, 132, 137–139, 143–144, 149–150, 155, 162, 163–164, 165, 170, 171–172; old-style campaigns and, 28–29, 31, 144–146; opinions of, 93; Republicans and, 46–48, 99–100, 114, 115, 121–122, 138–139, 143–144, 149–150; role of, 1–2, 4, 67, 77, 115, 139–140, 154–155, 158–159, 162, 163–164, 165, 170, 171–172. *See also* Advertising agencies; Campaign films, presidential; Image-making, presidential; Political consulting

Mediated Political Realities (Nimmo/Combs), 14

Meese, Edwin, 128

"Meet the Press," 148–149

Merchandising, campaign, 4, 39–43, 45, 47, 82, 85, 92, 134, 137, 164–169, 172; as cultural artifact, 177–180; Nixon and, 100, 106; Perot and, 162; Reagan and, 137–139, 143–144; spot ads and, 46–48; Stevenson on, 66. *See also* Military model

Messner, Tom, 139, 149–150

Military model, 31, 38, 135; of Kennedy film, 58; and merchandising, 43, 45, 47, 82; Mondale film and, 144, 146; Nixon film and, 66, 106

Miller, Scott, 155

Mitchell, John, 78, 85

Mitchum, Robert, 16, 172

Moe, Richard, 145

Mondale, Walter, 8, 137, 144–146, 163; campaign film techniques, 146–149, 157; and "Meet the Press," 148–149

*Moonstruck* (film), 156–157

Morality, 13, 14, 179; Carter and, 133; Goldwater and, 69, 72, 74; Kennedy on, 61

Morgan, Raymond H., 71

Motion picture industry. *See* Entertainment industry

MTV, 144

Mullins, Janet, 150

Music, and campaign films, 20, 35, 37, 65, 79, 114, 117, 121, 131, 133, 134, 140, 141, 144, 165, 172

Music videos, campaign, 144

Mussolini, Benito, 81

Mute tribunes, 26–27, 29

Myth, American, 6, 8, 11, 13, 83, 139, 143, 164; and presidential images, 6–14, 15, 19, 59–60, 87, 95–96, 103, 120, 132–133, 138, 158–159, 164–169, 172, 179; and propaganda, 25–26; rhetorical depictions of, 17–18, 131, 158–159, 165; visionary film and, 14, 62, 71. *See also* Ideology

Napolitan, Joe, 75, 80, 155, 156; on biographical film, 3

Narration, campaign film, 16–17, 37, 50, 66, 74, 82–83, 103, 114, 120, 123, 124, 147, 151, 152, 156–157, 172, 173; candidate's voice and, 151; domineering, 103–104; ineffective, 97;

non-manipulative, 54, 55, 165. *See also* Expository advertisement film format

*Nation*, 53

National Press Club, 124

National Resources Board, 131

NBC television, 37; and campaign film broadcasts, 53, 70, 72, 116, 143–144

News, television: convention films as, 56, 143–144; manipulation of, 5–6, 77, 91, 102, 162; public access to information and, 1, 91–92

Newspapers: old-style campaigns and, 27, 28, 30, 31; propaganda and, 52, 130–131; versus television, 1, 77

Newsreels, 33; calculated manipulation of, 34–35, 151; and campaign film distribution, 36; Eisenhower film and, 50; Kennedy film and, 58; reenactments in, 36; Roosevelt and, 35; Universal Pictures and, 35–36. *See also* Documentary format

Newton, Carroll, 63

*New York Post*, 52

*New York Times*, 30, 131

Nielsen ratings: campaign-film broadcast and, 144; *Campaigning with Stevenson* (film), 54; computer technology and, 138; convention coverage and, 78; *Report to Ike*, 50

Nixon, Julie, 102

Nixon, Pat, 50, 101

Nixon, Richard, 7, 8, 50, 60, 81, 84, 99–100, 126, 139, 170, 172; campaign film techniques, 16, 17, 36, 37, 56, 63–66, 85, 99–106, 134, 165; in Eisenhower film, 50, 52; and Ford pardon, 118; and Great Debates, 57–58; image manipulation and, 5, 12, 18, 49, 65, 78, 85, 91–92, 98, 114; and McGovern, 92–93; resignation of, 108, 111, 128

Nixon, Tricia, 102

Noonan, Peggy, 165, 166

Norman Craig Kummel agency, 56

Nostalgia, use of, 10–11, 83

November Company, 170

November Group, 99, 103, 114, 139

Objectivity, impression of, 15, 47, 113–114. *See also* Documentary format

O'Brien, Lawrence, 80, 93

O'Donnell, Terry, 119

Old Tippecanoe, 30

Omaha, Nebraska, 10

O'Neill, Tip, 132

*One Thousand Days* (film), 100. *See also* Kennedy, John F.

Oratory propaganda, 28, 30–32. *See also* Propaganda; Speeches

O'Reilly, Richard, 128

Oscar Awards, 19, 157

Parades, torchlight, 29. *See also* Campaigns, presidential

Paramount Pictures, 65; and *The Image Candidates*, 64. *See also* Nixon, Richard

Parker, George, 41

Party, political: advertising expertise and, 39, 40, 41–43, 46–48, 99–100, 117, 128–129, 132, 144–145, 163–165, 170; American Dream and, 8, 13, 131, 132–133, 169; Eisenhower and, 12; entertainment function of, 32, 177; imagery, 13, 20, 79; and motion picture industry, 36–37; and personal identity, 4; presidential candidates and, 27, 28–29, 32, 42, 46–48, 53, 74–75, 99–100, 101, 111–117, 132–133, 135, 137, 144–146, 161–162, 163–165, 169, 170, 178. *See also* Conventions, political party

Pathe, Charles, 33

Patriotism: entertainment industry and, 36, 156–157; image-making and, 31, 36, 60, 120, 131, 140, 141–142, 151, 153

Payne, Dan, 155

PBS, and campaign film broadcast, 171

Peanut Brigade, 126

Peck, Gregory, 16

Penetration, advertisement, 46–48

Pepsi-Cola advertisements, 140

Perceptions, 5; of Clinton, 163, 164; good vs. evil, 92–93; implied

objectivity and, 15, 108, 133;
incumbents and, 5–6, 91–92, 101–
106, 132, 140–144, 171; party
characteristics and, 13, 127–129;
persuasion and, 116, 143–144, 146–
147, 162, 163–164, 165, 170, 171–
172; of Reagan, 130, 132, 137;
statistical, 149; television and, 45, 77,
91–92, 95–96, 112–116, 123–124,
146–147
Perot, Ross, 161, 162
Perry, Joe, 51
Personality, 125–126; public perception
of, 2, 115, 146–147, 171. *See also*
Candidates, presidential; Character
construction, presidential
Persuasion: advertising experts and, 38–
43, 99–100, 143–144, 162, 163–164,
165, 170, 171–172; documentary
format and, 2–3, 16, 33–43, 103–104,
165, 166, 167–169; and motion picture industry, 36–37; old-style campaigns and, 26–27, 28–32; propaganda
and, 25–26, 28–32, 39–43, 115–116;
rhetoric and, 4, 131; television and,
46–48
*Philadelphia Franklin Gazette*, 27
Policy, government: corruption and, 149,
179; public relations and, 41
Political consulting: and campaign
strategy, 70, 77, 114, 115, 121–123,
128–129, 132, 139–146, 154–155,
163–164, 165, 170; establishment of,
41–42; merchandising model and, 47–
48, 51, 92, 100–106, 124, 137–139,
146. *See also* Image-making,
presidential; November Group;
Tuesday Team
Political information System (PINS),
128–129
Polls, opinion, 2, 42, 75, 78, 122, 138,
149; Caddell, 122–123, 127, 132;
Gallup, 115, 137, 149; Hart's, 146;
and issue determination, 57; old-style
campaigns and, 31; and party
allegience, 81; Roper, 91; Teeter's,
115; voter research and, 47, 93, 112–
116, 138, 161–162, 171; Wirthlin's,

127, 138. *See also* Market research
Populist campaigns, 13, 31; image-
making and, 13, 117–118, 123–127,
166, 168–169
*Portrait of a President* (film), 5. *See also*
Nixon, Richard
Poverty, images of, 18, 35
Powell, Jody, 122
Presidency: archetypal images of, 6–13,
88, 173; Catholicism and, 60; and
images of country/people, 13–14, 29–
30, 34, 50, 60, 61, 75, 95–96, 106,
124, 125–126, 138, 140–144, 152,
165, 166, 167–169; incumbent, 5–6,
91–92, 101–106, 132, 140–144, 149,
171; marketing principles and, 27–38,
39–43, 46–48, 117, 124, 127–129,
138–146, 163–165, 170–175, 178;
and motion picture industry, 36–37;
mute tribunes and, 26, 29; mythology
and symbolism of, 6–14, 31, 33, 60,
87–88, 97–98, 125, 132, 138, 140–
144, 151–154, 157, 165, 172, 179;
personal and party images of, 7, 13,
35–36, 59, 74–75, 93, 95, 98, 101,
115, 117–118, 123, 125, 127–129,
135, 140–143, 144–146, 151, 156–
157, 163, 178; and popular support,
27, 92–93, 111–112, 123. *See also*
Image-making, presidential
Presidential image-making. *See* Image-
making, presidential
Presley, Elvis, 173
Press agents, 41
Press bureau, 41
*Printer's Ink* magazine, 39
Print media, propagandistic, 28–29, 39,
40, 180; protest of, 41; theme
penetration in, 47
*Profiles in Courage* (Kennedy), 60
Progressive National Committee, 31, 35
Propaganda, 25–26; advertising experts
and, 38–43, 46–48, 99–100, 162,
163–164, 165, 170, 171–172; advertising techniques and, 38–43, 46–48,
164–169, 170–175; agitative, 25;
appreciation of, 53; and campaign film
technique, 32–38, 50–52, 92, 95, 102,

108, 130–131, 164–169, 170–175;
Creel Commission on Public
Information and, 41; Eisenhower and,
46–53; integrative, 25; and motion
picture industry, 36–37; and old-style
campaigns, 26–27; protest of, 41; and
television, 46–48, 50–52, 56, 64, 91–
92, 112–116, 164–169, 170–175;
wartime, 41. *See also* Persuasion
Prosperity, 13; and advertising boom, 47;
images of, in campaign films, 18, 61,
140–144, 149, 152
Protests, 77; anti-war activists and, 92–
93
Pryor, Arthur, 50
Pseudo-events, 29–32, 77, 107;
advertising experts and, 38–43, 100.
*See also* News, television
Psychology, behavioral, advertising
technique and, 39–40
Public relations, presidential: advent of,
33–43, 99–100; experts, 41, 71, 85,
143–144, 149–150, 162, 163–164,
165, 170, 171–172; and influence of
issues, 42, 48–49, 146; protest and,
41; and publicists, 41; television and,
46–48, 143–144, 149–154
Public Service Announcements, contrived
newsreels as, 33, 35
Puris, Martin, 170

*Quest for Peace* (film), 75, 100. *See also*
Johnson, Lyndon B.

Racism, in campaign films, 72, 73, 74,
105, 172; southern strategy, 74. *See
also* Ethnicity, in campaign films
Radio: campaign techniques and, 34; and
Great Debates, 58; television as
extension of, 53, 66
*Radio Patrol* (feature film), shots from,
65
Rafshoon, Gerald, 122, 132
Rather, Dan, 125
Reagan, Nancy, 9, 139, 142
Reagan, Ronald, 8, 9, 10, 108, 111, 127,
128–129, 137–139, 161, 165, 168,
172, 173, 179; assassination attempt,

11, 142; campaign film technique and,
15, 16, 19, 20–21, 129–131, 135,
140–144; and defense policies, 142,
161; and God, 11, 142; incumbency,
137–139; Normandy speech, 143; on
presidency, 12
Redding, Jack, 36
Reenactment strategies, 36, 37, 47, 49,
52
Reeves, Rosser, 46, 47
Reilly, John, 145
Religious inference, in campaign films,
62, 71, 133, 142; New Right and, 138
*Report to Ike* (film), 48, 49–53, 66, 179.
*See also* Eisenhower, Dwight D.
Republican party: advertising/media
experts and, 39, 40, 46–48, 50, 53,
55, 56, 57, 58, 63, 64, 70, 71, 85–86,
99–100, 128–129, 139, 140, 143–
144, 149–150, 152, 155, 170;
American Dream and, 8, 13, 120–121,
127, 138, 143–144, 169; and
campaign film techniques, 20, 34, 35,
36, 40, 46–48, 56, 71, 75, 85–86,
106, 117, 129–134, 139, 140–144,
150–154, 169, 171–174; convention
image-building and, 5, 140; family
values and, 9–10, 142, 151, 152, 170;
and industry, 106; and issue altera-
tions, 18, 74–75, 171–174; leader/
populist imagery and, 13, 140–144;
old-style campaigns and, 30, 31; and
political consultants, 41–42, 85–86,
114, 128–129, 139–140, 152, 170;
and publicity bureau, 41; television
and, 46–48, 55, 56, 57, 58, 85–86,
143–144, 149–154, 178; Thomas
Dewey campaign film, 3, 36, 37
Resor, Stanley, 39
Resume film genre, 4–5, 12, 162, 171.
*See also* Rhetorical genre
Rhetoric, 4; campaign film techniques
and, 17–18, 131, 162–163; myth and,
6
Rhetorical genre: biographical film, 4–5,
7–14, 162–163, 171; component
commonalities, 14–21; ideology and,
6, 13–14, 18, 131; resume film, 4–5,

12, 171; visionary film, 5, 14, 71, 171

*Richard Nixon: A Self-Portrait* (film), 78, 84–89, 101–106, 116, 165, 171

Rituals, campaign, 19, 158, 177–180; and elections, 14

Robards, Jason, 16

*Robert Kennedy Remembered* (film), 79

Rockefeller, Nelson, 84

Rogers, Ted, 63

Rogich, Sig, 139, 149–150

Rollins, Ed, 138, 170

Romney, George, 100

Roosevelt, Franklin Delano, 172; and campaign film techniques, 34–35

Roosevelt, John, 51

Roosevelt, Sarah, 51

Roosevelt, Theodore, 7–8, 31, 172, 173; and campaign film technique, 32

Roper poll, 91. *See also* Polls, opinion

Rosenberg, Julius and Ethel, 51

Rossen, Clay, 150

Sales techniques, presidential: soft-sell, 40, 76, 114, 162; TV spot ads and, 46–48, 76

*San Francisco Chronicle*, 131

*San Francisco Examiner*, 130

Sasso, John, 154–155

Savage, John, 128

Schwartz, Tony, 40, 80; The Daisy commercial, 76

Sears, John, 128

Senate, 12

Senate Foreign Relations Committee, 60

Shaffer, Paul, 100

Shakespeare, Frank, 85

Shapp, Milton, 80, 100–101

Silent Majority, 138

Skinner, Sam, 170

Slogans, campaign, 42–43. *See also* Campaigns, presidential

Smith, Al, 41, 51

Smith, Albert J., 33

Smith, Jean Kennedy, 58

*Snowblower* (film), 155–158. *See also* Dukakis, Michael

Sol Estes, Billie, 73

Songs, campaign film. *See* Music, and campaign films

Spanish-American War, 32, 33

Special effects, 20–21, 37, 74, 113, 114, 124–125, 151, 172. *See also* Expository advertisement film format

Speeches: and campaign tours, 1, 29, 30–32, 169; film clips of, 19, 51–52, 58, 59, 60, 121, 124, 143; Martin Luther King and, 165; party conventions and, 84, 123, 130, 155, 158; televised, 46, 49, 51–52, 53–54, 55, 57, 63, 78, 153. *See also* Candidates, presidential; Propaganda

Speech-writing, advertising experts and, 39

Spence, Roy, 145, 163

Spencer, Stuart, 114, 138

Spiegel, Ed, 101, 107, 116, 121–122

Spot advertisements, presidential, 2, 78, 80, 92, 116, 121, 134, 145–146; campaign film and, 3, 46–48, 50, 56–57, 72, 100, 123, 130, 144; The Daisy commercial, 76

Squier, Bob, 122, 132, 163

Squier, Eskew, Knapp and Ochs agency, 163

Statue of Liberty, 17

Steeper, Fred, 170

Stephanopoulos, George, 163

Stevenson, Adlai, 53; and campaign film techniques, 36, 46, 47, 66

Stock footage, 18–19, 34, 35, 37, 50, 165; reenactments and, 36; and visual leitmotif, 64–65; wartime, 11, 33, 51, 59, 61, 95, 97, 119, 120, 151

Storck, Shelby, 80, 83, 100

Strauss, Robert, 145

Structure, campaign film, 14–16, 32, 34, 50, 53–57, 58–66, 71–75, 82 84, 85–89, 94–99, 100–106, 116–122, 123–127, 129–134, 140–144, 146–149, 150–154, 155–158, 164–169, 170–174. *See also* Campaign films, presidential; Documentary format

Surveys, telephone, 138

Susnjara, Gary, 155

Symbolism: American myth and, 6, 10, 13–14, 15, 60, 61, 83, 87, 96, 120, 130, 131, 138, 143, 158–159, 164–169, 172, 174; heroes and, 11–12, 19, 30, 60, 120, 151, 152; motivational psychology and, 40–43; patriotic, 31, 32, 139, 143, 153, 156, 168–169; and presidential images, 6–14, 28–29, 46, 54, 60, 81, 87, 95–96, 103, 117, 119–120, 124–125, 130, 132, 133, 138, 143–144, 151–154, 157, 164–169, 172, 180; propaganda/persuasion and, 25–26, 27–31, 32–38, 39–43, 95, 103, 133; rhetoric and, 4, 6, 17–18, 131, 139

Taft, Senator Robert, 49
Talk shows, and presidential candidates, 162
Tax issue, 171
Ted Bates Agency, 46, 48
Teeter, Robert, 102, 114, 115, 138, 149, 170
Television image-making: advisers, 46, 67, 144–145; and campaign film broadcasts, 53, 81, 91, 143–144, 180; Carter and, 125–127, 132; closed-circuit, 56; and cultural artifact, 177–180; Democratic party and, 53–55; Dukakis and, 158; Eisenhower and, 46–53, 48–53, 56; and Great Debates, 56–57; inception of, 1–2, 37, 66; Kennedy and, 60; McGovern and, 95–96; Nixon and, 63–66, 85, 91–92; Reagan and, 137, 143–144; and realism, 2, 180; theme penetration and, 47, 51, 60, 61–62. See also Documentary format; Expository advertisement film format; Image-making, presidential
Testimonials, campaign film, 17, 49, 51, 102–103, 114, 132, 152; celebrity endorsements and, 39–40, 51, 117, 147, 156–157; enacted and prompted, 52; historical impetus for, 27; newspapers and, 130. See also Expository advertisement film format
Thatcher, Margaret, 155

The Christopher Hour (TV program), 58
The Democratic Faith: The Johnson Years (film), 79
The Dewey Story (film), 3, 36, 37
The Fighting President (film), 34–35. See also Roosevelt, Franklin D.
The Image Candidates (film), 64. See also Nixon, Richard
The Kennedy Story (film), 59
The Life of Calvin Coolidge (film), 3, 34
The McGovern Story (film), 10, 19, 94–99
The Man From Hope (film), 164–169. See also Clinton, Bill
The March of Time (film series), 36, 37
Themes, campaign, 42, 51; Bush and, 149–154; Carter and, 123, 124, 133; Clinton and, 161–163; construction of, 138; dissemination of, 52; Dukakis and, 155, 157, 158; Goldwater and, 72–73; Kennedy and, 60, 61–62; McGovern and, 92–94; Mondale and, 145–146, 148; Nixon and, 64, 102–106; Reagan and, 131, 133, 138, 140–144; and spot ads, 46, 76
The New Frontier (film), 16, 37, 58–63, 66, 71. See also Kennedy, John F.
The Nixon Years: Change Without Chaos (film), 37–38, 101–106, 120, 171
The Plow that Broke the Plains (film), 35, 95
The Presidential Campaign of Wendell Wilkie (film), 35
The Pursuit of Happiness (film), 56. See also Kennedy, John F.
The Reagan Record (film), 129–131
The River (film), 35
The Road to Leadership (film), 75. See also Johnson, Lyndon B.
The Selling of the President 1960 (film), 100
The Selling of the President 1968 (McGinnis), 85, 92
"The Time is Now," 131. See also Music, and campaign films
The Triumph of the Will (film), 64
The Truman Story (film), 36

*The Unseeing Eye* (Patterson/McClure), 92

*This Man, This Office* (film), 16, 132–134, 163, 173. *See also* Carter, Jimmy

Thomason, Harry, 163, 164

Thomson, Virgil, 35

Tkach, Dr. Walter, 102–103

Travis, Jim, 139, 144

Treleaven, Harry, 85, 86

Truman, Harry S, 36; and campaign film techniques, 35–37

Trust, as campaign theme, 161–162

Tuesday Team, 139, 140, 149–150. *See also* Reagan, Ronald

Udall, Morris, 132

Universal Pictures: and campaign "newsreels," 35; and *The Truman Story* (film), 36

*Upbuilding with Prosperity* (film), 34. *See also* Hoover, Herbert

USA network, 144

Value and Lifestyle Survey (VALS), 40

Values in Strategic Assessment, 138

Van Buren, Martin, 29, 149

Vance, Cyrus, 132

Van Voorhis, Westbrook, 37

Videotape technology, 19–20, 113. *See also* Special effects

Vietnam War, 76, 77, 84, 127; anti-war campaign and, 92–94, 98; images of, 19, 120; Nixon and, 103–104

Visionary film genre, 5, 14, 61–62, 171; Goldwater and, 71. *See also* Rhetorical genre

Vitagraph Newsreel Company, 33

Voice of God, 37, 55, 82. *See also* Narration, campaign film

Voters: and activism, 93; computer technologies and, 40, 91, 128–129, 138; entertainment of, 42–43, 177; identification with, 5, 155–156, 163–164, 165, 166, 167–169, 171; as marketplace, 42–43, 48, 91–92, 134; and motion picture industry, 36–37; old-style campaigns and, 4,

26, 32; propaganda and, 25–26, 33–43, 108; strategic persuasion of, 2–3, 25–26, 33–43, 46–48, 49, 103–104, 165, 166, 167–169; television and, 2, 46–48, 49, 91–92, 143–144; women, 106, 142, 147–148. *See also* Polls, opinion

Wallace, George, 76, 81

Wallace, Warren, 85

Walton, Russ, 71, 73, 74

Warner, Mrs. John, 51

Warren, Governor Earl, 51

Wartime, 11, 33; and anti-war demonstrations, 77, 92–94; and presidential imagery, 11, 19, 33, 36, 51, 59, 119, 151, 163; propaganda, 41, 95; stock footage, 19, 36, 51, 59, 61, 95, 120, 151

Warwick, Dionne, 124

Warwick and Legler agency, 40

Washington, George, 12, 50, 61, 172; as mute tribune, 26; virtue and, 13

*Washington Globe*, 28

Watergate, 108, 112, 121, 123, 127, 134, 162

Watson, John B., 39

Wayne, John, 51

Webster, Daniel, 27

*We The People* (film), 75. *See also* Johnson, Lyndon B.

"What Do You Get When You Fall in Love?," 124. *See also* Music, and campaign films

*What Manner of Man* (film), 19, 78, 80–84, 89. *See also* Humphrey, Hubert

Whig party, 29; and first national campaign, 30

Whistlestop campaign tours, 30–32. *See also* Speeches

Whitaker, Clem, 41–42

White, Theodore, 61, 81

"Why Not the Best," 124. *See also* Music, and campaign films

Wilhelm, David, 163

Wilkie, Wendell, 40

*William McKinley at Home* (film), 3

Wilson, Woodrow: and campaign film
     techniques, 34; and Creel Commission
     on Public Information, 41
Wirthlin, Richard, 127, 128, 138. *See
     also* Polls, opinion
*With the Landons* (film), 35
*With the Roosevelts* (film), 35
Wolper, David, 37, 75, 79, 100, 107
Women. *See* Voters

Works Progress Administration, 35
Wright, Jim, 132
WTBS, 144
Wyckoff, 64

*Yale Law Journal*, 166
Young and Rubicam Agency, 48

Zanuck, Darryl, 51

**ABOUT THE AUTHOR**

JOANNE MORREALE is Assistant Professor of Communication at Northeastern University. Her particular research interest is in campaign communication.